ECONOMIC DEVELOPMENT
IN THE TROPICS

Economic Development in the Tropics

B. W. HODDER M.A., B.Litt.(Oxon), Ph.D.(London)
Reader in Geography, Queen Mary College, University of London

METHUEN & CO LTD
11 New Fetter Lane, London EC4

First published 1968 *by Methuen & Co Ltd,*
11 *New Fetter Lane, London EC4*
© 1968 *by B. W. Hodder*
University Paperback published 1968
Printed in Great Britain by
Richard Clay (The Chaucer Press), Ltd,
Bungay, Suffolk

Distributed in the United States of America
by Barnes & Noble, Inc.

For Rosabelle

Contents

Figures

Tables

Preface

No one concerned with the study of any part of the developing world today can fail to consider in his analysis at least some of the problems and manifestations of economic development. Explicit or implicit in much of his work is likely to be some attempt to understand the nature and causes of poverty, backwardness, or underdevelopment, and to make some objective comment on the lines along which successful development might most logically be pursued. In so doing, however, he becomes aware of two distinct sets of problems. First, there are those practical problems which arise from the existence in a specific areal setting of a unique combination of natural and human resources, considered both quantitatively and qualitatively; for all applied problems of development are in part regional or local problems. Secondly, there are those problems of a more theoretical nature, relating to the aims, methods, and processes of development, which have received a good deal of attention from economists and other social scientists over the last twenty years or so. Both types of sets of problems seem to demand full consideration in any specific applied case of development. Just as there are dangers in the indiscriminate application of theoretical models and procedures to a particular case study, so any attempt to comment on development in an area without at least some acquaintance with economic development theory is likely to be both ingenuous and misleading.

I have tried in these pages to deal briefly, simply, and in a very preliminary way with some of the more important practical and theoretical problems of development in the tropical sectors of the developing world and, more specifically, to emphasize those issues which seem to me best able to provide the necessary interdisciplinary background for the study by geographers of economic development in these areas. I have therefore included at least some discussion of all material, whether 'geographical' or not, that seems to be relevant to an understanding of the problems of tropical development. The more theoretical material, however, has been

treated very briefly and introduced only where absolutely necessary; and on many occasions I have done little more than simply
to refer to the theoretical discussion in the literature and to indicate
the more significant areas of disagreement and intellectual controversy. Any reader wishing to delve more deeply into the theoretical
material or requiring a more rigorous treatment of any particular
line of inquiry will find this possible by following up the relevant
literature referred to in the text. As for the detailed factual and
descriptive material, this is most conveniently to be found in those
major regional geographical texts – by, for instance, James (1963),
Hance (1964), Spate (1967), and Fisher (1964) – upon which all
geographical thinking and writing on tropical development must
be based.

In writing this introductory book on tropical development I
have kept in mind the needs of undergraduates concerned regionally
or systematically with any part of the tropical world, and the rapidly
increasing number of graduates studying in the various Area Study
Programmes for Latin America, Africa, South Asia, and South-
east Asia. Much of the material and most of the ideas presented
here have grown out of a number of lecture and seminar courses,
and are set against my own experience in living and working in
various parts of the Asian and African tropics over a continuous
period of some twelve years. My first-hand experience of the
American tropics, however, has been limited to visits to Costa Rica,
Venezuela, and Trinidad during the summer of 1965, so that a good
deal of what I have to say is highly selective and possibly even
more biased by my own tropical contacts than I realize. Certainly
I am aware that much of what I have written here is controversial,
especially where I seem to have taken a perhaps unusually opti-
mistic standpoint over the potentialities for development in tropical
countries. On a subject so vast and ultimately so practical a good
deal of what one says must necessarily involve questionable hy-
potheses and over-simplifications. Yet I have thought it best to
give my own views on tropical development, finding this practice
to be more successful in stimulating discussion than is any attempt
to provide a comprehensive or systematic academic analysis of the
geography of tropical areas. And it is above all to stimulate further

thought, discussion, and field work in tropical lands that this book has been written.

My chief debt is to former undergraduates and colleagues of the University of Malaya (Singapore) and University of Ibadan (Nigeria), with whom I lived and worked from 1952 to 1963 and from whom I learned much of what I know about the tropics. The authorities of both universities also made it possible for me to travel in various other parts of South-east Asia and Africa. I also owe a great deal to the encouragement and help given to me over many years by Professor R. W. Steel, Professor C. A. Fisher, and Professor A. E. Smailes. A number of experts have been kind enough to read and comment on parts of the typescript; and for this I am particularly grateful to Dr B. W. Atkinson, Dr D. R. Harris, Dr N. Harris, Mr D. C. Ledger, and Dr A. Warren. Responsibility for any errors of fact or interpretation, however, remains mine alone. To the Central Research Fund of the University of London I am indebted for a grant enabling me to visit the American tropics during the summer of 1965. Much of the work of typing was undertaken by Mrs C. Hartley, Miss L. Bull and, in the final stages, by Mr G. Brannon, Senior Draughtsman in the Department of Geography, Queen Mary College, University of London.

Queen Mary College   B. W. HODDER
University of London
1967

Introduction: Some Definitions

Although there is still no generally accepted theory of *economic development*, all definitions imply that it involves raising living standards: it is, for example, 'a social process which results in a cumulative increase in levels of consumption' (Belshaw, 1956: xv). It can thus occur in all countries, including those already highly developed. But though many of the theories and applied problems of economic development may be the same for economically advanced as for developing countries, important differences of approach or attitude seem to be needed. The difference between the economics of developed and developing countries 'lies not so much in the problems which confront them (after all, both types are actively trying to raise real income per head) as in the assumptions which one "naturally" makes in considering the problem – and all too often fails to specify explicitly . . . For understanding the economic problems of underdeveloped countries one needs to develop a new set of instinctive assumptions' (Reddaway, 1963: 1–2). Again, the results of any analysis made of an economy in which the subsistence sector is negligible are likely to need modification when applied to those economies, common in the tropics, in which subsistence production is important. For a number of reasons, indeed, it may well be desirable to distinguish between economic development (associated with economically and socially backward societies) and economic growth (associated with advanced or developed societies). These pages will deal solely with economic development applied to countries at a relatively low level of development and in an environment – the humid tropics – which many writers believe to contain obstacles likely to complicate and even to frustrate the application of measures for economic development.

By *underdevelopment* is meant that condition, characteristic of developing countries, in which levels and growth rates of real

Table 1. Per capita *national income of chief countries wholly or substantially within the humid tropics*

	Per capita income 1962, $U.S.		Per capita income 1962, $U.S.
	Tropical America		
Brazil	129	Nicaragua	180
Guyana	218	Barbados	245
Colombia	222	Cuba	169
French Guayana	193	Dominica	205
Surinam	179	Dominican Republic	209
Venezuela	671	Grenada	187
British Honduras	195	Guadaloupe	166
Panama	376	Haiti	179
Costa Rica	291	Jamaica	373
El Salvador	176	Martinique	189
Guatemala	151	Puerto Rico	685
Honduras	182	Trinidad and Tobago	503
	Tropical Africa		
Dahomey	49	Malawi	49
Gambia	46	Moçambique	42
Ghana	179	Rwanda	40
Guinea	39	Rhodesia	156
Ivory Coast	89	Uganda	57
Liberia	43	Tanzania	50
Mali	37	Zambia	96
Niger	36	Angola	52
Nigeria	66	Cameroun	50
Portuguese Guinea	40	Central African Republic	41
Senegal	44	Chad	39
Sierra Leone	47	Congo Brazzaville	50
Togo	44	Congo Kinshasa	67
Upper Volta	39	Rio Muni	49
Burundi	29	Gabon	72
Kenya	72		
Malagasy	60		

Table 1.—continued

	Per capita income 1962, $U.S.		Per capita income 1962. $U.S.
Tropical Asia			
Ceylon	122	Singapore	406
India	69	Philippines	200
Pakistan	54	Portuguese Timor	112
Brunei	59	Thailand	88
Burma	50	Viet-Nam North	45
Cambodia	49	Viet-Nam South	53
Indonesia	49	Fiji	61
Laos	47	New Guinea	29
Malaysia	215	Papua	32

income and capital per head of population are low by comparison with Western Europe, North America, and Australia (Table 1). Data showing *per capita* national incomes are frequently used to distinguish between developed and developing countries, many of the former having annual *per capita* national incomes of £420 (1,000 dollars U.S.) or more, while the latter may show figures of well under £65 (150 dollars U.S.). A number of weaknesses in this concept must be noted, however. National income and population data are themselves often no more than the crudest of estimates. Furthermore, *per capita* national income normally refers to standard of living defined only in a quantifiable sense. Then *per capita* national income data are perhaps not fully relevant in a situation where subsistence production is important, perhaps dominant; and the average level of *per capita* income cannot show the distribution of national income among classes or groups (Bauer and Yamey, 1957: 16–24) – a consideration of some significance in a country like Venezuela where the extremes of income are very widely separated. The low *per capita* income figures for developing countries, moreover, are not to be thought of as always static, declining or only very slowly increasing. As Myint (1964) has noted, this viewpoint has affected most current theories of economic development and arises from notions about 'vicious circles',

B

the need for the 'big push', from the Malthusian spectre of population pressure in developing countries, and from popular notions of developing countries as closed, traditional societies. But in many developing countries – especially in Latin America – *per capita* income growth rates are very high indeed.

Other definitions of a developing country emphasize the potentialities for development, while another describes a developing country as one 'characterized by (i) mass poverty which is chronic and not the result of some temporary misfortune, and (ii) by obsolete methods of production and social organization, which means that the poverty is not entirely due to poor natural resources and hence could presumably be lessened by methods already proved in other countries' (Staley, 1954: 13). It is also possible to define underdevelopment on the basis of occupational structure, a developing country being said to have at least 50 per cent of its gainfully employed males engaged in agriculture, fishing, and forestry.

Perhaps the most satisfactory way of defining underdevelopment for the purposes of the present study, however, is simply to refer to certain characteristics which are commonly, though not invariably, found in a developing country in the tropics:

> (i) low life expectancy at birth, high infant mortality rates, poor health, and illiteracy;
> (ii) low *per capita* output, together with poverty and indebtedness;
> (iii) subsistence production generally important;
> (iv) economies non-diversified and geared to primary production;
> (v) little manufacturing industry;
> (vi) no large-scale application of scientific and technological methods to agriculture or industry;
> (vii) narrowness of markets.

Many of these and other variables have been mapped in a volume which aims at casting some light on the meanings of the terms 'development' and 'underdevelopment' by 'analysing them into some commensurable components and showing the world pattern of distribution of these components by countries' (Ginsberg, 1961: 5).

Yet it is easy to over-generalize about developing countries, ignoring differences between densely populated and highly populated countries and between countries at widely differing levels of economic achievement. Perhaps the first thing to bear in mind about developing countries, indeed, is that 'beyond the broad common fact of poverty it is rarely safe to make generalizations about them without first specifying the type of underdeveloped country one is considering' (Myint, 1964: 14); in such circumstances there is clearly no point in looking for a single theory to cover all developing countries.

With these reservations in mind it is worth noting that developing countries cover much of Asia, Africa, and Latin America, as well as many parts of eastern and southern Europe well outside the tropics. Shannon (1957) calculates that 63 per cent of the world's population is underdeveloped and covers 54 per cent of the world's land surface, and Fryer (1958) estimates that as much as 70 per cent of the world's population is underdeveloped. While those countries lying outside the tropics are not referred to here, it should be remembered that many of the characteristics and problems discussed are not in fact peculiar to *tropical* developing countries. It is significant that several United Nations documents define developing countries to include all countries in Africa, the Americas, and Asia, except the Republic of South Africa, Canada, the United States, and Japan.

The area with which this study is concerned is for the sake of brevity termed the *tropics*, but is in fact restricted to the *humid tropics*, defined for the purposes of this study as in Table 1, which lists those countries whose populations lie wholly or substantially within the humid tropics, so that a country like Niger is included (most of its population living in the southern humid tropical parts of the country) while Sudan is excluded (most of the population there living in the northern desert or semi-desert areas). There has been considerable discussion in recent years about the precise limits of the humid tropical region (Fosberg *et alia*, 1961; Garnier, 1961; Gaussen and Legris, 1963; Gourou, 1966). One way of defining the humid tropics is to refer to the A type climates of Köppen (1936). Gourou (1966) takes the mean temperature of 64·4° F (18° C) for the coolest month and the boundaries of those areas where 'cultivation is possible without irrigation' to delimit his humid tropical region, though he emphasizes the need to accept these limits cautiously and not always to adhere to them rigidly.

While these limits are perfectly satisfactory for all working purposes, more recent attempts have understandably been made to express the latter part of Gourou's definition – 'agriculture possible without irrigation' – more precisely. This is admittedly a rather unsatisfactory phrase because the need to irrigate is clearly dependent upon so many variables, such as choice of crop and methods of cultivation. Garnier (Fosberg *et alia*, 1961) has suggested criteria involving air moisture content and temperature. Garnier's view, briefly stated, is that humid tropical conditions may be identified by reference to a climatic situation in which the mean monthly temperature for at least eight months of the year equals or exceeds 68° F (20° C); the vapour pressure and relative humidity for at least six months of the year average at least 20 millibars and 65 per cent respectively; and the mean annual rainfall totals at least 40 inches (1,016 mm), precipitation being at least 2·95 inches (75 mm) for each of six months during the year. In the same paper Küchler puts forward his views based upon vegetation criteria.

The differences between the many suggested limits to the humid tropics are least in West Africa and America and greatest along the northern boundary of the Asian tropics, especially in India, and to a lesser extent in East Africa. These areal differences in the degree of coincidence of the various limits are explained partly by the contrasts between climatic patterns on the western and eastern margins of continents, and partly by the complications introduced by position and elevation. Whether or not to include the tropical highlands in the humid tropical area is arguable. Garnier excludes elevations of over about 3,300 feet (1,000 m) because such areas are not strictly 'humid tropical' in his sense. On the other hand, there does appear to be some justification for including at least the tropical uplands of intermediate altitudes, for it is usually inconvenient in practice to exclude the many upland enclaves such as those found in South-east Asia and Central America.

Much of the current discussion about the precise limits of the humid tropics is admittedly academic and of no relevance to the present study except in so far as it helps to clarify notions about the region and affects the possibilities of generalization. The environmental variations within the tropics are immense; and one of the chief conclusions arising from a comparative study of the tropical world is that it is rarely possible to formulate useful generalizations which are valid both for a country like Malaya, within the tropical rain forest or equatorial region, and for a country like Nigeria, most of which lies within the savanna tropics where differences between the wet and dry seasons profoundly affect the life and welfare of the people.

CHAPTER 1

Natural Resources and Tropical Development

The significance of natural resources. In assessing the role of natural resources in economic development, a number of writers strongly criticize the 'geographical school' (by which is meant the 'natural resource' school) of economic development studies for its crude determinism, its tendency to discuss physical factors at length but non-physical and especially economic factors hardly at all, and for appearing to ignore altogether the theoretical framework of economic development studies. Examples of this 'natural resource' school of thought can be found in the work of Semple (1911), Huntington (1915) and Parker (1961).

Some authorities would go so far as deliberately to disregard the role of natural or physical resources in economic development. It is argued, for instance, that economic growth is determined by capital – 'the engine of growth' – and is thus largely the result of an interaction between savings and the capital–output ratio (Harrod, 1948). Analyses such as this leave nature out of explicit consideration and give little if any attention to the role of natural resources, either qualitatively or quantitatively. While natural resources may receive some mention in theoretical analyses, their explicit consideration is commonly believed to be unnecessary (Kuznets, 1959; Meade, 1961). It is argued not only that land is a fixed factor but also that the old Ricardian model in which economic growth is limited by land – and especially by the poverty of natural resources – has been completely disproved by the experiences of nineteenth-century Europe and North America. Increasing returns and technical progress have always upset the Ricardian model. Even where countries have resource deficiencies, it should be possible for them to draw upon the resources of other countries, for instance by trade. Trade clearly opens up the possibility of breaking through

8

any constraints imposed by natural resource deficiencies and links growth more intimately and directly to population and capital accumulation, both of which leave a continuing potential for economic expansion (Barnett and Morse, 1963). Again, it is possible to compensate for lack of natural resources by the substitution of capital or labour skills and by social and economic improvements, including education – 'investment in human capital' – managerial capacity, and economies of scale (Kindleberger, 1966: 53–4).

Even the most cursory glance at natural resources – water, forests, soils, minerals, or power – reveals that there is indeed little correlation between the occurrence of these resources and the level of economic development in any particular tropical country. The presence or absence of naturally occurring material resources in no way immutably determines the economic development of a country. 'Since the changing fortunes of many countries and regions have not been connected with the discovery or exhaustion of natural resources within their territories, the fortuitous distribution of these resources certainly does not provide the only, and probably not even the principal, explanation of differences in development and prosperity' (Bauer and Yamey, 1957: 46–7). High productivity and prosperity can be achieved without abundant natural resources. While their possession may give certain initial advantages, plentiful natural resources are not necessarily associated with prosperity, nor are they a precondition for economic development.

It is true that many analyses grossly exaggerate the role of natural resources in economic development; and this is perhaps especially true of the work of geographers. In spite of his interest in the physical environment and in the broader aspects of man–environment relationships in specific areal settings, the geographer cannot afford to argue the overriding importance of the physical factors in development; he cannot associate himself with the school of thought which puts the emphasis upon natural resources and claims that the level of economic development in a country is somehow causally connected with its natural resource endowment; nor can the geographer afford to view economic development simply in terms of how far the natural resources in a country are developed or utilized. To abstract the purely physical factors in applied development studies is to falsify as surely as is to abstract the purely economic, political, or social factors.

On the other hand, it can be argued that there is no justification for ignoring natural resources altogether in any development analysis, and that there are real dangers in any tendency to underestimate the role of natural resources in tropical development. That any analysis of the applied problems of economic development cannot afford to accept natural resources as 'given' or 'fixed' is clear from the widely accepted need for the conservation of resources, both exhaustible and renewable: the problems of soil erosion and forest degeneration, for example, vividly illustrate the consequences of neglecting the utilization and conservation of resources. Again, the theoretical arguments for giving scant attention to natural resources in tropical development studies may fall down in practice; for while in theory tropical low-income countries can make up for the lack of certain natural resources by trade, capital, and skills substitution, in practice most of these countries do not have the external trading potential, capital, or labour skills to enable them to make up for limited natural resources in this way (Barnett and Morse, 1963). Then again, a good deal of the available empirical evidence supports the contention that natural resources are by no means an irrelevance, especially in the early stages of development. In Venezuela the *per capita* income is higher than in most other tropical countries, and this fact is clearly and causally connected with the exploitation of rich oil resources in that country. Oil is generally believed to be a dominant factor in explaining the relatively high *per capita* income in Venezuela, though several writers point out that the lack of natural resources of this kind cannot in any way help to explain the low income levels of most other Latin American countries.

Thus while the relative lack or abundance of natural resources is never a determining factor in economic development; and while the natural endowment is usually less important to this process than is the human contribution; natural resources may constitute an important factor in planning and decision-making as far as economic development in low-income tropical countries is concerned. This, at least, is the standpoint taken in subsequent chapters. The importance of natural resources to developing countries is relatively greater than to the developed countries of the world. In low-income tropical countries rich natural resources can have great significance as sources of exports and foreign investments, while poor resources may form some limitation to growth. The quantity and character of natural resources may well have an important initial effect on patterns of production and levels of income (Chenery, in Berrill, 1965).

The study of natural resources. Perhaps the most striking impression received from any study of the natural resources of the tropical world is the urgent need for more information about those resources. Such an impression remains true, not only for the assessment of mineral and power resources but also for the quantitative and qualitative analysis of moisture resources, vegetation, and soils. This point will be made several times in the following pages and is underlined by the reading of the current development plans of any tropical country. It is now widely realized that not enough is known about most of the natural resources of countries in the tropics, and that topographical, geological, hydrological, soil, and ecological surveys are vital prerequisites to any successful attempt at resource utilization. Though precise, accurate data are often very difficult and expensive to obtain, and though, also, it is true that these resources cannot easily acquire commercial value, further research into the various natural resources and their utilization is an immediate and basic need everywhere. Without such information, as has been abundantly proved on a number of occasions over the last two decades or so, all development schemes can be undertaken only with a serious risk of failure.

Yet while it is clearly convenient for the purposes of analysis to treat particular natural resources separately, it is perhaps worth pointing out that this is a somewhat arbitrary and misleading procedure. In any particular applied problem of economic development the interdependence of natural resources may be so close that it is impossible ever to single out any one factor or element as the crucial one for study. Water supply and hydro-electric power;

forests, soils, and vegetation: these are particularly obvious cases where the various kinds of natural resources are intimately dependent on one another. Furthermore, in any consideration of the applied problems of development of any of these natural resources, non-physical elements – human resources, economic factors or political considerations of one kind or another – are necessary to any full understanding. While it is convenient to write of the natural environment and natural resources associated with that environment as being quite distinct from the non-physical environment and resources, the truth is that all applied problems of economic development demand the examination of the 'total' environment, with its complex of resources and factors – natural, human, and capital.

Again, the quantity and quality of natural resources vary considerably from place to place, and it is perhaps not too much to say that every natural resource or group of resources poses a unique problem within the context of a specific area. This question of regional variation is of considerable geographical interest and is of great importance to development planning. The non-physical elements in the utilization of any natural resource are numerous, and may well be determining, but they operate within the limits and possibilities set by the nature and location of that resource. Mineral exploitation may be limited by difficulties of access. And in developing hydro-electric power potential, many of the best areas from the point of view of rainfall régime – that is, with rain all the year round – are associated in the tropics with the most difficult forest vegetation, the lowest population densities and low economic activity generally; many of the best potential sites from the physical point of view are therefore limited by their location.

Such areal differentiation in natural resource distribution is relevant not only to a continent or region but also to the political state within which the natural resources lie. In practice, the development of natural resources normally operates only within the context of a nation state, and the uneven distribution of mineral and power potential among different states is a matter of serious concern to those charged with planning. Many tropical developing countries, notably in West Africa and Central America, encompass only very small areas, and so may possess a narrow range and, perhaps, some important omissions in their pattern of natural resources. The territorial state context is also of importance here because some natural resources may be partly or even wholly private property: in the case of minerals, it may well be that the country in which the mineral lies will receive little or no financial benefit from its exploitation by concerns operating from another country (Barnett and Morse, 1963).

It is, indeed, an important principle in the relationship between natural resources on the one hand and economic development on the other, that standards of world comparison are not necessarily relevant to the level of or prospects for economic development in a country. In this sense a map of the distribution over the world of any natural resource is almost an irrelevance in economic development planning. What matters more to a particular country is the occurrence of these resources relative to its own size, population, and economy. This is most clearly illustrated in the case of mineral and power resources. In Asia, Brunei's economic development has been overwhelmingly the result of her production of petroleum which, though small by world standards, provides a large part of her national income. Similarly, although the production of natural phosphates in Togo (West Africa) is small by world standards, the discovery and exploitation of phosphates in Togo has proved to be probably the most important single event in that country's economic history, making it possible to add some 50 per cent to the value of its export trade within a few years.

.   .   .   .   .

While it is to some extent arbitrary to treat natural resources separately from the other factors of production in any analysis of the applied problems of economic development, there is perhaps more justification for doing this in the tropical world about which we still know very little and where the implications of natural resources for economic development have not yet been fully worked out. Yet even though it is necessary to emphasize our ignorance rather than our knowledge about the physical factors and natural resources of the tropics, it is also necessary to emphasize that there are no grounds for assuming that natural resources are anywhere a limitation to economic development or an excuse for the present relatively low standard of living in any part of the tropics: 'the Creator has not divided the world into two sectors, developed and underdeveloped, the former being more richly blessed with natural resources than the latter' (Bauer and Yamey, 1957: 46). The early traditional viewpoint of the tropics as having exceptionally rich natural resources and the 'modern' view of the tropics as poor or inferior in natural resources are equally false. The problem of natural resources is not that they are especially poor or inadequate in tropical countries but rather that the facts about these resources are little known and that their significance for economic development in any specific area is not fully understood. The standpoint adopted in the pages that follow is that any realistic analysis of an applied situation in tropical economic development must start from the assumption that the natural resource base is potentially adequate for substantial development, given sufficient knowledge about these resources and a ready adaptation of planning to the opportunities and limitations set by them. The next two chapters carry this point a little farther by discussing some of the characteristics and implications for development of the major natural resources of the tropical world.

CHAPTER 2
Natural Resources: Climate and Water Supply

Climatic types. The term 'tropical climate' popularly conjures up a picture of high temperature and humidity, constant rainfall, and unrelieved monotony. But of few parts of the tropics is this an accurate picture. Indeed, it is impossible to make any useful generalizations about the climate of the tropical world as a whole, not only because of the sheer size of the area but also because of complications introduced by the unequal distribution of land and sea, by great regional variations in relief and aspect, and by important positional differences in relation to extra-tropical areas.

At least three broad climatic types may be distinguished – the equatorial lowland, tropical monsoon, and tropical savanna climates (Table 2). The chief features of the true *equatorial lowland*

Table 2. *Three selected stations: rainfall and temperature*

	J.	F.	M.	A.	M.	J.	J.	A.	S.	O.	N.	D.	Year
Belem (Brazil)													
Temp., °F	78	77	78	78	79	79	79	79	79	79	80	79	79
Temp., °C	25·6	25	25·6	25·6	26·1	26·1	26·1	26·1	26·1	26·1	26·7	26·1	26·1
Rainfall, inches	7·6	13·4	17·0	17·8	11·8	9·0	2·3	2·8	0·6	0·5	0·6	2·6	89·6
Rainfall, mm	193	340	432	452	300	229	58	71	15	13	15	66	2,276
Kano (Nigeria)													
Temp., °F	71	75	83	88	87	83	79	78	79	81	77	72	80
Temp., °C	21·7	23·9	28·3	31·1	30·6	28·3	26·1	25·6	26·1	27·2	25	22·2	26·7
Rainfall, inches	0·1	0·1	0·1	0·4	2·7	4·6	8·1	12·2	5·6	0·5	0·1	0	35·1
Rainfall, mm	3	3	3	10	69	117	206	310	142	13	3	0	892
Bombay (India)													
Temp., °F	75	75	79	82	85	84	81	80	80	82	81	78	80
Temp., °C	23·9	23·9	26·1	27·8	29·4	28·9	27·2	26·7	26·7	27·8	27·2	25·6	26·7
Rainfall, inches	0·1	0·1	0·1	0·1	0·7	19·1	24·3	13·4	10·4	2·5	0·5	0·1	71·2
Rainfall, mm	3	3	3	3	18	485	617	340	264	64	13	3	1,809

climate are a mean annual rainfall of over 60 inches (1,594 mm), no true dry season, high relative humidities, and uniformly high temperatures. Belem (Brazil) is an example of a station with this kind of climate. It will be noted that the rainfall is by no means evenly distributed throughout the year. More commonly, definite double maxima occur, and there may even be a near approach to a short dry season. This kind of seasonal rhythm of rainfall is responsible for most variations within the type. In general, however, conditions are ideal for rain formation throughout most of the year in the equatorial lowlands. These are primarily areas of rising air, a fact which results in part from the lifting of trade-wind air masses along the inter-tropical convergence zone, and in part from local convection in the warm, humid, unstable doldrums air. Yet this climatic type is not solely a reflection of latitude, for several places on the equator, such as parts of East Africa and the coastal fringes of Equador and Peru, do not experience these conditions, whereas other places some way from the equator, notably the east coast of Malagasy, experience typically equatorial lowland climatic conditions.

In the *tropical monsoon climate*, rainfall seasonality is very well marked, though annual total amounts of rainfall may be even greater than in the equatorial lowlands, and this to some extent makes up for the rainfall's restricted duration throughout the year. This climatic type may be looked upon as resembling the equatorial lowland type in that the total amount of rainfall is large, though in its annual distribution the pattern of rainfall more nearly resembles the tropical savanna, or tropical wet-and-dry climate. As for temperatures, these commonly reach higher maximum figures than in the equatorial lowland zone, but the mean annual range is much greater, reaching to as much as 15° F (8° C). The tropical monsoon climate occurs chiefly in Asia on the Malabar coast, the coast of Burma, southern Ceylon, and in much of the Philippines, but is also significant on part of the western Guinea coast of Africa and in the lower Amazon valley.

Bombay experiences a tropical monsoon climate, but it will be noted that there is no simple division of the year into a wet, cooler season and a dry, hotter season. It is, in fact, more accurate to talk of the tropical monsoon of the Malabar coast as having four seasons. From December to March the south-east monsoon winds are blowing off the coast, rainfall is slight and temperatures relatively low; April and May comprise the transitional hot period when rainfall is slight, but temperatures and relative humidities are very high; from June to September the south-west monsoon is blowing, rainfall is heavy, relative humidities are high, but temperatures are reduced; and finally, during October and November, when the monsoon is retreating, rainfall is slight, humidities remain high, and temperatures increase (Spate, 1967).

Taken together, the equatorial lowland and tropical monsoon climatic types affect barely 10 per cent of the world's land surface, whereas the third main climatic type – the tropical savanna climate – alone covers over 10 per cent of the land surface of the world.

In the *tropical savanna climate*, illustrated in Table 2 by data for Kano (Nigeria), the rains, which are not of monsoonal origin, are concentrated into one or more parts of the year so that there is at least one definite dry season of variable duration, increasing in length and intensity with distance from the equator. The annual rainfall is less than in equatorial or monsoonal regions and may be as little as 20 inches (508 mm), though an average rainfall of 24 inches (610 mm) is sometimes taken as the minimum annual rainfall for the humid tropics. As for temperatures, the mean annual range is considerable, often exceeding 20° F (11° C).

This division of the humid tropical climate into three types is a useful conventional classification, but it tends to exaggerate the sharpness of the transition from the equatorial lowland type into the savanna or monsoon types. The transition is in fact gradual, sometimes complicated and often very difficult to describe. Furthermore, this three-fold classification of tropical climatic types tends to oversimplify the whole question of the extent and timing of the monthly humid and non-humid periods. In spite of the limitations of expressing seasonality in statistical terms, there is much to be said for using a classification like that of Lauer (1952), whose work depends upon the use of De Martonne's index of aridity in compounding the formula $20 \rightleftharpoons \dfrac{12p}{t + 10}$ to calculate indices for separate months, where 'p' represents the average monthly precipitation in millimetres and 't' represents the average monthly temperature in ° C. On this basis, Lauer classifies the humid tropical climates into five types: *equatorial*, in which there are 12 months with an index over 20; *equatorial with one dry period*, in which 7 months have an index over 20; *equatorial with two dry periods*, in which 5 months have an index over 20; *tropical dry winter*; and *tropical dry summer*. This classification indicates the diversity of climatic types within the tropics and emphasizes what is probably the most important criterion for any classification of tropical climates in economic development analyses – the length and timing of the humid period.

Climatic characteristics. Anomalies in rainfall seasonality are common throughout the tropics and the theoretical incidence of rainfall in relation to the movement of the overhead sun is in practice the exception rather than the rule. Thus in Guyana the two rainfall maxima coincide not with the highest but with the lowest altitudes of the noonday sun. Then there are local 'dry' areas in northern Venezuela, north-eastern Brazil, southern Burma, and in West Africa (southern Ghana and Togo). These anomalies are often explicable in terms of relief, the irregular distribution of land and sea, or the effects of ocean currents. Generally speaking, Africa's climate is modified in this way less than are the other two sectors because of the relatively small contrasts in relief, the compactness, and the relatively straight coastline of that continent.

The variation of rainfall from year to year may be considerable and unpredictable, and is of particular relevance to agriculture and water supply. As a general principle, annual reliability of rainfall increases as the rainfall decreases, and this being so it is most strikingly illustrated from the drier fringes of the savanna tropics. At Maiduguri in northern Nigeria the average rainfall for the forty-two years up to 1957 was 25·7 inches (653 mm), but it has in some years been less than 15 inches (381 mm) and in others over 35 inches (889 mm) – a significant degree of variation where the total rainfall is so critically low. Some of the most interesting work on rainfall reliability has referred to East and South-east Africa (Manning, 1956; Kenworthy and Glover, 1958; Kenworthy, 1964; and Gregory, 1964).

Another important characteristic of rainfall in the tropics is its high intensity, though really high degrees of intensity – over 2 inches (50 mm) an hour – are only common over short periods of less than one hour. In the humid tropics generally, local falls of 2–2·5 inches (50–64 mm) in one hour can be expected once in two years, and the maximum falls over a full hour recorded in Java and Singapore are 3·7 inches (94 mm) and 4·7 inches (119 mm) respectively (Beckinsale, 1957). Nevertheless, even very short periods of high intensity falls can have serious effects on water supplies, soils, and crops. Moreover, though rainfall intensities for periods of up to one hour may be no higher in tropical than in middle latitudes, intensities for longer periods are significantly higher (Mohr and van Baren, 1954).

As for temperatures, these are more striking in their uniformity than in their height, but everywhere plant growth is possible throughout the year. In the equatorial lowland tropics the mean monthly range of temperature is rarely more than 5° F (8·3° C). In the savanna tropics both the seasonal and diurnal ranges are much greater. Nevertheless, maximum temperatures are lower throughout the humid tropics than in the dry tropics or sub-tropics, especially near the coasts or where other water bodies, such as lakes or stretches of forest, act as thermal regulators and so limit temperature ranges (Richards, 1952).

The differences in relative humidity patterns between the equatorial lowland climate on the one hand and the tropical savanna and monsoon climates on the other are of great importance from the point of view of human energy, comfort, and health: relative humidities are continuously high in the former, but show strong seasonal variations in the latter. Diurnal variations are considerable everywhere, however, relative humidities usually being lowest in the early afternoon and highest in the very early morning, when they may reach 100 per cent.

Although it is a common belief that the tropics suffer from severe wind storms, such winds are confined to certain very localized areas; except under certain seasonal and local influences and in the neighbourhood of cyclones, wind speeds are generally under 10 mph (16 kph). The regions that suffer most from tropical cyclones are, in fact, largely outside or on the edge of the humid

C

tropics; these cyclones normally form only outside the belt between 7° N and 7° S and are most common in the West Indies and Central America, Malagasy, the west and east coasts of India, the west coast of Burma, the east coast of the Indochinese peninsula, and in the northern Philippines. Apart from tropical cyclones, which are important here chiefly because of the damage to life and property they can inflict, there are other winds of local importance, such as the *harmattan* of West Africa, which blows as a cool, dry wind towards the Gulf of Guinea from the Saharan fringes during the November to February period, and brings cooler weather with very low relative humidities to much of the West African interior, and occasionally to as far south as the coast itself. Though the *harmattan* can affect the distribution of crops by exerting a marked desiccating effect, and may be one of the most important factors determining the nature of vegetation in any given area, its importance is more often seen in terms of human comfort.

In contrast to common notions, solar radiation is not necessarily greater in tropical than in temperate latitudes; indeed, near ground levels in the equatorial lowlands clouds may reflect over half the solar radiation incident upon them. Bernard (1945) has noted that in the central Congo Basin the mean and maximum values for total radiation seem to be no higher than those recorded in temperate regions during the summer months, and he ascribes the relatively low total radiation in this part of Africa to the high content of water vapour and to impurities such as smoke from bush fires in the lower atmosphere. Even where light intensity is greater in tropical than in temperate latitudes, this advantage is offset by the greater length of days in middle latitudes during the growing season.

Differences in the timing and total amount of solar radiation can affect the hardness and composition of grains and crop yields. Thus the highest yields of rice are produced not in the humid tropics but in such mid-latitude countries as Japan, Italy, and Spain. This is due partly to longer hours of sunshine, which greatly benefit the photosynthetic processes of rice plants. Even within the tropics rice yields produced in the rainy season may be lower than those produced during the dry season when the percentage of cloud is less.

The length of day varies but little within the tropics, but what variations there are can be most significant agriculturally, for even the smallest differences in length of day may be enough to provide stimulus for flowering. In Malaya the photosensitivity of padi varieties affects very much the suitability of any one variety for a particular area. Rice, in fact, provides an outstanding example of a crop affected by photoperiodism, and Jagoe (1952) shows that short periods of extra illumination, coincident with daylight, which maintain a daily light period of more than 21 hours 30 minutes, inhibit or very greatly delay inflorescence development in three typical and widely grown varieties of Malayan rice. Indeed, what evidence there is seems to suggest that tropical plants are more sensitive to small changes in the length of day than are plants of higher latitudes, though internal as well as environmental factors probably play some part in explaining other widely different types of behaviour found among tropical plants (Tempany and Grist, 1958).

The main climatic factors relevant to this study of tropical development are rainfall, atmospheric humidity, temperature, light intensity, and light duration. In the tropics, rainfall rather than temperature determines seasons, and it is the amount and timing of rainfall which forms the chief criterion for distinguishing the various tropical climatic types. On the other hand, it has been demonstrated that in the geographical distribution of crops, temperature determines the limits north and south of the equator within which particular crops can be grown; rainfall and atmospheric humidity determine the distribution of plants within particular zones; while light intensity and the duration of illumination profoundly influence plant behaviour. Moreover, much of the literature refers to climate considered as an abstraction, although the limitations of using average rainfall, temperature, and similar data as a basis for agricultural planning are now widely recognized. The local climate, or the actual meteorological conditions occurring in a particular year over a strictly limited area are of more agricultural significance than are the theoretical abstractions of climate. Finally, the micro-climate and eco-climate, referring to the conditions immediately surrounding a plant, are probably of especial importance under tropical conditions. Further applied research in micro-climate and eco-climate is urgently needed.

Water supply. At first sight, it might seem paradoxical that the tropics – at least the humid tropics as defined in this study – should suffer from difficulties in water supply: after all, the humid tropics are sometimes defined as hot, wet lands where agriculture is possible without irrigation (p. 6). Yet water is probably the most important single determinant of tropical land use. The supply of moisture for agriculture is commonly unsatisfactory – either too much or insufficient – and this is often due to some of the climatic characteristics already noted.

The unequal distribution of rainfall throughout the year is most obviously a problem in the savanna or monsoon tropics where there are distinct and sometimes prolonged dry seasons and where the moisture balance between rainfall and evapotranspiration losses is so crucial agriculturally. Yet even in the equatorial tropics, certain parts of the year are normally drier than others; and this seasonal fluctuation of rainfall is often the climatic variable of greatest agricultural significance. The variability of rainfall can also have serious effects locally, even in an equatorial country. In north-western Malaya, for example, rainfall variations resulted in a lean year for peasants in 1949; in Kedah only 25 per cent of the anticipated rice crop was realized, and in the Kota Star and Kuala Muda districts there was a mass exodus of padi planters searching for employment. In Perlis, too, the early onset of the seasonal dry spell caused the complete destruction of approximately 43,430 acres (17,590 ha) of padi (Hodder, 1959). This kind of disaster is very common and many examples could be cited from at least some part of the Indo-Pakistan subcontinent in most years. In many parts of the humid tropics croplands are unirrigated and so depend chiefly on the direct rainfall. What irrigation works there are have in many cases only a supplementary effect on water supply in conserving and distributing rain-water. If the rains come too soon or too late these irrigation works can do little to save the situation.

Problems in water supply are also caused by high rainfall intensities which have two main effects as far as water supply is concerned. In the first place, much of the water is lost by rapid run-off; and it is unfortunate that in many tropical areas the very rains which are sufficient in amount to contribute significantly to soil moisture are those in which rainfall intensities are high. Secondly, local variations in rainfall are great. Even within a small geographical area some districts may be short of water while others are adequately supplied or even suffering from a surplus of water.

Yet another factor affecting water supply in tropical countries is the tendency for rainfall to be interspersed between periods during which insolation is intense, so that rates of evaporation and transpiration are high and the balance of moisture available for agricultural purposes consequently reduced. And in many areas, as has been noted in Ceylon, the difficulties already inherent in a markedly seasonal rainfall are enhanced by the fact that 'drought comes in the hottest and windiest time of the year, so that loss by evaporation is very high' (Farmer, 1957: 46). Similarly, in the northern parts of West Africa the rainless months are frequently accompanied by the drying *harmattan* wind.

The limitations of using only rainfall data to measure moisture conditions have encouraged the search for formulae leading to moisture indices, and the importance of considering evaporation and transpiration in assessing moisture resources has been emphasized by Thornthwaite (1948) and others. Garnier (1958, 1960, 1961) has illustrated this for West Africa, making use of the concept of potential evapotranspiration, and from his work it is possible to obtain some idea of the problems involved in the utilization of moisture resources in West Africa, at least in so far as these problems are climatically derived. Without irrigation, Garnier concludes, full advantage of the favourable temperatures for growth cannot be taken anywhere in the region because there is some period of moisture deficit in all parts of West Africa. Over more than half of Nigeria, for instance, mean annual rainfall is less than mean annual water need, a fact which limits the possibilities of irrigating all the year round and suggests the need for careful selection of localities for irrigation schemes.

Finally, the supply of water may be affected by hydrological changes. This factor has been discussed for the Rima Basin of northern Nigeria where recent increases in flood heights in the lower Rima Valley were found to have been caused by a 'deterioration of channel conditions due to excessive aggradation, itself the result of an increase in the quantities of sediment carried by the major tributaries' (Ledger, 1960: 113).

Difficulties in the supply of water for the growing of crops, then, are due to the characteristics of the rainfall – seasonality, variability, high intensity; to evaporation; and to hydrological changes. But the significance of these factors depends to a large extent upon other physical considerations. The characteristics of the land on which the rain falls – its porosity and permeability, topography, soil, and vegetation – also influence the moisture balance and may be agriculturally more important than the characteristics of the rainfall itself. Thus in Malaya the choice of localities for vegetable growing is influenced not so much by climatic considerations as by the available sites suitable from the point of view of relief, drainage, accessibility, and soil type: a clay, for instance, is usually preferred to a lighter soil because although the clay may be more difficult to work it does retain water.

Analyses of the amount and depth of groundwater resources have as yet received little attention compared with the work devoted to surface water resources. In India it has been estimated that only about 20 per cent of the available underground water resources are at present being utilized. For West Africa, Archambault (1960) has shown that underground water resources may well be of vital significance in agricultural and settlement development planning. In particular, the pockets of deep weathering in the basement complex – so widespread in West Africa – have been found to contain relatively stable water levels that can be tapped by wells. This phenomenon also often explains the existence of subterranean water supplies beneath the bed of dried-up surface streams over basement complex, notably granite, rocks. Groundwater resources are not only associated with water-bearing sedimentaries.

The relationship between forest vegetation and rainfall is controversial, but is unlikely to be very close. On the other hand, forests do undoubtedly have a significant effect, particularly in areas of marked relief, on water supply by reducing the amount of water entering streams as direct runoff. The encouragement of indigenous forest is normally included in all recommendations for the conservation of water supplies, and some writers give this point much emphasis. There is little doubt that a change from natural vegetation to cultivation normally results in 'an increased run-off, higher peak flows, reduced dry season flow and more erosion, the extent of the change depending upon the method of cultivation' (Ledger, 1960: 115).

Finally, the development and utilization of water resources may depend as much on economic, social, and political factors as upon the amount of water available. The type of crop grown is a matter of some significance because the major tropical crops – rice, rubber, coconuts, oil palm, yams, bananas, maize, sugar-cane, peppers, millets, manioc, and vegetables – have widely differing moisture requirements in amount, distribution and reliability. Although tropical rainfall is not as effective in providing soil moisture as might be supposed from total precipitation figures, water supply is often a 'problem' in the tropics only because the crop chosen is not wholly suited to the particular set of climatic, edaphic, or topographical conditions under which it is grown. Shortage of water may also be simply an expression of unsuitable methods of cultivation. Lim (1954) has noted this in the Krian district of Malaya where there is a wasteful and inefficient use of irrigation water resulting from the attempt to simulate deep swamp conditions to which the Banjarese immigrants from Celebes are used; these farmers appear to regard such conditions as an essential precondition for cultivation. All crops, however, may suffer from an excess of moisture at times and from insufficient moisture at others. The ideal conditions, in which the right amount of water is available in the right place at the right time, are only rarely achieved under natural conditions in the humid tropics.

The scarcity of information on the water resources of the tropical world reflects in part these numerous and complicated variables. Very little research, moreover, has yet been devoted to the accurate assessment of water resources in most tropical countries, either on the surface (Ledger, 1964) or underground. It is now generally realized, however, that development planning depends so much upon this information being available that a number of countries are undertaking large-scale research into their surface and underground water resources and the problems of their utilization.

For the Third Five-Year Plan of India it was estimated that the annual rainfall is equivalent to about 3,000 million acre-feet of water for the whole country. Of this amount, one-third is lost immediately by evaporation. Of the remainder, 1,350 million acre-feet flow into the river systems; 350 million acre-feet stay in the topsoil, thereby contributing directly to soil moisture; and 350 million acre-feet move down through the soil into some form of underground water storage. It is recognized, however, that much of the theoretical potential of 2000 million acre-feet can never be utilized. Of the surface water flow into rivers, for instance, it has been estimated that only one-third can be harnessed for irrigation because of local topography, flow characteristics, climate, and soil conditions – all of which impose limits on usability. At present only about 36 per cent of the usable flow of surface water is being utilized. Of the 300 million acre-feet which percolate down into porous strata and represent the annual enrichment of underground water, under 20 per cent is being utilized; and the actual amount of underground storage of water at any particular time may well be several times the annual enrichment figure of 300 million acre-feet. Geophysical investigations are now being undertaken to determine the depth of the bed-rock in various parts of the country.

Even in tropical monsoonal and savanna India, clearly, potential water resources are far from being inadequate over the country as a whole. During the next twenty to twenty-five years it is hoped that the amount of water utilized for irrigation will go up to '350–400 million acre-feet or 60 per cent of the annual supply from both surface and underground resources. That will leave adequate quantities of water for meeting probable domestic supply, industrial needs and the requirements of more power generation' (Indian Govt., 1961: 189). Assuming further hydrological and geological survey work in India and assuming, also, continued research into the various factors in water supply noted earlier in this chapter, water resources need not form any insuperable barrier to agricultural development in India.

The same conclusion probably holds true for all humid tropical countries. Indeed, in certain areas, such as East Pakistan, it is not so much a question of whether there are sufficient water resources, but of whether there is not too much water, at least for part of the year. In all countries of the humid tropics, however, the real problem is not how much water is theoretically available, but how to utilise and control the water already known to exist. Water storage is commonly necessary, and everywhere there is an urgent need for more data on rainfall, river flow, evaporation, transpiration, seepage or leakage rates, and silt-carrying capacities in flood, in order to secure the greatest storage volume with the least possible loss of water. The effective improvement, development and utilization of land for agricultural development in the humid tropics is to a great extent dependent on the provision of adequate irrigation or water-control measures.

Methods of water control. Traditional indigenous methods of water control, though widespread in the tropics, often do very little to reduce the hazards of cultivation. In the small riverine areas of southern Asia, for instance, brushwood dams are built across rivers and a portion of the flow is directed to the adjoining padi fields. Elsewhere, peasants seek out swampy areas where losses of water are usually made good by seepage and surface run-off from higher ground. But brushwood dams are frequently swept away by floods, and habitually swampy areas are by their very nature subject to prolonged flooding which may result in the partial or total loss of crops. In the great alluvial deltas of southern and south-western Asia different indigenous forms of irrigation by inundation are common, and throughout the Asian and African tropics various forms of the *shadouf* are in use. Other indigenous irrigation works, of particular importance in peninsular India and in Ceylon, include the tank, described by a number of writers. Typically, the tank is a modest affair consisting of an earthern embankment, or *bund*, blocking the line of a stream, or closing the outlet of a natural depression in which rain collects; in places it may take the form of a hollow in the ground fed by a channel cut from a neighbouring stream. Tanks, old and modern, can be seen at their best in the dry south-east of peninsular India, especially in the Madura-Ramnad country, and in Ceylon. The essential function of the tank is simply 'to correct the vicissitudes in the rainfall of a given season and to husband it so that it may be used to best advantage' (Williamson, 1931: 87). A rainfall régime that tends to foster the growth of a semi-aquatic crop such as rice – namely, heavy seasonal rainfall – favours the use of the tank, so that next to the canal proper it is the preferred type of irrigation work among rice cultivators.

Although popular attention is often concentrated on the large-scale schemes for irrigation and water control, most of the control of water for irrigation is concerned with small, humble indigenous works, the great majority of which are constructed and maintained by the cultivators themselves with or without assistance from government authorities. Minor irrigation schemes of this kind require comparatively small capital outlays, yield quick results, and can be executed speedily with local materials and labour. On the other hand, the protection afforded by them is liable to be cut short in drought years when protection is needed most: for example, tanks cannot store water when there is a failure of rainfall in the locality. Major and medium schemes, though much more expensive, do benefit large and extensive areas, give much more assured protection in years of scarcity, and can also be designed to serve a multiplicity of purposes. Nevertheless, small works are and will for long continue to be of fundamental importance, and many reports have emphasized that governments should devote more attention to them. In his report on the water resources of parts of Africa, Debenham (1948) was concerned to recommend the small, generally inexpensive local scheme rather than the grandiose and costly plan, whether it be for water supply, drainage, or hydro-electricity; he also stressed the importance of securing the full co-operation of the African peoples themselves, and was especially anxious that more action be encouraged at the village level, whether or not more ambitious and large-scale water schemes are put in hand by the central government. Indeed, 'the physical conditions of Africa south of the Sahara offer little scope for the development of a series of large-scale projects of irrigation such as those which have produced so dramatic a change in the economy of India, Egypt, and the Sudan' (Hailey, 1957: 1010).

Of the large-scale schemes for water control, perhaps the greatest interest has focused on the method of irrigation by large-scale impounding. Examples of this are numerous – the Niger Bend (Sandsanding) Scheme in West Africa, the Limpopo Scheme in Mozambique, the Krian Scheme in Malaya, La Ferme and La Nicoline Schemes in Mauritius, and the recent huge Mangla and Tarbela dams project on the Jhelum and Indus rivers respectively – but the greatest development in recent times has undoubtedly been in the monsoon countries of India, Pakistan, and Ceylon, where the need for water control is so urgent. East Pakistan is a good illustration of an area where the water problem is normally one of too much water rather than too little. Annual floods ordinarily occur over a third of the cultivated area, some of them of severe proportions: the 1954 floods, for instance, damaged 10,000 square miles (25,900 km²), destroyed crops, houses and livestock and deeply affected the lives of 12 million people. In this and similar regions adequate drainage is necessary to prevent the deterioration of the land by a rising groundwater table and consequent waterlogging. Anti-waterlogging measures such as drain-lining of irrigation channels in selected reaches have been taken up in the various development plans in Pakistan.

Of growing importance in recent years has been the construction of multi-purpose rather than single-purpose schemes of water control: the Volta Scheme of Ghana, for instance, involves the drainage of swamps and the provision of irrigation water as well as hydro-electric power; and the Niger Dams Project of Nigeria (Ledger, 1963) is similarly designed for multi-purpose benefits. There has also been an emphasis in recent years on unified river basin development, as in the Brahmaputra Scheme of East Pakistan. Agriculture, drainage, water power for industry: all are in varying ways fundamentally dependent upon the supply of water and may well affect each other's needs and supplies. Whether for irrigation, water power or drinking water, the planned regional and integrated planning of water resources is essential to economic development.

Even an equatorial lowland country, with a heavy rainfall distributed over most of the year, may suffer from water shortages, both for agriculture and for drinking. Other areas may suffer from too much water at times, too little water at other times. The explanation of this characteristic lies chiefly in the way the rain falls – its seasonal variability, unreliability, and torrential nature; the high rate of evaporation and transpiration; and the characteristics of the land on which the rain falls. All these factors affect the moisture balance available for agriculture and the amount of water available for drinking. In the monsoonal and savanna tropics, water supply is often the most important single problem awaiting solution.

The difficulty of this problem, however, depends to some extent on human activities. A farmer may court disaster by making a bad choice of crops, or by adopting unsuitable farming methods. On the other hand, by intelligently adapting his activities to the local effective moisture conditions, the farmer can make the most of his natural resources. As for drinking water, the siting of wells is especially important in the equatorial lowland environment with its high water table and in the conditions of generally poor sanitation. The bulk of the rural population of the tropics must for long continue to depend upon wells and streams for their drinking water. In the sphere of water supply the intelligent co-operation of the individual must go hand in hand with attempts to deal with the problem by the construction of irrigation and water control works and the construction of reservoirs and pipe water units. Here again, as in so many aspects of tropical life, the crucial need is for more basic data about moisture resources and the problems of their utilization in any one specific development area. Everywhere, however, the provision of a more reliable supply of water for agricultural, industrial, and domestic purposes must be looked upon as one of the most important concomitants of social and economic progress (Hodder, 1959: 109).

CHAPTER 3

Other Natural Resources

Vegetation. The theoretical distribution of vegetation types in the tropics is based chiefly upon climate and suggests a progressive change from tropical rain forest to tree, bush and grass savanna as the dry season increases in length and intensity away from the equator. But other ecological factors – edaphic, physiographic, and biotic – confuse the picture everywhere, in some cases drastically.

Tropical rain forest is a most impressive vegetation type, but it covers a smaller area than is often supposed. Three separate formations – the American, African, and Indo-Malayan forests – may be distinguished and important differences exist between them. The most widespread development of tropical rain forest today is found in the Indo-Malayan forest region; the largest area of continuous forest is in South America, and the least in Africa. In any region where rain forest is potentially the climatic climax 'only a part of the area is actually covered by mature forest. There may be large expanses where it has not yet developed – swamps, lakes, river margins, and estuarine mudflats occupied by seral communities in process of development towards the climax. There may also be bare rock and young volcanic lava where soil is gradually forming, and here, too, stages in the development of mature forest are found. In some tropical regions there are areas where local peculiarities of soil or topography make the development of typical rain forest impossible, even though the climate is suitable' (Richards, 1952: 7). On the other hand, the rain forest may extend beyond the usual climatic limits where local soil or drainage conditions are favourable.

The true rain forest is remarkable in many ways, but perhaps its most important characteristic, on which many other features are directly dependent, is the richness of its tree flora. On average the height of trees is greater than in most temperate forests, but they vary widely and there is much stratification of the forest. The trunks of the main trees are normally clear until the canopy is reached, though many trees are massively buttressed and there is an abundance of woody climbers and epiphytes. The forest interior is gloomy and oppressive. Climatic conditions there vary very little, evaporation is only slight so that humidity is always high, and air movement may average as little as a mile (1·6 km) a day.

The tropical rain forest is often thought to limit development. Most important, it is believed to be a serious barrier to movement and settlement, but in fact 'it is the slippery clay soil and the abundance of fallen logs and branches which make progress in the forest slow and laborious, rather than the thickness of the vegetation' (ibid.: 5). In its primary state the rain forest is not difficult to penetrate, whereas in the secondary (second-growth) forest, movement is often very difficult indeed. One of the greatest problems of development in the tropical rain forest areas, in fact, is that as soon as the forest is cut down it begins vigorously to re-establish itself as jungle, with dense and often impenetrable undergrowth, especially along river banks or in clearings where a good deal of light reaches the ground. The suggestion that the rate of growth of vegetation in tropical lands is more rapid than elsewhere is not strictly correct, for true growth involves the accumulation of new material, and the conclusions of workers in this field suggest that the mean net assimilation rate is more or less constant everywhere. Where there is a difference – and this is most relevant there – is in the rate of regeneration after cutting or burning (Njoku, 1955).

In the monsoon forests the vegetation is thinner, trees are generally smaller and there is less diversity of vegetation forms. There are many woody lianas and herbaceous epiphytes but fewer woody epiphytes. Deciduous species are common and there is a well-marked leaf fall from many trees, especially at the beginning of the dry period. Many of the same difficulties of utilization, movement, settlement, and control arise here as in the tropical rain forest. But the tropical monsoon lands are characteristically the longest settled and most densely populated areas of the tropics, so that the natural forest has been very severely disturbed by human activities.

In the tree, bush, and grass savanna lands of the tropics movement and settlement become easier. Tropical tree and bush savannas are most extensive in Africa, but the bulk of these are probably derived from former forest, a point which gives emphasis to the need for forest conservation. Most of the savannas are also probably man-induced by cutting and burning over a long period. Grassland is very rarely the climax vegetation in the wet tropics, except where elevation or water-logging prohibit tree growth. According to Richards (op. cit.), all lowland tropical grasslands and 'open' savannas are either biotic climaxes due to edaphic conditions unfavourable to trees, or stages in a hydrosere. Whereas the boundary between the rain forest and deciduous forest is probably a true climatic limit, and is determined mainly by seasonal drought, it is doubtful whether any tropical grassland is a true climatic climax.

The present economic value of tropical forests is not great. In 1938, the total world exports of timber amounted to 43 million cubic yards, of which the tropics contributed only 4·4 million (Asia 1·8 million, Africa 1·4 million, and America 1·2 million). Since then the relative importance of the tropics in timber exports has hardly changed at all, the tropics producing about the same proportion – 10 per cent – of the world's roundwood. The reasons for this include the predominance of hardwoods, often very difficult to cut and transport, and for which world demand is much less than for softwoods; the tendency towards a mixed species composition, pure stands rarely occurring naturally in the tropical rain forest; the slow rate of forest growth (as distinct from regrowth); and inaccessibility. Several writers have distinguished concentric zones of progressive exploitation in tropical forests, zones which are especially noticeable in the most highly populated regions of India, the Indochinese peninsula, and Malaya; the transport distance determines the zones in which the exploitation of each category of species remains profitable. As for the monsoon forests, the percentage of precious hardwoods is usually higher than in the rain forest and, in Asia, includes the teak (*Tectona grandis*). The chief value of this tree lies in its straight, branchless trunk, its hardness, and its durability, but it is peculiarly liable to the ravages of shifting cultivation by burning and in many areas has been almost removed from the landscape: in northern Thailand, for instance, only 45 per cent of the forest land is now productive because of such burning. The largest indigenous teak forests have been carefully preserved, extended or, as in West Africa, where teak is not native, planted on a very large scale. Finally, what forests there are in the savanna lands are for the most part not economically productive and are only of local importance for fuel.

Nevertheless, in many countries of the tropics the forest must be looked upon as potentially the chief natural resource, not only for timber but also for fuel, cellulose, resin, gums, camphor, and rattans. Moreover, many of the obstacles to the exploitation of tropical forests are likely to be overcome; and the future development of timber production in the tropics will probably involve the creation of 'artificial communities composed of relatively few valuable species either by planting or by sylvicultural treatment of existing primary, depleted, or secondary mixed forest' (Richards, op. cit.: 7). Aubreville (1937) has suggested schemes of cutting and planting to transform mixed rain forest into commercially useful stands in fifty to a hundred years. In these artificial or planned forests, inaccessibility is much less of a problem in that a definite network of outlet roads can be constructed. The problem of protecting felled logs against attacks by insects and fungi is also being tackled.

There is already a need for tropical forest conservation. The consequences of widespread forest destruction at the present rate are many: the loss of forest products, the loss of protection against soil erosion and excessive run-off, and the less well understood effect on moisture resources. Here is a great natural resource rapidly being wasted away through ignorance, though the importance of forest resources in economic development planning is now widely recognized. In India, for instance, the Third Five-Year Plan estimated that the annual requirements of industrial wood including pulp materials, which amount to 4·5 million tons at present, will increase to about 9·5 million tons by 1975. The demand for paper and rayon grade pulp, in particular, is likely to expand considerably with the growing population, increasing literacy and rising standards of living. As new plantations take twenty-five to thirty years to develop, in the ordinary course of events annual production may not increase beyond 5·5 million tons by 1975, leaving a gap of as much as 4 million tons.

For many immediate and practical economic reasons, forest conservation and reafforestation projects are clearly very necessary elements in the economic development policy of most tropical countries. Furthermore, Richards and others claim that deforestation has adverse effects on the course of plant evolution in the world as a whole, because the tropical rain forest has always played a role as a source of supply of genetical material in the evolution of new forms of plant life.

Soils. According to many writers, soil poverty is a fundamental and often intractable limitation to economic development in the tropics. The luxuriant vegetation associated with rain forest for long suggested that tropical soils were rich. It has been found, however, that the lush virgin tropical rain forest exists partly because it has been able to take back from the humus and shallow topsoil the equivalent of the nutrients it sheds upon the surface in leaves, branches, and trunks. The yearly production of organic matter is indeed very great, possibly exceeding 100 tons an acre, and the turnover is rapid, being assisted by the elements of fungi, bacteria, termites, and animals. Moreover, the forests of the humid equatorial regions may have started when 'the soil was not so poor, when rocks had not weathered so deeply, so that there was not such a scarcity of plant nutrients in the surface soil within the reach of the roots of the forest trees and other plants' (Carter and Pendleton, 1956: 506).

The general scarcity of plant nutrients in the surface soil of humid tropical areas is usually the result of intensive and extensive leaching. Where rainfall is normally in excess of evaporation, as it is for at least part of the year in the humid tropics, there is a net downward movement of water in the soil. This sweeps plant food

D

downwards and leaves the surface soil an impoverished mixture of altered mineral particles. In more precise terms, leaching involves leaving the sesquioxides of aluminium and iron at or near the surface and carrying downwards silica and some aluminium silicates; these are relatively soluble in rain-water, particularly in combination with organic compounds.

This whole process is aided by the rapid chemical action, notably oxidation, induced by high temperatures. Indeed, the main difference between temperate and tropical weathering may be said to be the stepping-up of tempo in the tropics: 'in hot climates temperatures are higher by 18°–36° F (10°–20° C) and all chemical reactions proceed at two to four times the speed usual in temperate climates . . . If one bears in mind that there is no interruption by winter, one will hardly err in estimating that over the whole year and in relation to temperate climates the intensity of weathering in the tropics is increased at least tenfold' (Vageler, 1953: 16). Another writer has shown that the seasonal renewal of groundwater movement is of equal importance in tropical areas of strictly seasonal rainfall; such areas 'may be described as subject for part of the year to equatorial soil processes where surface evaporation is nearly nil and for part to desertic soil processes in which soil evaporation is at a maximum' (Dobby, 1954: 74).

Insufficient is yet known of the chemical and physical characteristics of tropical soils for any classification to be wholly satisfactory. The tentative classifications of Robinson (1949) and Aubert (1954) emphasize the importance of soil moisture and soil drainage. For the geographer, however, perhaps a more illuminating classification is that of Charter (Brammer, 1956) who classifies tropical soils into orders based on the factors which predominantly determine soil characteristics. The most common soil type in all three regions of the tropics is the reddish savanna soil and tropical red earths or 'latosols' which are particularly well developed in tropical America. These are all laterized soils, with molecular ratios of silica to alumina of about 1·33–2·00, and come under the climatophytic soils of Charter. Mohr and van Baren (1954) distinguish laterites formed under conditions of continuous rainfall from those formed under conditions of intermittent rainfall.

Whichever classification of tropical soils is used, however, it must be emphasized that these soils are no more homogeneous than are the soils of temperate lands. Moreover, the degree of leaching depends very much upon the age and situation of the soil: immature soils formed from geologically recent volcanic material will be relatively little leached and may have an inherently high level of fertility. There is also a marked difference between, on the one hand, soils of upland regions and, on the other, the alluvial soils of valleys, coastal regions, and flood plains of rivers. The latter soils, being usually less leached and more fertile, have a wider range of agricultural possibilities. Upland soils, however, are often inherently poor, except where they consist of immature volcanic soils, and on this account their agricultural uses are limited. Only where the dry season is more defined or where slope characteristics and soil texture are favourable is the possibility of development really significant.

All laterized soils of the humid tropics, moreover, are not necessarily infertile. Even true laterites may be fertile, as in parts of Uganda or in Cuba, where the richest soil – the red clay of Matanzas – is loose laterite (Dumont, 1966: 30). And although termites in the soil may have a bad effect in destroying organic matter such as humus in tropical soils, many writers have pointed out that termites have value and importance in the tropics in rapidly breaking down dead organic matter on and in the soil. In tropical regions termites may take the place of earth-worms in preserving fertility (Adamson, 1943); and though termite mounds are inconvenient and may be less fertile than their surroundings, on poor soil they may form patches of relative fertility. De Schlippe (1956) has noted this in Zandeland, where cowpeas and sorghum are often confined to old termite mounds and so may be classified among patches of ecologically specialized crops.

Furthermore, the texture of laterized soils is often very good indeed – that of a loam. It is particularly important that this good structure, with its particles integrated into small crumbs permitting an adequate entry of air and water, should be preserved. Exposure of the organic matter in the surface to tropical conditions may lead to structural deterioration of a soil. It is for this reason that western methods of deep ploughing and turnover of soils may be found unsuitable.

Efforts to correct the earlier popular misconception that tropical soils are extremely fertile – a traditional opinion based on the luxuriance of tropical rain forest vegetation – are possibly in danger of going too far in the opposite direction. The popular view of tropical soils nowadays is that they are generally poor: 'the fertility of 8 or 9 square miles of average land south the Sahara and north of the Union of South Africa is equivalent to that of 1 acre of Iowa soil' (Kindleberger, 1966: 64). But there is no evidence for postulating inferior fertility in tropical soils. Rather does it appear that many tropical soils are capable of being very productive as long as each type of soil and land is treated in the most effective manner. Moreover, what is meant by inherent fertility in temperate lands is of a different nature and may have less agricultural relevance in the tropics. Providing that two soils have all the elements of plant food in fair amounts, the superior richness of one may make but little difference. It is also worth noting that local methods of agriculture and means of usufruction of the soils have an influence in maintaining tropical soils at a certain degree of fertility. Conclusions based on investigations with temperate soils are not always readily applicable to tropical soils. For instance, one of the most important tropical crops – wet rice – does not require 'fertile' soil in any normal sense of the term: what it does require is a soil capable of holding standing water. Again, judged by European standards, and in terms of temperate crops, tropical soils are deficient in calcium. But most tropical crops do not need much calcium and in some cases tropical soils contain so much calcium that artificial acidification is required. Comparisons between tropical and temperate soils can only have validity if their relations to crops, local agricultural methods, and other environmental elements are fully considered.

There is already sufficient evidence to make it possible to refute the general contention that tropical soils are a serious or permanent limitation to the agricultural development of the tropical world. Yet much remains to be learned about tropical soils, and in particular about their significance in the ecological complex. In many situations it may be misleading to consider the soil factor in isolation; and in this connexion the work of Milne (1935) on soil catenas, of Charter (1957) on soil/crop relationships, and of Coulter (1964) on tropical agricultural and soil surveys, is of especial interest. Furthermore, as one geographer has demonstrated, there is a need for more study of the relationship between soils and land use, in which 'several facets of the biogeographical system may be in such delicate equilibrium that disturbance of one may bring about the collapse of the whole structure . . . In order adequately to plan agricultural development some assessment of the impact of new crops and techniques upon the ecosystem must be made, an end which may be achieved by study of the relations of the ecosystems at present existing, and by detailed investigation of individual mechanisms within them' (Moss, 1963: 165).

Soil erosion. The partial or complete removal of the thin covering of living soil is a phenomenon that has profound effects upon potentialities for agricultural development in many tropical lands. But before discussing soil erosion, two points must be made. First, normal denudation, or geological erosion, is a beneficial and indeed important process in soil formation: most of the fertile alluvial plains in tropical countries, for instance, are the result of this kind of long-term process. In the second place, large areas of the tropics suffer only slightly if at all from soil erosion in its more serious manifestations, especially where the density of population is low and where large areas are still covered by forest.

Two main types of soil erosion may be distinguished here: soil erosion by water, common throughout the tropics, and wind erosion, which is much less important, being confined to the drier fringes of the humid tropics during the dry season. Soil erosion induced by water flow may take one of two forms: sheet erosion, in which water passes over a smooth slope and flows down in a sheet, irreparably removing a thin layer of topsoil over an area; and channel erosion, in which gullies develop. The latter is a more impressive kind of erosion, and may bring about local desiccation by lowering the water table; but agriculturally it may have less significance than sheet erosion.

The severity of soil erosion induced by water flowing down a slope is influenced not only by the degree of slope but also by the amount, distribution, and intensity of rainfall, the physical characteristics of the soil, and the vegetative cover; moreover it commonly occurs in association with one or more of a number of human activities, especially agriculture, stock rearing, and mining.

In relating agricultural activities to the intensity and extent of soil erosion, confusion may arise from the failure to distinguish clearly between the processes of soil deterioration – the *in situ* deterioration of soils – and those of soil erosion, or the actual physical removal of soil. Soil deterioration may occur in many irrigated areas where soil erosion is unknown – for instance, in many irrigated rice fields in India where waterlogging induces salinity and alkalinity. On the other hand, it is true that there is a distinct connexion between these two processes: 'the maintenance of soil fertility is always the *sine qua non* of soil conservation' (Tempany and Grist, 1958: 92). Moreover, the rate of soil erosion depends not only on the slope and on the duration and rate of flow of water but also upon the soil structure, which is itself part of the process of soil deterioration. As several authorities have observed, tropical soils are for the most part characterized by low silica–alumina ratios and appear to be less susceptible to erosion losses than do the soils of temperate climates.

Nevertheless, the clearing of land for agricultural purposes is always liable to initiate or aggravate erosion unless care is taken. Clearly, the amount of topsoil which is removed by water erosion – itself precipitated by the clearing of the natural vegetation – must depend upon several factors: the time interval between exposure of the soil and the establishment of a new vegetative covering; the slope of the ground; and the type of crop. It has been established that perennial tree crops are better than arable crops at preventing soil erosion, and that those arable crops which form a more or less continuous cover – such as grass, lucerne, leguminous crops, sugar-cane, sweet potatoes, and pineapples – are better at preventing erosion than are those arable crops, such as maize, cotton, tobacco, and cassava, which are characterized by separate stems readily permitting the passage of moving water (ibid.). Wet padi farming is normally very satisfactory in this respect, and those parts of tropical Asia with flooded rice fields are not commonly associated with severe erosion problems though, as noted above, soil deterioration may occur.

When fully established perennial tree cultivation may be good for protecting the soil, but severe erosion problems arose in the days when clean weeding between the trees was practised. In Malaya, for example, the early days of rubber planting led to the realization that clean weeding is not always desirable in a tropical context and may well precipitate soil erosion. Local reluctance to clean weed between trees is not an indication of laziness or backwardness. A tropical garden with its untidy jungle of mixed trees and shrubs around the house is satisfactory in that it does not leave the soil exposed to torrential rain and does imitate fairly successfully the natural rain forest ecology in which the soil is not too severely exhausted or subjected to erosion. As Pelzer (1957) has noted, the steady continuous use of unirrigated land offers one of the most difficult agronomic problems in the humid tropics because of the difficulty of preventing soil erosion or soil depletion. This arises more especially where high population density demands continuous cultivation, as has been demonstrated in south-eastern Nigeria by Grove (1951) and Floyd (1965). In connexion with tree crops, too, the early stages of growth afford little protection to the soil and similar precautions are required as for arable crops. When tree crops are fully grown the aim should be to imitate conditions in the natural forest by avoiding clean weeding and by maintaining ground covers and mulching. Much attention has been given to the establishment of protective cover crops; and a large number of creeping covers, some leguminous and others non-leguminous, have been developed for this purpose. During replanting on slopes, efforts are commonly made to reduce the risks of soil erosion by such practices as bench terracing. The cultivation practices of peasant cultivators have often been criticized by observers, and there is little doubt that improved methods of agriculture have a part to play in reducing erosion. But it is as well not to ignore the fund of experience which lies at the root of many indigenous practices. For example, mound cultivation in Africa has been frequently criticized; but in practice the erosion effects are slight and compensated for by the beneficial effects mounding has on moisture retention and root growth.

For arable crops the uses of rotation in controlling erosion are many and include the possibility of enabling erosion-conducing crops, such as cassava, to alternate with erosion-preventing crops like sugar-cane. Inclusion of most kinds of grass cover in rotation is desirable not only because of the direct protection it affords against soil movement but also on account of the effect it exercises in promoting soil structure. Rotations, however, are by themselves inadequate to effect complete control unless they are accompanied by measures to maintain fertility, suitable cultural methods and, where necessary, measures to protect the soil in other ways.

Stock rearing is responsible for soil erosion in many parts of the tropics. Where there is overstocking, sometimes together with over-cropping, the vegetative cover is not given a chance to establish itself, bare patches appear, and the soil is easily broken up by the hooves of the animals. In Kenya, the Ukamba and Kumasi reserves are so badly overgrazed that, as early as 1938, 37 per cent of their area was eroded down to the subsoil; and on a reserve capable of supporting a maximum of 60,000 cattle there were distributed some 250,000 cattle, 269,000 goats, and 60,000 sheep (Hailey, 1957). Africa is perhaps the classic instance of a continent suffering from soil erosion caused by overgrazing, and defective livestock management there is in general responsible for greater losses from erosion than is defective cultivation. The reduction of stock numbers has been tried in many territories – notably in Malawi, Rhodesia, Tanzania, Lesotho, Uganda, and Swaziland. But the solution probably lies more with the 'substitution of mixed farming or alternate husbandry for purely arable farming or grazing, cultivation of soil-conserving crops, restrictions on the use of pastures or numbers of livestock, protection of forests and reafforestation' (Tempany and Grist, 1958: 100). As a later chapter will show, however, the whole problem of overstocking is in many areas intimately bound up with cultural habits.

Other ways in which soil erosion can be initiated or increased include mining. And here, especially, the problems of erosion and silting are seen to be only different facets of the same problem: for instance, muddy water containing eroded soil in suspension has a greater abrasive action than has clear water. In Nigeria, Grove (1952) has discussed the relationship between mining and soil erosion on the Jos Plateau, and Ooi (1955) cites mining as one of the chief causes of soil erosion and silting in the Kinta Valley of Malaya. By skinning the ground surface (lampanning), the exposed hillsides are easily eroded and large quantities of silt are discharged into the river systems, leading to sedimentation, the raising of river beds, and flooding. In a village a mile or so from the confluence of the Tumboh and Kinta rivers, mining activities followed by erosion led to the mouth of the Tumboh being silted, and the overflow from the river converted the padi lands of the 2,000 inhabitants of Kampong Bulan Bidai into a swamp. The steamer service between the village and Telok Anson had to be abandoned, the population began drifting away, and by 1937 only 400 people were left.

The dangers of soil erosion are real and serious in almost all tropical countries. In India it is estimated that about 200 million acres (81 million ha) of land, or almost a quarter of the country's land surface, is suffering from soil erosion; and it is argued that it will not be possible to maintain yields of crops on dry lands, much less to increase them, if the soil is allowed to deteriorate through soil erosion in this way. Erosion problems are likely to intensify everywhere in the tropics as the distribution of population widens and as more of the vegetative cover is interfered with.

Mineral and power resources. Of the minerals, iron ore is present in some form or another in most parts of the tropics, where there are in fact many instances of ancient iron (lateritic) workings and smelting. But today it is produced in significant quantities only in Venezuela, India, and Brazil. Reserves, however, are believed to be considerable. Brazil at present produces only about 4 million tons a year from the south-eastern part of the country, where a great steel industry has been built at Volta Redonda, but reserves there

are estimated at about one-quarter of the world's present consumption of iron ore. Reserves in Venezuela and India, too, are
good. At present the Indian production comes from the northern
Orissa and Raipur districts of the Central Provinces, but in the
south-west (Singhbhum) there is an area with a continuous thickness of 700 feet (229 m) of haematite containing more than 60 per
cent iron. As for Africa, recently discovered iron deposits in
Rhodesia are considered to be very great; and in Liberia, too,
deposits are considerable. According to latest estimates, indeed,
Africa may well have the largest total potential reserves of iron ore
of all the continents.

Tropical Africa also has the greatest current production of
copper; and if the south-central African copper belt, extending
from Zambia into Katanga, is regarded as a whole, it is easily the
second largest single source of world supply today. These African
beds are unusually uniform in metallization, and some of the ore
is fit for direct smelting. Of the many other minerals, the tropics
have a wide range, notably of bauxite (Guyana and Surinam, with
very large reserves elsewhere in Jamaica, Brazil, India, and Thailand); tin (Malaya, Indonesia, Bolivia, and Nigeria); cobalt
(Katanga and Zambia); columbite (Nigeria); uranium (Katanga);
chromite (Rhodesia, India, and the Philippines); and lead and zinc
(Burma).

Of the mineral fuels – coal, petroleum, and natural gas – anthracite and bituminous coal is produced in significant quantities only
in India; and only 3·5 per cent of the total world production of coal
occurs in tropical countries. For lignite the percentage is even
lower – some 0·3 per cent. The reserves of anthracite and bituminous coal in India are believed to be fairly good, the most productive coalfields lying in west Bengal and east Bihar, and an
annual production target of some 97 million tons has now been
achieved. The most productive parts of the chief coalfield in India
lie in the Damodar valley belonging to the basin of the Hooghly,
where about nine-tenths of the coal raised in India is produced.
All the coal resources of the Indian subcontinent, with the exception of some Punjab lignites, lie in India and not in Pakistan.
Elsewhere in the tropics, Rhodesia and Brazil are the only other

countries producing over 2 million tons a year, and nowhere are proved reserves great.

The tropics produce about 22 per cent of the world's crude petroleum, but only in the American and South-east Asian tropics is there any large production at present, the bulk of it coming from Venezuela. As yet, the production in tropical Africa is insignificant by world standards. There are only small areas in the region over which favourable geological conditions – notably certain types of sedimentary basins – are believed to exist. The only known area of any promise in the interior of tropical Africa is in western Uganda, where oil seepages are present in the extensive Lake Albert rift valley. The remaining regions of promise in tropical Africa are mainly on coastal plains around its outer margins. Production is now under way in Nigeria, and drilling is taking place in Angola, Tanzania, Cameroun, and Ghana. At the moment most of the world's proved reserves of over 250,000 million barrels occur outside the humid tropics in the Middle East, and reserves in Indonesia, Venezuela, and Colombia are small by world standards of comparison. Nevertheless, in aggregate tropical countries contain some 30 per cent of the world's oil reserves, and recent experience in southern Nigeria emphasizes that the difference between actual and potential production is in no case more important than it is with petroleum. Natural gas normally occurs wherever oil is found, but has also been discovered elsewhere. At the moment Venezuela has a large and rapidly expanding production of natural gas, and prospects for developing this in Nigeria and Borneo also seem bright.

Any consideration of mineral resources seen in relation to economic development in the tropics must clearly take into account much more than the simple figures of production by countries or regions. In the first place the size of the reserves is of particular importance in any discussion of these capital or 'wasting' resources; and enough has been said to indicate that while actual production of many minerals may be small in tropical countries compared with temperate countries, the reserves are substantial, though basic geological and mineralogical survey work is often only just beginning. Secondly, technological developments and changes in the consumption and world price of minerals are continuously affecting both the current production and the possibilities of exploiting reserves, so that all prognostications about the value of mineral reserves must be viewed with caution.

As for power, while in temperate countries thermal sources of power are likely to dominate for the foreseeable future, in tropical countries most immediate industrial developments are likely to depend upon the supply of power from hydro-electric stations, many of which are included in multi-purpose schemes involving water-control, storage, and irrigation facilities.

Hydro-electric power forms potentially perhaps the greatest power resource of the tropical world. As far as present utilization is concerned, however, whereas the rate of utilization of potential water power is 60 per cent in Europe, it is only 3 per cent in South America, 5 per cent in Central America, 13 per cent in Asia, and as little as 0·1 per cent in Africa. Water power has advantages over other sources of power in that it is a renewable as distinct from a capital resource, and requires no storage of fuels, such as coal or oil. Its chief disadvantage is the high cost of capital installations.

Of the three sectors of the tropics, Africa is particularly well endowed, possessing some 40 per cent of the world's potential hydro-electricity. The continent is the only area with considerable stretches of internal drainage, and remarkably little of it is really low-lying, even in the Congo Basin. On the Congo River the most striking instance of modern hydro-electric power development could take place if the plans, initiated under the former colonial governments, are ever put into effect. Less than 100 miles (160 km) from the coast, at the Inga Rapids where the Congo falls 300 feet in a 15-mile 'awesome span of sustained violence', it is hoped to create an African Ruhr. It is believed that Inga could eventually produce 25 million kW – ten times the production of the Grand Coulee and as much power as is now consumed annually by the whole of Western Europe. Moreover this power could be produced at the cheapest rate of any large installation in the world. The Inga Scheme could easily do for the Congo what the Owen Falls (McMaster, 1956), Kariba (Reeve, 1960), Volta and Niger Dams (Ledger, 1963) schemes are doing for other parts of the continent.

In tropical America a number of important hydro-electric schemes have been begun, the largest being at Guri on the Caroni River above its junction with the Orinoco in Venezuela. When completed, this will be the largest scheme in the humid tropics and provide power not only for the programme of rapid industrialization in Guayana (eastern Venezuela) but also for most of the Venezuelan industrial and domestic market. Again in South America, mention must be made of the proposed Great Lakes Plan to create five large, artificial lakes in the interior in order to assist economic integration in the continent; the lakes would enable timber and mineral exploitation to develop and provide hydro-electric power for industry in the northern half of the continent.

The problems of developing hydro-electric power in a country are many and complex, stretching far beyond such relatively simple physical difficulties as irregular stream flow. Some of the factors can be illustrated from the case of India. Many of the Indian projects, such as the river valley projects of Bhakra-Nargel, Hirakud, Chambal, Tungabhadra, and Nagarjunasagar, provide both irrigation and power and are designed to help rebuild the agricultural economy as well as to pave the way for the rapid industrialization of the country. Over the country as a whole, however, a total hydro-electric power potential of about 41 million kW has been assessed as technically and economically feasible and the additional generating capacity installed during the Second Five-Year Plan averaged about 0·45 million kW per annum. By 1975–6 the aggregate installed generating capacity in the country may be of the order of 15 million kW. According to present estimates roughly half this capacity could be provided from hydro-electric projects and the balance will come mainly from thermal stations. In order to achieve these targets, however, new hydro-electric sites will need to be investigated speedily and work commenced in time to take advantage of subsequent plans. The Indian Third Five-Year Plan clearly appreciated the interdependence of natural and human resources and their factors in power development. In deciding upon particular methods of power generation for different areas, the key factors taken into account were: the capital cost per kilowatt of installed capacity; the foreign exchange component; the cost per kilowatt-hour generated; the period required for construction; the impact on other allied development activities such as coalmining, washeries, irrigation, and the exploitation of natural gas; and stimulus to the development of technological methods. In India the average production costs per kilowatt-hour of electricity for hydro, coal-fired, and diesel power stations are in the ratio of 1·2, 3, and 25 respectively.

A good deal of research is now being directed into the economics of large river-development projects. Serious doubts are now frequently cast on the wisdom of investing large sums of scarce capital in huge multi-purpose projects; and many authorities would now agree with Hanson that 'the creation and operation of a multi-purpose river project presents an under-developed country with the most difficult of all assignments in the sphere of public enterprise' (Hanson, 1960: 333).

. . . . .

There seem to be no grounds for assuming that the climatic vegetation, soil, mineral, or power resources of the tropical world are not potentially adequate for greatly increased economic development. Certainly there can be no question of explaining the present generally low level of agricultural and industrial development in terms of inadequacies in these resources. Admittedly the problems of resource utilization are considerable, but in most cases they arise from insufficient basic information. In all countries there is an urgent need for an intensification of climatic vegetation, soil, and geological survey and mapping, and for a much closer study of the relevance of all natural resources to the general processes of economic development.

CHAPTER 4

Human Resources: Qualitative Aspects

Much thinking and writing on the quality of tropical peoples in relation to prospects for economic development is riddled with prejudices and misconceptions. In the more extreme cases it is argued, either implicitly or explicitly, that many tropical peoples are innately incapable of participating fully in western-type economic life and even that they are inferior human types. Some writers argue that the enervating climate is such as to produce indigenous peoples who are lazy and both physically and mentally incapable of sustained effort. The standpoint taken here, however, is that all thinking and writing on the qualitative aspects of human resources in tropical lands must start from the assumption that there is no innate incapacity of the kind described above. The real problem, it is argued, is how to encourage the human skills, attitudes, and efficiency of economic organization which alone can provide the 'political, social and institutional framework which exploits the impulses to expansion' within an economy (Rostow, 1960).

At this stage it might be useful to look at a few examples of the issues and problems which need consideration and fuller study before any attempt can be made to induce the kind of change so frequently required.

Some social and institutional issues. A number of writers argue that existing institutional relationships and attitudes are inadequate in most tropical countries. Certainly, conventions and taboos of a number of kinds may restrict economic opportunity in many ways, including the use of resources. Probably the most striking prejudice of this kind hampering economic development concerns livestock, for both in Asia and in Africa there are some classes or communities which take a non-commercial attitude to livestock, fail to exploit their cattle to best advantage in terms of work, meat and milk, and carry excessive numbers of animals. Under Hindu laws, for instance, beasts of inferior quality cannot be killed or restrained from breeding, even though the numbers of animals may be so excessive as to be an obvious drain on the farmers' resources and on the land (Lewis, 1955: 43). There may be a similarly excessive accumulation of cattle in order to achieve social distinction or to discharge obligations, such as the bride price (Prescott, 1960). Then there are prejudices against manual work, against having economic relations with strangers, against changing occupations, and against migration. Other conventions include those relating to family life, especially the place of the woman in the economy, the control of agricultural practices by priests, and the caste system (Bailey, 1958).

The extended family, sometimes known as the joint family, is a common feature of the economic and social life of many tropical countries, especially in Africa and South Asia, and entails hospitality on a lavish scale to family members and the indiscriminate maintenance of distant relatives. Property and income are pooled and inherited as such; and expenditure is not accounted for individually. A man may thus have obligations towards a much larger number of people than in communities in which the concept of the family is more restricted. In appropriate circumstances, admittedly, the extended family system has many virtues. But at a later stage it can form an obstacle to economic progress in that a man is likely to be much less willing and able to rise in the income scale, and to save and invest, when he knows that he will have to distribute his gains among his relatives (Bauer and Yamey, 1957: 64–6).

In considering whether the attitudes to work of tropical peasants are restrictive on economic development, it is often pointed out that tropical peoples generally work shorter hours than do their counterparts in temperate latitudes. But the definition and measurement of the employed labour force in many tropical countries is complicated by several factors, including the place in the labour force of women and children, who sometimes make important, even decisive, contributions to economic activity. Again, and particularly in subsistence or semi-subsistence agriculture, the demands of labour vary greatly with the seasons. The study of daily and seasonal work cycles in tropical countries is as yet little advanced, but several interesting facts have already been revealed. Ooi (1959) shows that Malay padi planters work hard for only part of the year and that the rubber smallholder works in total only very short hours; for peasant smallholders and fishermen in Malaya the normal working hours per day are 3·5–5·1 hours. Similarly, in the West Indies it has been found that the individual agricultural labourer works 5 hours a day for 4 days a week on the average: that is, for some 20 hours a week. And A. Richards (1939) noted that the Bemba of Northern Rhodesia work for 5–6 months in an agricultural year, averaging only about 4 hours a day. This is a common enough feature of tropical countries, but should be taken to express endemic under-employment and simple agricultural systems rather than any inability or disinclination on the part of the farmer to work longer hours because of laziness, climate, or dietary deficiencies. Furthermore, the difficulty of getting tropical peasants to work very hard does not prevent them seizing opportunities to use better seeds, fertilizers, or more profitable crops: it has not 'prevented the Gold Coast farmer . . . from switching from subsistence production to creating the largest cocoa industry in the world, over a short space of time; or prevented the farmers of Uganda or of Indonesia from taking enthusiastically to cotton or rubber respectively' (Lewis, 1955: 41). All the evidence seems to suggest that changes in the attitudes of tropical peasants to work can only be effected by making the peasant want to work harder and giving him the opportunity to do so. This is very much a problem of changing his attitudes towards cash incentives. There are many instances of peasants responding to increases in the rate of earnings by producing or working proportionately less, because they need only a money income sufficient to pay for their fixed and limited wants. In economic terms this phenomenon is expressed in a backward-bending supply curve as distinct from the more normal upward-sloping curve of labour (Berg, 1961). In primitive societies, extra income beyond the conventional level may not be enjoyed as much as in more advanced societies because of the limited ranges of possible uses. Extra money has to be spent not so

E

much in acquiring new goods of a type not owned before, as in buying more of the same – more drink, more cloth. As Bauer and Yamey (1957) conclude, however, there are no grounds for postulating a ceiling to economic development imposed by inflexibility in habits of consumption (p. 86). Imitation is doing its work, replacing the old forms of compulsion in labour which, while necessary to development by western entrepeneurs in tropical countries, was nevertheless not likely ever to cause any fundamental or radical change in indigenous attitudes to work. The tropical peasant is continually acquiring new wants, and is showing himself increasingly willing to work to satisfy them without compulsion (Lewis, 1955: 38–9).

In examining the role of social factors in tropical economic development emphasis is perhaps too often put on the limitations imposed by these factors, but though there is admittedly much in the attitudes of tropical peoples that may curb economic growth, there is also much in their social organization which can serve its cause. In Nigeria, for instance, the people have strong local loyalties; 'they are closely tied to the immediate family or clan; they support local "unions" (clubs); and they take pride in local achievements. The banding together of families, clans, and village communities in producers' co-operatives, in the savings clubs of the Yoruba and in the thrift societies' of the Ibo strangers in northern Nigeria: these are practical and promising illustrations of self-help. Furthermore, 'respect for elders and acceptance of their counsel, if not carried to the point of becoming an impediment to learning new ways, make for social restraint and stability. Respect for learning in any form and the authority enjoyed by *mallams*' (learned men) of the northern parts of Nigeria, and by teachers and even students in southern Nigeria, suggest a 'key role which the teaching profession can play in developing new attitudes, and in the adoption of new institutions and techniques'. Many Nigerian social traditions, attitudes, and institutions, indeed, have positive value in a period of rapid change and advancement, and the same holds true for probably all tropical countries. The real problem is how to make use of these existing and powerful forces in any particular line of development, and how to ensure that they assist rather than obstruct its cause. Thus the International Bank report on Nigeria recommends that full support should be given to the co-operative movement as a vehicle for economic development in the country, 'for it is a form of economic organization fully compatible with Nigerian tradition and social sentiment' (International Bank, 1954: 10–11).

As for the role of education in the economic development of tropical countries, on which there is already a substantial literature, a good deal of controversy exists over the form such education should take. Balogh (1966: 90) argues that the input of conventional education is fatal from the point of view of balanced progress; and certainly the experience of India and several African independent countries would seem to give strong support to this view. According to Balogh three commonsense principles need to be adopted: that education should be in close harmony with the technical and administrative requirements of the country; that education should not create a disaffected intellectual proletariat; and that education should be in close touch with the life of the community as a whole.

There is a wide range of opinion about the role of social or cultural factors in economic development. While some writers believe their role to be negligible or only marginal, others, like Hagen (1962), regard social and cultural factors as causal and decisive; and Balogh (1966) claims that these social factors often do not provide a framework in which the profit and price mechanisms can operate so effectively as in developed societies. For this reason economic models based on the assumption of an efficiently working price mechanism are dangerous. Other less extreme viewpoints are expressed by Rostow (1953; 1956), Hoselitz (1952), and many others, who regard social and cultural factors as but two of the many variables affecting economic development. The question as to which of these points of view is correct is clearly of real practical significance for planning and policy-making in those countries of the tropical world where social and cultural forces appear to play a relatively substantial role in human life and activity. Case studies to support each of the various viewpoints can no doubt be found. Yet it may be unwise to try to make general conclusions about so diffuse and complex an issue. On *a priori* grounds, as Kindle-

berger has urged, it seems difficult not to reject both of the extreme points of view: 'sociocultural determinism is no more likely
an explanation of the course of economic development than is
economic determinism of social history' (Kindleberger, 1966:
38–9). The standpoint taken in the present study is that social or
cultural factors are normally important in any analysis of contemporary applied problems of economic development in a tropical country, but that they need nowhere form a decisive drag on
or permanent impediment to development.

The political framework. The essential interdependence of political,
social, and economic factors is only too clearly demonstrated in
almost every tropical country today. Economic and social progress
is dependent upon political stability, but so, equally, is political
stability dependent upon social and economic progress. The
political factor, however, operates in varying ways and is commonly open to a great many interpretations. In Ghana, for
example, it is possible to argue that the overthrow of the Nkrumah
régime – with all the implications this has for economic development in the country – was due largely to the oppressive form his
administration had taken; but it can equally be argued that the
Ghana coup of 1966 would never have occurred had not economic
distress in the country – itself partly the result of low world cocoa
prices – become so severe and so apparent to the peoples of Ghana.
In Rhodesia the 1966 imposition of mandatory sanctions against
the existing government of that country was undertaken with the
aim of bringing about political change. In Malaysia the political
factor has changed the form and emphasis of economic development planning from one based on maximizing production on a
national basis to one based on economic integration, though this
has itself been gravely upset by the secession of Singapore from the
Malaysian Federation. In many of the Latin American republics,
too, political instability seems to be a factor limiting the cumulative
processes of social and economic endeavour; yet at the same time
that political instability is itself caused or fostered by social and
economic backwardness.

The political factor is also of fundamental importance here because most parts of the tropics have at one time or another experienced external political, usually colonial, control and thus the impact of materially advanced cultures. In tropical Asia the British held what are now the countries of India, Pakistan, Burma, Malaya, and parts of Borneo; France controlled Indochina; Holland Indonesia; and the United States the Philippines. In tropical America the chief external powers were Spain, Portugal, France, Britain and Holland; while in tropical Africa, Belgium, Germany, and Italy have at times also played their part in the general processes of colonial expansion. Differences in colonial policy between the various powers have left their mark in a number of ways; and it is probably not too much to say that the whole extent and nature of economic development in tropical countries has until very recently been conditioned by external interests and policies.

Then again, while it is true that governments in the past may have kept direct intervention in the economic systems of tropical colonial territories at a minimum, governments nowadays have almost everywhere an unquestioned responsibility for stimulating progress in most spheres of economic and social development. In considering the role of government in economic development, Lewis (1955) distinguishes nine categories of function: building public services, influencing attitudes, shaping economic institutions, influencing resource utilization, influencing income distribution, controlling the quantity of money, controlling fluctuations, ensuring full employment, and influencing the level of investment.

The way in which political changes take place has profound effects upon the direction and scope of economic development and must deeply affect future prosperity. For whatever the geographical basis to economic development, and whatever the conclusions reached by economic theorists for a particular country at a particular time, in the last analysis it is governmental action and planning that determine the direction and scope of economic policy. According to a number of economists, indeed, government planning has now replaced the market as the engine of economic development throughout the developed world (Kindleberger, 1966: 150; Galbraith, 1967) and must presumably eventually fulfil the same critical role in developing countries.

Climate and human comfort and energy.[1] In any discussion of the qualitative aspects of the human resources of the tropical world the suggestion is commonly made that the tropical climate is responsible for much of the present low quality of manpower in low latitudes. Indeed, it has for long been widely accepted that the tropics, particularly the humid tropics, provide far from ideal conditions for man to live in, and that they are associated with ill-health, laziness, inefficiency, and marked physical, mental, and moral degeneration. This viewpoint is remarkable in that primitive man, with his lack of natural protective covering and profuse endowment of sweat glands to enable him to tolerate high levels of warmth with impunity, was originally almost certainly a tropical animal. Moreover, advanced civilizations have existed in the tropics – not only in the tropical highlands, as with the Aztec civilization, but also in the rainy forested lowlands of Ceylon, Cambodia, Java, Guatemala, and Yucatan. On the other hand, most of the world's ancient civilizations were located in subtropical or warm temperate lands, especially in those fertile areas near to the 70° F (21·1° C) annual isotherm; and Huntington (1915) contends that it was in these areas that what might be called 'intrusive' civilizations of the very low latitudes originated. According to this viewpoint, only special advantages of location or soil made it possible for civilizations to flourish in the tropics.

Certainly the tropical climate seems to be far from stimulating. Yet the improvement of life in the tropics must not be obstructed by an unquestioning acceptance of traditional ideas about the ill-effects of the climate on comfort and energy. Many of these ill-effects have been found to be due to disease, poverty, ignorance, and poor diet. Moreover, it has been found possible by intelligent adaptations to avoid or at least mitigate many of the direct ill-effects of the climate. It is important to try to understand the real nature of the climate–man relationship; to distinguish clearly between fact and fancy; and to adapt one's way of life to the peculiarities of the climate.

[1] Much of this section is substantially the same as pp. 91–9 of my *Man in Malaya* (1959).

In any examination, however brief, of the relationship between
climate and mental and physical energy in the tropics, no simple
causal relationships can be found. Man's capacity for mental and
physical energy and even his physical comfort are affected by a host
of variables – nutrition, cultural habits, religion, standards of
living, and psychological factors. Though much remains to be
learned about this branch of knowledge, and many of the conclusions drawn can only be tentative, the subject has already been
given a firm scientific basis. No attempt can be made here to discuss those relationships of a more specious nature: between climate
and civilization, climate and suicide, climate and crime, climate and
intelligence, or between climate and the number of men of genius.
All such relationships involve climatic factors whose role may only
be indirect and so strongly neutralized by other non-climatic
factors that the influence of the climate becomes almost intangible.
Thus the decline of the Mayan civilization in Central America,
though attributed by some writers to climatic changes involving
the return of a hot, wet climate, was more probably due to a great
number of factors, notably soil degradation. Even in skin colour,
though it is true that pigmentation is usually heavier in tropical
than in temperate skins, the relationship is greatly complicated by
ethnic variables: the Malay with his Mongolian origin, for instance, has a much lighter skin than has the African living under
similar climatic conditions in Africa.

There is little agreement about the ideal climate. Huntington,
basing his conclusions on the statistical analysis of the frequency of
deaths in different countries, in different conditions of temperature
and relative humidity, tries to express quantitatively what he believes to be the optimal climatic conditions for mental and physical
work: these are, for physical work, an outside mean daily temperature of about 64° F (17·8° C) and for mental work a mean daily
temperature of 40° F (4·4° C). For both physical and mental work
the ideal relative humidity is 75–80 per cent. Seasonal variations in
temperature, he says, are desirable, but should not be too great.
Brunt (1943), on the other hand, believes that for a healthy and
active life the climate should be such that the mean temperature of
the hottest month shall never exceed 75° F (23·9° C). Brunt has

also specified that the ideal outdoor climate is one in which a man lightly clothed can walk at 3 miles per hour (5 km per hour) in sunshine, without sweating, and rest in bright sunshine or stand in the shade or outdoors doing light work, with light air movement and without body cooling; the optimum for these prescribed conditions is 67° F (19·4° C) for a lightly clothed man, when the relative humidity is near 50 per cent. Another writer states that the temperatures between which a man is at his most efficient are 60° F (15·6° C) and 76° F (24·4° C), according to the relative humidity (ideal 40–70 per cent), the amount of clothing worn, and the amount of body movement; a slight air movement only is assumed (Markham, 1947). Mills (1942) puts the upper limit of comfortable conditions, assuming a low wind speed, at an average temperature of 80° F (26·7° C) with a relative humidity of about 58 per cent; at higher humidities conditions are 'sultry'. The importance of relative humidity in all these concepts of the ideal climate has led to attempts to express comfort in terms of wet bulb temperatures. Taylor (1946) has suggested that wet bulb temperatures between 45°–55° F (7·2°–12·8° C) indicate 'very comfortable' conditions; between 55°–65° F (12·8°–18·3° C) conditions are 'sometimes uncomfortable'; between 65°–75° F (18·3°–23·9° C) they are 'often uncomfortable'; and over 75° F (23·9° C) conditions are 'continuously uncomfortable'.

All writers on the subject, however, imply that the humid tropics have too hot, too humid, and too monotonous a climate for optimal physical and mental energy. Many settled parts of the tropics have average temperatures over 10° F (5·6° C) higher than Huntington's optimal temperature for physical energy and twice that of his optimal temperature for mental energy. And even the coolest months in many parts of the tropics never have an average temperature as low as the maximum prescribed by Brunt. Significance attaches to certain of the tropical highland areas in this respect, for there is some considerable white settlement dependent upon the lowering effect of altitudes on temperature. This is especially so in parts of Central America and in East and Central Africa; but there are also many hill stations elsewhere, as in India where they commonly lie between 6,000 feet (1,830 m) and 7,500 feet (2,286 m).

It is easy to exaggerate the monotony of tropical climates in its effect on human comfort and energy. Thus the wide seasonal humidity contrasts so characteristic of parts of the tropical savanna climate (in which relative humidities may drop to below 10 per cent during the dry season and rise to over 90 per cent in the wet season) are not normally found in the equatorial region. All seasonal climatic changes have their effect on human comfort and energy, though much of this effect is probably psychological. It has been observed of the monsoon in India, for instance, that 'in the rains temperatures are lower, and feel lower than they are. Gratifying as this initial coolness is, however, after a few weeks of eternally cloud-sealed skies the absence of sun has a depressing psychological effect' (Spate, 1967: 55). Something of the same effect may be experienced along the West African coast during the wet season, especially around July. The feeling of monotony in tropical countries can also be relieved by diurnal temperature ranges which can be considerable outside the equatorial region, though even there the diurnal temperature variations may be of real human significance, varying with latitude and distance from the sea. Furthermore, it must be recognized when considering the monotony of the tropical and in particular the equatorial climate that man there is extremely sensitive to climatic changes so small that they would go unnoticed in temperate countries; it is not unusual for newspapers in tropical lands to publish accounts of 'heat waves' when the increase in the average daily air temperature is no more than 2° F (1·2° C).

The tropical climate is indeed far more tolerable than climatic abstractions and traditional notions would suggest. It is necessary to take account, among other things, of automatic and conscious efforts to adapt human activities as completely as possible to the climate in which man has to live and work.

As for *automatic responses*, man in the tropics is almost continuously faced with the problem of how to dissipate heat from the body, and this may be effected chiefly by convection, conduction, radiation, or evaporation. But sweating leading to evaporation is in the tropics perhaps the most important automatic response, for the increased activity of sweat glands is a sign that the cooling of the body by convection and radiation alone is insufficient to maintain an even body temperature, and that evaporative cooling, which takes place when sweat evaporates from the body surface or from clothing in contact with the skin, is also necessary. Indeed, sweating is one of nature's safeguards, though it can lead to a complex of maladies resulting from loss of the salt contained in sweat which commonly contains between 0·2 per cent and 0·5 per cent of salt. But the more moist the air the less easily can moisture be evaporated into it from the body surface. Allowing for a person weighing about 130 lb (59 kgm) and for the specific heat of the human body of 0·8, about 0·22 pints (0·1 litre) of water must be evaporated from the body to reduce the average body temperature by about 2° F (1·2° C). This amount of sweat can easily be produced on the body in the humid tropics by exercising for an hour. The limits of evaporation, however, are passed in still air when the wet bulb temperature exceeds 88°–90° F (31·1°–32·2° C), even when a man is unclothed and doing no work: the surrounding air is then so saturated that no more moisture can be evaporated into it. Though wet-bulb temperatures of this order rarely occur with very high temperatures, the effectiveness of evaporative cooling is widely restricted by the high relative humidities experienced in the tropical wet or equatorial areas, and in the savanna and monsoon tropics during the wet season. The increase in comfort during the dry season in these latter areas is due very largely to the drop in relative humidities, though discomfort from excessively low humidities may then occur.

Partly because of limitations to the effectiveness of evaporative cooling, man's ability to acquire any considerable degree of acclimatization to tropical climates is now generally doubted. The processes of acclimatization, admittedly, include more than the increased activity of sweat glands: acclimatization also consists in a loss of weight with a corresponding increase in conductance and of the ratio of skin area to total weight of body. Yet it is believed that the development and maintenance of true acclimatization to heat is prevented by the lack of stimulating changes of temperature. It has been found, for instance, that Europeans who live in the humid tropics for many months, or even all their lives, do not show those changes in the blood usually associated with true acclimatization to heat. There is little doubt that many tropical peoples withstand poorly not only cooling but also warming. The consensus of opinion is that frequent changes in environmental temperatures in the wet tropics are usually insufficient to allow the processes of true acclimatization to operate satisfactorily.

It may be objected that most of the above remarks, while possibly true of Europeans, are not applicable to indigenous peoples in the tropics. Admittedly, most of the experimental evidence refers to Europeans, but according to most authorities it is unlikely that there is any significant difference in physiological responses between races. The normal temperature of man is the same in all latitudes, and all available evidence suggests that the differences between racial types in physiological response to work at high temperatures which can be attributed to racial factors alone are small. According to the most recent conclusions, 'European workers in hot industry, or Europeans who have lived in, say, Singapore for a hot season or so, Africans in Nigeria . . . Australian aborigines, and Indians and Chinese in Malaya – all these show precisely the same capacity to acclimatize to heat. This, of course, is not really surprising, as on other grounds, genetic and palaeontological, we are aware that modern man is one interfertile species and that the origin of the hominids was certainly in an equatorial region' (Weiner, 1966: 375).

On the other hand, there may be very significant differences between races in psychological response and in their readiness or opportunities to make intelligent adaptations to the climate; indeed, it may well be that the key to the whole problem of comfort and energy in the tropics lies in this direction. Little is known about the psychological aspects of the problem as yet, but tropical fatigue certainly constitutes a serious obstacle to social, economic, and political development. Monotony, boredom, and dissatisfaction undoubtedly affect a man's physical and mental vigour through their effect on his nervous system, and this may be because the climate requires continual loss of moisture from the body so that the nervous system supervising this never or rarely exercises its opposite function – the conservation of heat.

Many of man's *conscious responses* to the climate in the humid tropics are based on the appreciation of two facts: that moving air carries warmth away from the body more effectively than does still air; and that even the slightest air movement acting upon a body damp with sweat will accelerate the rate of body cooling by accelerating the rate of evaporation from the body. Thus if a man sits fully clothed in a room with all windows shut in a tropical climate, he will undoubtedly soon feel warm. If he turns on an electric fan he will feel cooler. If by the time he turns on the fan his body and clothes are damp with sweat, then he may quickly feel uncomfortably cool. The fan, and such more primitive methods as the *punkah*, are based on the principle that movement of air is the great reliever of oppression in the tropics. A breeze can have a similar cooling effect, but only if a house is properly located and designed will maximum benefit be gained from whatever movement of air there is. An open type of house is called for in wet equatorial lowland areas, located where it can be reached by any local breeze. Innumerable subjective observations could be made to support the contention that small differences in siting, aspect, and location of houses can produce appreciable differences in body temperature and comfort. A satisfactorily quantitative statement, however, must await more integrated and comparative research in physiological climatology.

A distinction must be made here, however, between the house type of the lowland equatorial tropics and the house type of the savanna and monsoon tropics. Whereas in the wetter tropics one of the chief ways of promoting coolness in a house is by opening it up to any air movement, in the drier tropics coolness is obtained more by the heavy construction of houses and by the small number and size of windows. In West Africa, for instance, outside the rain forest and mangrove coastal zone, the house type is quite distinctive: walls are thick and made from puddled mud and there are few openings for ventilation. The reason for this kind of contrast is interesting and illustrates human responses and adaptations to differing climatic conditions within the tropics. In the first place, most of West Africa has a distinct dry season, a broad range in relative humidities and sharper diurnal contrasts than are experienced, say, in Malaya. Apart from the availability of materials, which may have some bearing on the question, the house in West Africa must be less open partly to keep out the dust, but primarily to produce more even temperatures: the thick walls protect the house during the day from intense insolation, especially during the dry season, and warm the house during the night. Mud is cheap, easily obtainable, has good insulating properties, and can be remarkably durable.

It is true that wholly suitable house designs and locations must for long be restricted to a very small section of the population. Even new housing in towns is normally of inadequate design and far too congested. On the other hand, present concepts in the design and location of tropical urban housing may become outmoded if the practice of air conditioning becomes widely available to a large section of the population in towns. In a fully air-conditioned house the ideal design is quite different from the design for a house without air conditioning: windows are fewer and smaller, and rooms are smaller and less airy. Air conditioning depends for its success not so much upon moving the air as upon lowering air temperature and relative humidity. As the standard of living rises, air conditioning is becoming more common to the extent that a small but still increasing section of the population sleeps, eats, and works in its artificial climate. However, the European must not too glibly assume that all indigenous peoples would like air conditioning, even if they could have it. There is still a certain amount of prejudice against the practice, though it is difficult to see why if central heating is necessary in England, air conditioning should be considered unnecessary in the tropics.

A further adaptation a man can make to climate is in his clothes. According to their colour, thickness, texture, and tightness of fit, clothes can raise or lower the threshold levels of warmth at which a man begins to sweat or feel uncomfortable. Thus 'in Singapore a lady wearing a thin dress which leaves her legs and arms bare, and light sandals on her feet, may be much more comfortable than her husband in a linen shirt with collar and cuffs and in long trousers and leather shoes' (Glaser, 1955: 1). In this whole question of suitable clothing it is important to appreciate that in the dissipation of heat from man the most important parts of the body are the hands, feet, and ears: that is, those parts of the body where the total surface area is great in relation to the total volume or weight and where the supply of blood to the skin is richest. Clearly, then, the practice of wearing socks and western-type leather shoes in the wet tropics is illogical, for it restricts the feet, especially the toes, as cooling agents. As for colour, it is in accordance with the principle that tropical clothes should have good reflective power and poor absorptive power that they should be white or at least bright in colour. Following on what has been said above, too, it is logical that they should allow good ventilation: clothes should be loose in texture and loose fitting.

Because the highest temperatures are reached in the early afternoon – usually about 2 p.m. – it might be expected, by analogy with certain European countries, that the afternoon siesta would be common. This practice varies with the country, or more precisely with the European power that controls or formerly controlled it. Whereas the siesta is fairly common practice in most Latin American tropical countries and in those other parts of the tropics where French, Spanish, or Portuguese control has been exerted, the siesta is not commonly associated with the former British possessions in the tropics. This, of course, affects the distribution of work throughout the day.

It is frequently stated that the humid tropics have a climate which is not conducive to mental and physical energy: 'warm, wet climates are inimical to sustained mental work'; or 'labour in the tropics is unlikely to be as efficient as in temperate areas'. There seems to be no evidence to support such statements, however. Rather must it be insisted that by increasingly intelligent adaptations it will prove possible to negate the ill-effects of the wet tropical climate on human activities. The difficulties of life in the tropics are cultural rather than climatic (Bates, 1952; Simey, 1946). It will be realized that the pattern of living in most tropical countries has been almost slavishly transported from Western European or North American countries. The whole concept of civilized living – in diet, housing, clothing, the distribution of work throughout the day, and recreational habits – must be reassessed against the realities of the natural environment. In relating tropical climate, human comfort, mental and physical energy to economic development, it must be assumed that with continued research in applied physiological climatology, improvements in medical knowledge and services, and an improved diet and standard of living, there is no reason why anyone should not be as active and efficient in the tropics as elsewhere in the world. The real problem is to find out how to live and work at one's best in any particular tropical country as distinct from anywhere else. It is not enough simply to avoid infections, increase food production, create industries, and improve social services. Tropical peoples must also consider how they can so adapt themselves and their activities to the climate that they can work, think, and live at their best.

Tropical diseases. Many writers have concluded that health is the chief problem in the settlement and development of tropical countries. Yet here again it must be assumed that the tropics can be made as healthy as anywhere in the world, and so to look upon unhealthiness as only a temporary impediment to development. Many of the so-called tropical diseases have at one time or another existed in temperate latitudes, and certain parts of the tropics – notably some of the small island territories – have already been made very healthy.

Disease, nevertheless, is very much a force to be reckoned with. In Nigeria malaria is still a most important problem and one with which surprisingly little progress has yet been made: probably one-third of all Nigerian children die before they reach the age of five, and the bulk of these die from malaria. In Ghana, Hunter (1966) has shown how rural settlement has advanced and retreated in association with the incidence and spread of river blindness (onchocerciasis). In Malaya, now certainly one of the healthiest countries in the tropics, it is nevertheless reported that there are still areas 'where 50–90 per cent of the population shows signs of malaria, where worm infestations are more or less universal, where yaws is prevalent, leprosy not uncommon and smallpox a constant threat. Tuberculosis, venereal diseases, malnutrition, and a host of lesser ailments, though preventable or curable, are still widespread causes of sickness, disability, and premature death more or less throughout Malaya' (International Bank, 1955: 400). The main diseases now mainly tropical are anklyostomiasis, blackwater fever, cholera, dengue fever, diarrhöeal disorders, guinea-worm, filariasis, dysentery, liver abscess, malaria, sleeping sickness, tetanus, yellow fever, and most skin diseases. There is space here, however, to deal very briefly with only a few of these.

Malaria still plays an important role in restricting economic and social development. It is true that in many tropical countries malaria has lost its menace as the chief killing disease, though official figures of deaths from diagnosed malaria are thought to be very much lower than the true figure. Malaria has in many areas been reduced by control measures and personal prophylaxis to an endemic burden of sickness. In most malarious areas the sickness rate is far higher among children than among adults, and the signs of repeated malaria indicate the hazards of the slow immunizing process whereby adults gain their immunity. Although the number of deaths from malaria has been greatly reduced, the disease is still a serious consideration because of its restricting effects on energy, initiative, and the development of positive good health. Agriculture, for instance, may not receive all the care it needs.

Approaching the study of malaria from the geographical point of view it is easy to find a correlation between the distribution of malaria and the distribution of population. In Malaya, for instance, the well-established, densely populated padi areas on the flat coastal plains, urbanized areas like Singapore, and the western interior foothill belt of rubber and tin-mining settlements are relatively free from malaria. In the sparsely populated interior, on the other hand, the incidence rises rapidly. The incidence of malaria in the peninsula is highest in narrow, isolated, and relatively sparsely populated valleys of the interior. But such remarks do not establish a simple causal relation. It is not true that the pattern of population distribution is in any way determined by the distribution of malaria. The absence of malaria in populated areas is often the effect rather than the cause of settlement, anti-malarial measures being best developed in the more populous districts.

The high moisture and temperature conditions essential for the breeding of anopheline mosquitoes are found almost everywhere in the humid tropics. Attempts have been made to fit annual rainfall curves to the incidence of the disease itself, but so far little success has been had in this direction though rainfall undoubtedly does influence malaria by affecting the height of the water table. More success in establishing climatic correlations has attended attempts to relate malaria incidence and wet-bulb temperatures, though research in this direction is handicapped while climatic data are used from widely spaced stations. The natural conditions immediately surrounding the insect – illumination, humidity, temperature, and air movement – differ from regional averages. The micro-climate has more epidemiological significance than the regional climate, though some general conclusions are possible – for instance that low temperatures inhibit the development of the plasmodium in the fly.

In the application of anti-malarial measures in rural areas of the tropics, the pattern of settlement is an important consideration. Anti-larval measures, used with such success to protect the population in towns, villages, and estates, may be prohibitively expensive in rural areas where the population is widely scattered. Consequently, whereas in Western European countries rural life is popularly associated with healthy living and town life with unhealthy living, in the tropics the converse is generally true: the healthiest spots are the towns where control measures and personal prophylaxis are more easily available and enforceable. The scattered distribution of dwellings also makes it difficult to capture mosquitoes because there is no focal point in settlements towards which they are attracted. Another difficulty in the application of anti-malarial measures is that since the various species of vectors have different environmental requirements, malaria control measures must necessarily differ from place to place. The real key to malaria control in any one area is a knowledge of the vector species and its breeding habits in that particular area; 'the problem is first, last, and always, a local one, success depending upon knowledge of the habits of the particular species of *Anopheles* concerned and the local peculiarities of topography, population, and climate' (Malayan Government, I.M.R., 1950: 173).

The control of malaria, as of other diseases, tends at first to raise

F

the birth rate and lower the death rate, thereby helping to boost the rate of growth of population. On the other hand – and quite apart from humanitarian motives – experience has shown that the control of malaria in the long run reduces the endemic burden of diseases other than malaria, releases energy and initiative, and in general raises the prosperity of the people. This is a feature which, though perhaps not immediately apparent to a visitor to a tropical country, is really more significant to the present study than is the serious and dramatic outbreak of malaria in a country. Continuous contact with tropical peoples emphasizes how insidiously the lack of positive good health can affect attitudes towards work, individual initiative, energy, and capacities for sustained work or thought.

Human sleeping sickness (*trypanosomiasis*) in Africa is caused by *Trypanosoma gambiense* or *T. rhodesiense* and conveyed to man by the bite of the tsetse fly (*Glossina*). Both species finally invade the central nervous system, causing the classical symptoms which have resulted in the disease being called sleeping sickness. *T. gambiense* is widespread, from West Africa through Central Africa to Uganda, western Kenya, and the shores of Lake Tanganyika. *T. rhodesiense* may occur here, but is typically found in the rest of Tanzania, Rhodesia, Zambia, and Mozambique. The tsetse species of greatest significance are *G. palpalis*, *G. tachinoides*, *G. morsitans*, *G. swynnertoni*, and *G. pallidipes*. Like the various malaria vectors, each species of tsetse has special climatic and other environmental requirements which determine its distribution: thus *G. palpalis* is almost invariably restricted to the humid vicinity of rivers or streams with heavily shaded banks, while *G. morsitans* can survive in arid thorn scrub, provided it can secure shade in thicket.

The detailed distribution of trypanosomiasis is influenced by several factors. During the wet season there is a high density and wide distribution of the fly because conditions are generally suitable; but in the dry season, although their density is low, they tend to concentrate in foci where local climatic conditions are favourable. These foci usually contain pools of water on which man also is dependent, so that close and regular contact is established between the human and fly populations.

The distribution of trypanosomiasis is also influenced by the human population density. According to experimental work in Nigeria, where the population density is below 20 persons to the square mile (8 per km²) sporadic cases may occur, but population densities of 20–100 per square mile (8–38 per km²) have the highest incidence of trypanosomiasis. Over 100 per square mile (38 per km²), fly–man contact decreases because agricultural and other activities disturb the environment and make it unsuitable for the fly. Flies readily follow man, animals, and vehicles for long distances, so that improved communications often result in the carriage of infected flies into uninfected areas. Clearly, then, the reduction of contact between man and *Glossina* must be achieved, and this can be achieved by concentrating the human populations or by so altering the environment that the fly departs or dies.

In Nigeria the range of the tsetse fly (*G. palpalis* and *G. tachinoides*) extends from the coast to the open savannas of the north. Only small parts of the extreme north, parts of the Cameroons and the Jos Plateau are fly-free. With the exception of small foci in the south, however, human sleeping sickness is confined to northern Nigeria, and more especially to the Middle Belt, though this relative freedom of the south does not extend to the animal population. The provinces most severely affected are the southern areas of Katsina, Zaria, Plateau, and Benue, which together account for 70 per cent of all cases in northern Nigeria. The problem was attacked by the clearing of vegetation along streams and around settlements with varying degrees of ruthlessness, thereby destroying the pockets of shade and humidity sought by the fly; by the setting up of dispensaries from which mass treatment could be organized; by the prophylactic use of modern drugs in selected populations; and by large-scale resettlement schemes involving the concentration of population, as at Anchau. Originally one-third of the population at Anchau had sleeping sickness and in some villages up to one-half of the population was infected. It was reported that nothing could be done before the population was concentrated; and the Colonial Development and Welfare Fund gave money for a scheme of rural development in which economic development was to form an essential part.

The greater incidence of human sleeping sickness in northern

Nigeria has been shown to reflect the greater man–fly contact there. Near Kaduna, for instance, *G. palpalis* survive in the late dry season by concentrating at a few permanent pools in the stream bed. When the pools are utilized by an African village as its sole source of water, man becomes the primary host and is thus heavily exposed to Gambian sleeping sickness. In the humid forested areas of southern Nigeria, however, there is normally a low degree of man–fly contact. Under humid conditions, *G. palpalis* is widespread and barely riverine in habitat. Whereas man in southern Nigeria may be dependent upon stream or other water points, the fly there is not (Page and McDonald, 1959).

Yellow fever is confined to western and central Africa and the northern half of South America. The parent source of this infection is primarily in monkeys, but transmission to man is effected by certain species of culicine mosquitoes, especially the *Aedes aegypti*. This mosquito is common in the whole inter-tropical belt, and usually breeds in the immediate vicinity of human habitations; in small shallow collections of water in old tins, bottles, coconut husks; and, in fact, in almost anything that will hold water. The disease usually arises from the introduction into an area of an infected person. Consequently those areas which have the vector have to guard carefully against the immigration of people from yellow fever countries. Most of the measures are decreed by international conventions, and very strict control is exacted at all airports or seaports in contact with endemic areas.

The incidence and mortality of *tuberculosis* is increasing rapidly in many tropical countries as communications improve and as people congregate in larger communities; it is more of a social than a medical problem, being associated more especially with overcrowding. It has also been introduced in its more malignant forms by European contact, notably in the Congo where the disease spread along lines of communication and through European settlements into rural areas.

In many of the more advanced tropical countries tuberculosis is now probably the most important single disease in public concern. In Malaya, overcrowding is very common in the types of dwelling known as shophouses, which are believed to constitute the most potent single factor in the production of the high rate of tuber-culosis in the country. Over 50 per cent of the urban population of Malaya live in shophouses, the rooms of which are commonly divided into one-family cubicles, leading to very high floor-space densities and producing units of accommodation in which there is often no direct access to light and fresh air. In Sarawak, too, the Dyak longhouse is believed to be an important cause of the high rate of tuberculosis.

Diet and nutrition. The effects of a low dietary on social and eco-nomic development are undeniable, though difficult to isolate or measure. Chronic disease in association with malnutrition produce a cumulative effect, since 'it leads to severe debility, which inter-feres with the individual's capacity to work and hence lowers his production and earnings' (F.A.O., 1966: 12). Poverty and ignor-ance are probably the chief causes of malnutrition, and in areas where chronic hunger appears to exist, as in parts of tropical Asia, the problem is 'not one of planning for optimum requirements and an optimum diet, but for minimum requirements and minimal diet on a bare subsistence level, and the problem has to be ap-proached from a practical point of view and carefully related to prevailing agricultural standards' (ibid.: 14). Hunger, too, is by some authorities believed to be a direct cause of high crude birth rates; de Castro (1952), for instance, holds the view that hunger, especially when associated with low animal protein consumption, leads not to depopulation but to overpopulation.

The three main energy-producing foods are carbohydrates, pro-teins, and fats, the last having the highest calorific value; whereas one ounce (28 gm) of dry carbohydrate gives 113 calories in the body, and one ounce (28 gm) of dry protein gives about the same amount, fats are twice as good a fuel, one ounce of fat giving 255 calories in the body. It is believed that the minimum calorific intake per head per day should be about 2,500, though it is held by some authorities that a marked increase in energy and initiative cannot be expected until a minimum level of 3,000 calories per head per day is reached. Davey and Lightbody (1956) recommend 2,500 calories for the average peasant doing a moderate day's work

in the tropics, where metabolism is lower than in temperate countries, though in Malaya the recommended allowance for peasants
doing manual work has been put as low as 2,100 calories per day.
In tropical countries the average figure is usually under 2,500 and
in some cases under 2,000. Being average figures, large numbers of
the population must exist at even lower figures, and conditions may
well be much worse in countries for which data are lacking.

Bearing these facts in mind, it is useful to look at Table 3, which

Table 3. *Net food supplies* per capita *in selected countries* (kg per annum)

Country	Year	Cereals	Pota-toes, etc.	Sugar	Pulses and nuts	Meat	Milk	Fats and Oils	Cal. per diem	% animal	Prot. in gm
Brazil	1962	113	157	39	30	28	4	9	2,920	15	69
Colombia	1961	70	116	51	6	32	4	6	2,080	18	46
Venezuela	1963	194	66	18	11	25	7	12	3,130	17	98
Rhodesia	1962	201	10	12	16	26	29	4	2,890	18	79
Malagasy	1962	160	123	7	5	15	1	1	2,160	12	48
Uganda	1961	61	475	13	27	10	3	2	2,340	11	40
Ceylon	1963	118	30	13	29	2	2	4	1,920	5	42
India	1962–3	134	10	17	21	1	5	4	1,940	6	50
United States	1964	66	46	40	7	103	17	22	3,120	40	92

Source: United Nations, *Yearbook of Statistics*, 1965; F.A.O., *Yearbook*, 1965

also shows the contribution of different types of food to the total
per capita calorific intake in selected countries. Such a table has, of
course, many limitations, and it is impossible to draw any definite
conclusions from it. Certain ideas, however, are suggested by
these figures.

The dominating importance of cereals – commonly rice in much
of Asia and millets, wheat or maize elsewhere – is very evident. As
a carbohydrate, rice is one of the poorer foods in calorific value,
weight for weight, but it has a high yield and so is best adapted to
areas of high population density, such as occur in parts of Asia.
However, much of the rice is polished before eating, a process
which removes some of the nutritive value. Rice may be artificially
enriched with vitamins and minerals, and the nutritive value of
ordinary rice may be raised by the addition of this enriched rice in
appropriate proportions. Two potentially valuable supplements
are thiamin and iron, the former to prevent *beri beri*, caused by lack
of the vitamin *B* complex, and the latter to prevent the very common iron-deficiency anaemias. But prejudice against a rice having

a different flavour or appearance from that to which people are accustomed is very real and difficult to overcome.

Rice, together with the other cereals, potatoes, and starchy roots such as yams, provide the bulk of the carbohydrates in tropical diets, and Table 3 indicates how high a percentage of calories is provided by such foods. In Pakistan something like 75 per cent of the calories are provided by cereals alone; and cereals, potatoes, and roots commonly provide at least 50 per cent of the calorific intake in tropical countries. Sugar, too, is a source of carbohydrate, though its consumption is strictly limited in most tropical countries outside the Caribbean area.

Taken together, the cereals, potatoes, roots, and sugar are tropical foodstuffs rich in carbohydrates but relatively poor in protein and fats. According to Davey and Lightbody (1956) the average tropical peasant doing a moderate day's work should take 2,500 calories per day which should be made up of 1,650 calories of carbohydrate, 400 calories of protein, and 450 calories of fats. From Table 3 it is clear that, though in many cases even the carbohydrate requirements are inadequate, tropical diets are most strikingly deficient in proteins and fats. This is particularly true of tropical Asian countries which come off badly in almost all dietetic comparisons.

In view of what has already been said, the figures for fats and oils are interesting, even though fat needs may not be identical in tropical and temperate countries. The average person in the United States or the United Kingdom takes over four times the amount of this valuable fuel than does his counterpart in most Asian and African countries, and substantially more even than most tropical American countries. Even more striking is the set of figures for meat, milk, and eggs. In this connexion, however, it should be pointed out that animals are comparatively wasteful converters of food and are often the first to go when food gets scarce. Furthermore, tropical climatic and vegetative conditions do not in general favour livestock production, and in many parts of the tropics there are religious objections to eating animal flesh so that inferior vegetable protein has to take its place. Yet at least 30 per cent of the recommended 400 calories of protein should be first-class protein of animal origin if certain deficiency diseases such as deoedema or kwashiokor are to be prevented. The ideal minimum animal protein intake per day *per capita* is 1·25 oz (35 gm), but most tropical countries have an average consumption figure well below this.

One important fact that does not come out of the data given in Table 3 is the fluctuation of calorific intake, both in amount and in composition, throughout the year. Much of the dietetic problem in tropical countries, in fact, is of a seasonal or temporary nature. Throughout most of the tropics, and especially in the savanna or monsoon tropics, one frequently encounters references in the literature to the 'hungry season', the 'hunger gap', or 'the hungry months'. Miracle (1958) has argued that this concept may well be an exaggerated one – at least the notion that it occurs regularly. Clark and Haswell (1964) go farther and contend that the whole hunger problem of the tropical underdeveloped world is grossly exaggerated. These authors examine F.A.O. and other data on food requirements and calorific intake, and conclude that there is only a 15–20 per cent and not a 50 per cent deficit as is so often supposed.

Much remains to be learned about many aspects of the health problem in tropical lands. In this field, as in so many others, the chief and urgent need is for more reliable basic data. Continued research in public health, tropical medicine, and entomology is as necessary as it ever was. To some extent, admittedly, any improvement in the general health situation must depend on economic and social development: a decrease in prosperity will affect, for instance, the dietary of the population. But equally, without positive physical and mental health there can be no question of making the fullest possible use of the natural resources and economic opportunities of the tropical world (Hodder, 1959: 133).

. . . . . .

While accepting that many tropical peoples possess attitudes and traditions that can militate against their ready absorption into a rapidly developing or industrializing society, neither the available evidence nor common experience suggest that there is any inherent physical or mental incapacity for this kind of change.

Rather must it be assumed that the quality of tropical labour is potentially as good as anywhere else in the world. It must also be assumed that tropical labour can be made as efficient as any other kind, given a full understanding of the exact nature of resistance to change in any specific area, and given also that attempts to induce the required change take into account the limits and opportunities set by any particular situation. Sociological, social, anthropological, psychological, medical and educational research, and technical education: it is on such bases that any programme for improving the quality of tropical labour in a rapidly developing society must be built.

CHAPTER 5
Human Resources and the Population Problem

Population data. In perhaps no field of tropical studies are accurate basic data so necessary yet so scarce as in the field of population analysis. This applies not only to the simple totals of population but also to the demographic structure – birth and death rates, age and sex ratios, migration statistics, and the like. According to the available data it seems that rather over one-third of the world's population lives in humid tropical countries today, but tropical countries are not generally densely populated, though many post-war development theories seem to assume that densely populated countries are the prototype of all developing countries. In fact, however, the notion that they are crowded lands is true only of parts of the Caribbean and especially of parts of the Asian tropics. The really high densities of population in the tropics, moreover, commonly occur in one of two main types of area: the small islands associated with plantation economies, such as the West Indies, Mauritius, and Ceylon; and the long-settled, usually large, agricultural countries such as India whose present high density is partly a result of successful development in the past. Countries like India were able to support a high density of population before it started growing in the modern period. In the plantation islands, on the other hand, migrant labour was brought in to add to the indigenous population; high population densities subsequently developed, being helped 'by the relative ease with which diseases such as malaria can be wiped out from the islands' (Myint, 1964: 32).

Beyond presenting Table 4 no attempt is made here to give any detailed regional account of the population distribution. Tropical Asia, it will be seen, alone contains over two-thirds of tropical peoples and a quarter of the world's population. Outside Asia the tropics accommodate only about 8 per cent of the peoples of the

Table 4. *Population numbers and density of tropical countries* (1964 estimates)

	Population in thousands	Density per km²
Tropical America		
Costa Rica	1,387	27
Cuba	7,434	65
Dominican Republic	3,494	72
El Salvador	2,824	132
Guatemala	4,305	40
Haiti	4,551	164
Honduras	2,209	20
Jamaica	1,739	159
Mexico	39,643	20
Nicaragua	1,597	11
Panama	1,185	16
Trinidad and Tobago	949	185
Barbados	242	563
British Honduras	103	4
Cayman Islands	9	34
Guadeloupe	306	172
Leeward Islands	141	149
Martinique	310	281
Netherlands Antilles	205	213
Puerto Rico	2,584	290
St Pierre and Miquelon	5	21
Turks and Caicos Islands	6	15
Virgin Islands (U.S.)	41	118
Windward Islands	334	158
Bolivia	3,647	3
Brazil	78,809	9
Colombia	17,482	15
Ecuador	4,881	17
Peru	11,298	9
Venezuela	8,427	9
Guyana	629	3
French Guiana	36	1
Surinam	324	2
	201,136	

Table 4. – *continued*

	Population in thousands	Density per km²
Tropical Africa		
Burundi	3,000	110
Cameroon	5,103	11
Central African Republic	1,320	2
Chad	3,300	3
Congo Brazzaville	826	2
Congo Kinshasa	15,300	7
Dahomey	2,300	20
Gabon	459	2
Gambia	324	29
Ghana	7,537	32
Guinea	3,420	14
Ivory Coast	3,750	12
Kenya	9,104	16
Liberia	1,041	9
Malagasy	6,180	11
Malawi	3,900	33
Mali	4,485	4
Niger	3,237	3
Nigeria	56,400	61
Rwanda	3,018	115
Senegal	3,400	17
Sierra Leone	2,240	31
Togo	1,603	28
Uganda	7,367	31
Tanzania	10,325	13
Upper Volta	4,750	17
Zambia	3,600	5
Angola	5,084	4
Equatorial Guinea	526	10
Mauritius	722	387
Mozambique	6,872	9
Reunion	382	152
Sao Tome and Principe	58	58
Rhodesia	4,140	11
	182,774	

Table 4. – *continued*

	Population in thousands	Density per km²
Tropical Asia		
Burma	24,229	36
Cambodia	6,120	34
Ceylon	10,965	167
India	471,624	155
Indonesia	102,200	69
Laos	1,960	8
Malaysia	8,537	57
Pakistan	100,762	106
Philippines	31,270	104
Singapore	1,820	3,133
Maldives	96	322
Thailand	29,700	58
Viet-Nam (North)	18,400	116
Viet-Nam (South)	15,715	92
Brunei	97	17
Portuguese Timor	543	36
Ryukyu Islands	927	422
Total	729,965	

Source: U.N. *Demographic Yearbook, 1965*, New York, 1966

world. There are clearly wide contrasts in population density between tropical Asia on the one hand and tropical America and Africa on the other, as well as between different parts of the same sector. There are also wide differences in the pattern of population density: thus the peripheral, coastal distribution of population in tropical South America contrasts with the relatively more even distribution in tropical Africa. Within each country, too, the spatial distribution of population is always an important factor in development: no economic development plan for Venezuela, Nigeria, or Malaya, for instance, could afford to ignore the great range of population densities found within those countries. Finally, in dealing with this question of population distribution, account must be taken of the urban–rural distribution. While it may be true that in tropical countries the role of urban economies in national development is less than in most developed lands, towns in all tropical countries are nevertheless important centres of economic power. The distribution of the larger towns of over 100,000 population reveals a general correlation with the most densely populated areas; there are almost two hundred towns with populations over 100,000 in tropical Asia as against eighty in tropical America and thirty-six in tropical Africa. Even more striking is the distribution of cities of over one million inhabitants. While the ten 'million' cities of Asia are spread over a large area, the three in tropical America are on the extreme outer fringes of the tropical zone. There are not as yet any 'million' cities in tropical Africa.

In discussing the regional distribution of population, attention must also be directed to the question of population mobility or migration – either rural–urban or rural–rural. And, as Prothero (Steel and Prothero, 1964: 190) points out for Africa, population mobility today is one of the most important factors in African demography and influences the character of the population in many parts of the continent: 'it is of immediate practical concern to governments in the conduct of administration and in promoting economic and social developments'. Whether movements of population should be encouraged and directed by governments in any positive way is very much a matter of opinion. But certainly the present distribution of people in many tropical countries seems to act as a brake on economic development. In particular, it is perhaps difficult to spend long in the tropics without being forced to the conclusion that one of the chief restrictions on development is underpopulation. In very few parts of the tropics does the density of population seem to be too high for successful economic progress. For most areas, in fact, it is perhaps fair to suggest, as Brookfield (1960) has done for New Guinea, that a measure of planned redistribution of population is necessary if the benefits of economic development are to be more widely diffused; in particular, the concentration into urban and rural areas of at present widely scattered populations is perhaps a precondition of development.

Racial and tribal composition. The racial composition of the population is very relevant to any analysis of tropical economic development, for foreigners have in the past played a particularly important role in tropical lands. Apart from the specialized services
contributed by Europeans during and since the colonial period, the
work of the immigrant Chinese in South-east Asia; of Indians in
Mauritius, the West Indies and East Africa; of Lebanese and
Syrians in Brazil; of Lebanese and Chinese in the West Indies;
and of Lebanese and other Levantines in West Africa – all have
done much to further the growth of the exchange sector of underdeveloped countries, 'and to promote their economic growth generally. They have accumulated capital, provided skills and aptitudes
not present or developed among local people, and have pioneered
in the development of trade, transport, and industries. By per-
meating the economy more extensively than the establishments
and activities of the large-scale European mercantile, industrial,
mining or plantation concerns, their influence has generally been
more widespread and has affected large numbers of local people
directly' (Bauer and Yamey, 1957: 107).

The Chinese immigrants and settlers in South-east Asia are
especially numerous and have been the subject of several studies.
Their contribution to economic development has been striking and
they play a particularly important part in the economic life of
Malaya. In Sarawak, too, where most of the non-indigenous
peoples are Chinese, they occupy the more densely populated
coastal and lower valley strips in the relatively well-developed west.
As in many parts of South-east Asia, the Chinese provide the chief
urban element in the Sarawak population, the capital, Kuching,
being 60 per cent Chinese; the Chinese dominate, too, in business,
the whole internal trade of the country passing at some stage or
another through the hands of Chinese merchants. In most parts of
the world, though the numbers of foreign immigrants may now be
very small indeed, such immigration, selective as it is nowadays,
continues to have an economic significance out of all proportion to
its actual volume.

Yet while the traditional functions of non-indigenous peoples
are still frequently important factors in the economic development

of individual countries, the analysis of economic development prospects must now also take account of the far-reaching social and political implications of the resulting plural societies, the problems of minorities, and the European settler problem. While in Africa, especially in East and Central Africa, the problem of the European settler is or has been dominant, in other parts of the tropics more attention is focused on the Chinese, Indian and similar problems: thus in Guyana and Indonesia racial tensions disrupt stability. Yet even within relatively homogeneous racial groups the problem of tribalism is often an equally serious matter for economic development planning. In Nigeria, for instance, the major human groups – Hausa, Fulani, Yoruba, and Ibo – are, in fact, linguistic and cultural rather than racial groups, but they do, nevertheless, form an important divisive factor in the Nigerian population. The geographical distribution of the tribal groups emphasizes and perpetuates these differences, being associated with one or other of the three main population nuclei in the north, west, and east respectively. There is also a large number of smaller but still distinct groups, some of which, like the Kanuri, Ibibio, and Tiv, total over half a million each. In Nigeria, as in so many tropical countries, the internal diversity of tribal groups, languages, and cultures is a fact of fundamental importance for economic development planning.

Population growth. In relating population to economic development in any tropical country the rate of population growth is commonly a more important factor than is the size, density, or distribution of that population. Of the three variables that directly affect change in population numbers – births, deaths, and migration – the first two are nowadays by far the most important. In many countries population growth has in the past been very much a question of migrational surplus: in Malaya, for instance, the population growth up to about 1900 was almost exclusively a function of migration; and until recently Trinidad's population increased for the same reason. Today, however, migration is generally a negligible factor in population growth throughout the tropics, though labour migration – often of a temporary or seasonal nature –

is still an important consideration in any analysis of the problem of labour supply, especially in parts of the African tropics.

In spite of the limitations of crude rates, it is worth emphasizing that rates of natural increase in tropical countries are not generally so high as is commonly supposed. Only in a few cases, such as Malaya and some of the Central American countries, is it over 3 per cent (Table 5). On the other hand, the potential for population growth is admittedly very high indeed, for the present figure is kept down – at least in most African and a few Asian countries – chiefly by high crude death rates. As these death rates are brought down, the large potential seems certain to assert itself. Almost all development programmes, indeed, must take account of the fact that the rate of population growth will accelerate as the control of diseases and improvements in maternity, child welfare, and hospital facilities lower death rates. Lewis (1955) distinguishes three sets of factors in the fall of death rates: the effects of better nourishment; better environmental improvements, especially in health; and modern hospitals, clinics, and similar institutions. Lewis calculates that each of these three groups might be responsible for a reduction of 1 per cent over a ten-year period: in other words, taken together, they can bring down the death rate from 4 to 1 per cent in a decade. How dramatically some of these factors can operate may be illustrated from Ceylon where the death rate fell by 34 per cent from 1946 to 1947 as a result of the use of DDT against endemic malaria: from 1945 to 1952 the death rate was reduced from 22 per thousand to 12 per thousand.

This argument varies from one country to another. In Burma the present relatively low rate of population growth is caused by a high death rate, the infant mortality rate of 130 per thousand being one of the highest in the world; Burma, consequently, has a large potential for reducing her death rate and so must face the fact that her rate of population growth must rise rapidly. The Philippines, on the other hand, can reasonably hope for no significant increase in her relatively low rate of natural increase because this is not a function of a high death rate.

On the basis of available vital statistics, and ignoring for the moment the effects of migration, it can be said that the population

G

Table 5. *Crude birth and death rates for selected countries* (1964)

	Crude birth rates/1,000	Crude death rates/1,000	Rate of natural increase
Tropical America			
Costa Rica	40·8	8·8	32
El Salvador	46·5	10·5	36
Guatemala	43·5	16·8	26·7
Jamaica	39·4	7·9	31·5
Mexico	45·3	9·5	35·8
Puerto Rico	30·2	6·6	23·6
Trinidad and Tobago	27·6	6·1	21·5
Brazil	40·0	11·0	29
Guyana	39·9	7·6	32·3
Colombia	43·0	14·0	26
Surinam	43·0	7·6	35·4
Venezuela	47·0	9·0	38·0
Tropical Africa			
Central African Republic	48·0	30·0	18·0
Congo Kinshasa	43·0	20·0	23·0
Gambia	38·7	21·0	17·7
Ghana	47·0	24·0	23·0
Kenya	50·0	20·0	30·0
Senegal	43·3	16·7	26·6
Togo	55·0	29·0	26·0
Uganda	42·0	20·0	22·0
Zambia	51·4	19·6	31·8
Tropical Asia			
Brunei	43·0	6·4	36·6
Burma	50·0	35·0	15·0
India	38·4	12·9	25·5
Indonesia	43·0	21·4	21·6
Malaya	39·1	8·1	31·0
Pakistan	43·0	16·0	27·0
Singapore	29·9	5·5	24·4

Source: U.N. *Demographic Yearbook, 1965*, New York, 1966

of the humid tropics is increasing at an average rate of something between 2 and 2·5 per cent in tropical Asia and Africa, and between 2·5 and 3 per cent in tropical America. In other words, something like 30 million people are being added every year to the population of the humid tropics.

One of the most important demographic implications of this high or potentially high rate of natural increase is a large number of children in proportion to the population of working ages. Whereas the age median in the United States is twenty-nine, in South-east Asia it is about eighteen. The proportion of the population under fifteen years of age varies from 37 per cent in Burma to 43 per cent in the Philippines or Congo Kinshasa, so that the percentage of the total population thereby excluded, at least in theory, from the effective working population in tropical lands is about 40 per cent, whereas in many developed countries the figure is between 22 and 30 per cent. In practice, however, this theoretical burden of child dependency is lightened by the low age at which children enter the effective working force. For this reason a large family is frequently regarded as an economic asset.

The high proportion of children in the total population limits capital formation: the needs of the whole community have to be satisfied by a small working population so that little is left for the purposes of investment. Moreover, where infant mortality rates are high, an unusually large part of the investment made in the bearing and rearing of children is wasted because so many of them never live long enough to enter the adult labour force. Something like a quarter of the Indian national income is spent in maintaining those who die before they reach the age of fifteen, as compared with a figure of about one-fifteenth in Great Britain. All such figures are useful criteria of the quality and texture of life in a country.

The population problem. In most contemporary discussion on the economic development of tropical countries in America, Africa, and Asia, great emphasis is placed on the 'population problem'. Much is being written of the problems of population pressure and overpopulation, of the 'population explosion', and of the urgent need to limit births (Villard, 1963). Certainly anyone attempting to examine the problems of development in any tropical country cannot fail to see how important to his analysis is the population problem in all its manifestations; yet so diffuse is this whole question that it is difficult always to be precise, either about its meaning or about its implications for development.

Much of the discussion about the relationship between population distribution and density on the one hand and economic development on the other centres around the question of population pressure, and is based on the assumption that some areas are overpopulated and that others are underpopulated. To express it another way, it is believed that there are too many or too few people in some areas to allow the fullest economic development. Implicit in any discussion of this kind, too, is the concept of optimal population.

A close examination of almost any particular case study usually reveals important limitations to these ideas. Population pressure is such a relative term – relative to natural resources, the extent of division of labour, the standard of living, techniques of production, and total economic structure – that it is useful only within the framework of a rigid and specific set of variables. Simple density figures are particularly suspect as an indicator of population pressure. Moreover, there is the paradox that 'a country may be overpopulated relatively to its agricultural resources, but underpopulated relatively to its capacity for industrial development. Some very small countries, like Jamaica or Mauritius, face the problem that their populations are much too large in relation to agricultural development and at the same time much too small to support a wide range of industrial development' (Lewis, 1955: 87).

It can also be suggested that a high density of population is a necessary precondition for economic development in many tropical countries. Without following too closely the hypothesis that moderate physical obstacles to material advance have supplied the main stimulus to the growth of civilizations, there is little doubt that the most striking adaptations of human societies to the limitations of their tropical environment have been achieved in areas where population density was so high as to make life impossible without some such adaptations.

Much has been written on this question; but from the point of view of the present study it seems that too much emphasis is commonly placed upon the problem of population pressure in any consideration of economic development in tropical countries. In particular, the term 'population pressure' is too often used loosely as a synonym for high density of population, poverty, or distress. But poverty or distress – relative to conditions in western developed countries – are characteristic features of tropical developing countries almost everywhere, whether heavily populated or not. The use of the term population pressure is generally valid only when the distress or poverty is seen to result directly from there being too many people in an area – too many in the sense that fewer people would result in an improvement in the standard of living. In fact, however, such a relationship can rarely, if ever, be demonstrated; and, in practice, it is to be doubted whether it exists anywhere. Furthermore, it is perhaps not too much to suggest that population pressure in the sense of there being too many people in an area for the available natural resources – whether land or any other kind of natural resource – is a rare phenomenon in tropical under-developed lands. This is so, partly because of the remarks already made about natural resources – that it must be postulated that in no country is the lack of natural resources a limitation to economic development – but also because the whole concept of population pressure rests upon the stability of factors which are essentially dynamic variables. Natural resources (either by trading, applied research, or technological developments); capital supplies; and population numbers and density (by the normal operation of the variables of births, deaths, and migration) – all are continually changing phenomena.

Another idea commonly advanced in any discussion on population pressure in many developing countries of the tropics is the concept of 'disguised unemployment'. This suggests that 'surplus' labour in agriculture (and even in industry) can be extracted from their present occupations without affecting present production and can be put to use in the construction of productive capital goods like roads or irrigation works. In recent years, however, this idea has come in for a good deal of criticism, and the few available case studies suggest that the idea rarely works in practice. Furthermore, the disguised unemployment argument focuses attention, as does so much of the current discussion on population pressure, away from the central problem – how to raise productivity. As Myint (1964) has put it, the exponents of the disguised unemployment idea have tended rather to concentrate on 'how to increase the mere volume of unskilled work by extracting the surplus labour from agriculture, and have made a great point of saying that this can be done without improving the techniques of production' in the agricultural sector (p. 90). But the central problem of how to raise productivity remains.

The whole concept of pressure of population or overpopulation in relation to economic development seems, in fact, to be a vague, ambiguous, and even sterile idea. It is certainly responsible for a great deal of misunderstanding about the nature of development problems in tropical developing countries.

On the other hand, there seem to be firm grounds for asserting that the *rate* of population growth is central to any study of tropical development: in its simplest terms, the chief problem of tropical development is how to increase production at a rate substantially higher than the rate of population growth. The Malthusian position on this is well illustrated in the low-level equilibrium trap (Fig. 1), discussed by a number of writers, in which any short-term rise in *per capita* income is quickly exceeded by a more rapid gain in population numbers (A). In this context Leibenstein (1954) emphasizes the need for a critical minimum effort to escape this trap (B).

In terms of capital, as noted earlier, a high rate of population growth is costly. Assuming that about 3 per cent of the national income must be saved to provide capital for a 1 per cent increase in population (U.N., 1955), it follows that in some countries up to 10 per cent or so of the national income must be saved for demographic investment – merely to cope with the additional population without any increase in the average standard of living. In Singapore and Malaya, for instance, the population is growing at the rate of 3–3·5 per cent a year, so that these countries require a net domestic capital formation rate of 9–12 per cent merely to provide the increased population with a *per capita* endowment of capital assets every year. According to many writers, in fact, all developing countries need to save not less than 10 per cent of their national income as a precondition for any kind of development, and without such a rate of savings Rostow (1956) has argued in his stage theory that the 'take-off' as an automatic and self-generating growth can-

Fig. 1. The low-level equilibrium population trap (after Leibenstein, 1954; Nelson, 1956; and Kindleberger, 1966).

not occur (Fig. 2). In similar vein is the oft-quoted remark that 'the central problem in the theory of economic growth is to understand the process by which a community is converted from being a 5 to a 12 per cent saver – with all the changes in attitudes, in institutions and in techniques which accompany this conversion' (Lewis, 1955: 225–6). According to Myint (1964) there are several conceptual weaknesses in this general proposition that all developing countries need to save at least 10 per cent of their aggregate national income to achieve economic development. Nevertheless, even the most cursory examination of domestic capital savings in tropical countries makes it clear that these savings are generally insufficient, relative to the rate of growth of population, to allow any significant increase in the average standard of living – or in other words, to allow economic development. While some of the tropical American countries – Venezuela, Puerto Rico, Trinidad and Tobago – have annual growth rates in gross domestic product of over 6 per cent, most other countries – notably Honduras and Nicaragua in the Americas; Malawi, Nigeria, and Uganda in Africa; and Malaysia and Pakistan in Asia – are achieving rates of growth of gross

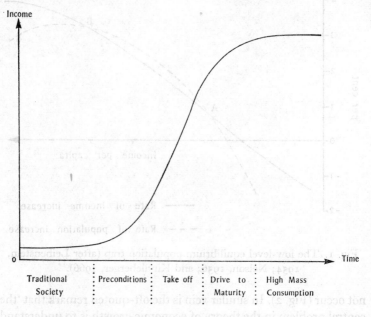

Fig. 2. Rostow's stages of growth
(after Rostow, 1960 and Kindleberger, 1966).

domestic product barely sufficient to keep pace with the rise in population.

What measures can be used to meet this problem? There are two main lines of approach – one demographic, the other economic. The demographic approach includes a direct attack on the natural increase by the use of birth-control measures. The value of these in reducing birth rates is very much a matter of opinion. Until very recently, only a minority supported the large-scale artificial restriction of births on the grounds that it was for long unlikely to be effective in tropical developing lands where educational and economic standards are still low, and cultural, particularly religious, prejudices are difficult to overcome. More recently, however, an increasing number of writers have come out in support of propagating birth-control methods as potentially perhaps the most effective means of achieving economic prosperity. The development of the oral contraceptive and the popularization (in some parts of India, for instance) of voluntary sterilization have brought direct birth control much nearer as a practicable proposition.

However, without in any way dismissing the demographic approach to the population problem, it must be pointed out that the more fundamental and difficult task is to make people in the developing countries *want* to use birth-control measures. More important still, the recent upsurge of interest in birth control as a means of inducing economic growth in developing lands is perhaps a rather dangerous trend because birth control seems to be becoming accepted as the latest and most fashionable of a series of panaceas. In a sense, however, to reduce the rate of population growth, while undoubtedly desirable, is simply to apply a negative solution, for by itself a declining birth rate can do nothing to increase production. An excessive preoccupation with how to reduce the birth rate is thus concentrating attention on the wrong thing. Furthermore, it normally fails to take account of the fact that the rate of natural increase will inevitably tend to stabilize itself when death rates reach the levels already reached in the developed world. Again, by western analogy and by analogy with Japanese experience, birth rates may ultimately fall as economic development – expressed in terms of a rising *per capita* income, urbanization, education, occupational changes, and the weakening of religious ties (Spengler, 1952) – proceeds. Finally, any such reduction of birth rates as envisaged by the supporters of large-scale birth-control programmes would, if successful, have serious long-term repercussions on population age structures. The demographic–economic problem as it has been posed here is very much more than simply a demographic problem. Its solution, therefore, must not lie solely in demographic terms.

As for the economic approach to the demographic–economic

problem, this is directed at developing production at a rate greater than the rate of population growth; and under this heading lie two important measures – the increase of agricultural production and the development of industrialization. Both of these will receive more detailed treatment in later chapters of this book. Some of the demographic implications of such development, however, may be briefly noted here.

The increase of agricultural production implies both its areal extension and its intensification. The areal extension of agricultural land, or agricultural colonization, normally has one or more of three aims: to increase the total food production, to relieve population pressure in the area from which colonists come, and to encourage economic development in the area to which colonists go. Thus in Indonesia, official support for agricultural colonization in the islands outside Java is designed to increase the total amount of food produced within Indonesia, to relieve population pressure in Java and, finally, to assist in the development of the more sparsely peopled islands. Although pioneer agricultural settlement may possibly be successful in raising the total amount of food produced within a country, and is sometimes successful in promoting economic development in the new area, there is no evidence that the redistribution of population for agricultural colonization in the tropics has anywhere appreciably lessened population pressure in the country of origin. The numbers involved have never been large enough over a short enough period. In 1953 the Indonesian Government moved some 50,000 colonists from Java to sparsely peopled islands, chiefly Sumatra and Borneo. Such a figure constituted less than one-tenth of the natural increase in Java during that year.

Furthermore, migration may even increase distress in the area of origin because of its effects on the age and sex structure, for migration commonly involves the younger, more active male section of the population. This has been demonstrated in Togo, where it has been shown that far from relieving population pressure, the emigration of Cabrais into central Togo commonly increases distress in the Cabrais country. Of the population present in Cabrais country in 1957, for instance, the female dominance was striking, notably in the fifteen to fifty-nine age group, upon which the bulk of the farm work relies. This disparity, giving a total sex ratio of 120 females to 100 males, is almost wholly the result of emigration.

All schemes for agricultural colonization have to face the dilemma that if the shift of population is large enough and speedy enough to reduce significantly population density in the place of origin, then the rate of immigration into the new area is likely seriously to strain its capacity for absorbing people. And unless it is planned and controlled it can hinder rather than assist development.

As subsequent chapters will attempt to show, the extension and intensification of agricultural production is very much a matter of applied research. Taken together, the extension and intensification of agricultural production constitute important measures to meet the demographic–economic problem in tropical countries. The nature and relative emphasis of these measures must, of course, vary from one country to another, depending on population density and the present pattern and intensity of land use: in densely populated Java the emphasis is on intensification by various means whereas in Sumatra the extension of agricultural land is of first importance. In some countries a combination of these measures is emphasized. Thus in the Philippines the increase of food production from 7·3 million tons in 1955 to 11·3 million tons in 1959 was partly accounted for by the extension of agricultural land – about 5 million acres (2 million ha) of public land was distributed during the five years; production increases, however, also arose from improved farm practices, soil conservation, improvements in irrigation, and the use of fertilizers.

As for industrialization, meaning not only the development of primary and secondary manufacturing industries but also the mechanization of agriculture, one of the commonest arguments for promoting industrialization in underdeveloped countries is that it will be accompanied by urbanization which, by western analogy, brings about a decline in fertility. Certainly the relevant social transformations are more easily effected in towns than in rural areas. But on the other hand, such a decline in fertility must lag well behind the expected decline in death rates previously referred to, so that no immediate reduction in the rate of natural increase of population could be expected. Analogies between western countries and the countries of the tropics are dangerous because the potential for population expansion in tropical countries is in most cases greater than it ever was in western countries at the early stages of their industrialization. Several writers have shown that the increase in population in Western Europe followed, not preceded, the industrial revolution, whereas in the developing countries today the population explosion is preceding the true industrial revolution. The situation in the developing countries today, then, makes any general increase in prosperity more difficult than it was in England around 1780, or in France around 1820.

Urbanization is also held to reduce population pressure on the land, for urbanization is frequently a function of migration from rural to urban areas. Gourou (1966) has advised relieving the rural density in overcrowded tropical Asia by this means. But such an urban drift can lead to increased pressure of rural population because here again there is often a disproportionately large number of young adults in these peasant migrants to the towns, because such migration hastens the decline in rural industries, and because it may lead to a decline in food production in the rural areas. Moreover, urbanization often leads to severe problems of population pressure in the urban centres themselves. As in many parts of the world, the large cities and towns tend to grow more quickly than the medium-sized and small towns. It is chiefly from the large cities that most of the broader benefits of industrialization can be expected to radiate. And although town planning can help to meet the problem of housing in such centres, it can do little to affect the problem of employment arising out of urban population pressure; certainly one of the most distressing features of many large tropical cities is the squalid, congested nature of much of the housing, exemplified in Singapore's 'Chinatown', in the slums of Rio de Janeiro, or in the *ranchos* of Caracas.

Industrialization has one important demographic disadvantage compared with agricultural production as a measure to cope with the demographic–economic problem in tropical lands: it is less effective at absorbing labour. The application of those western technological devices aimed at saving labour may appear unsuitable, even illogical, in a tropical context with its problems of under-employment. The high population density in those parts of the tropics most likely to attract and stimulate industrial development must limit the pace of introduction of any labour-saving machinery. This disadvantage applies not only to manufacturing industry but also to the mechanization of agriculture. Consequently, such measures as seed improvement and the scientific use of fertilizers should perhaps play a larger part in schemes for intensifying agri-cultural production than should the more expensive and labour-saving measures of mechanized agriculture. As subsequent chapters will show, however, the problem is much more complicated than this.

The whole population issue is immensely diffuse and contro-versial, and it has only been possible here to refer to a few of the major problems relevant to this study. A number of important considerations have been touched upon only very briefly. For in-stance, little has been said of the absolute size of the population base, although this is important for three reasons. In the first place, a country with a huge population base presents in many ways a more formidable problem than does a country with a small popula-tion, even if the latter's population is increasing at a faster rate. The 11 millions being added to India's population every year clearly pose more serious issues than do the 40,000 extra Togolese. Secondly, the varied problems of economic development in those developing countries with large populations today are both more urgent and more difficult than in the developed world where large populations grew up after, and as a consequence of, economic development. Finally, as will become apparent in the following chapters, the lines along which countries attempt to solve their demographic–economic problem are to some extent affected by the size of the total population. While the size of a domestic market is, of course, a function of more than simple population totals, coun-tries like India and Brazil clearly offer more favourable environ-ments for setting up those heavy industries which depend for their success upon economies of scale. On the other hand, countries like

Ceylon and Trinidad, with relatively small populations, are believed to be handicapped in their industrial development by the smallness of their domestic markets.

Much remains to be learned about demographic–economic relationships, more especially in the developing lands of the tropics. Much of what has been said above is controversial, and it is always difficult to be quite sure that one is entirely free from cultural prejudices and is not affected by too facile analogies with western experiences. There is no doubt, however, that all tropical countries have a population problem in some form or another, and that this problem must be fully considered in all plans for economic and social development. It has been argued above, however, that the central problem of economic development in all tropical countries is what has been called here a demographic–economic problem – how to ensure that production rates of increase consistently outstrip the rates of increase of population. It has been argued that the solution lies less in attempting directly to control population growth than in a rapid increase of production. The chapters that follow concentrate attention on how to achieve this, beginning with agriculture.

CHAPTER 6

Types of Tropical Agriculture

Of all possible lines of development in tropical developing countries, perhaps the most important and certainly the most widespread relate to the improvement of agricultural production. Any comparative study of agriculture in the tropics, however, reveals striking regional differences in agricultural practices and types of agricultural enterprises; and these differences make it impossible to generalize about tropical agriculture, especially where this concerns problems of and potentialities for development. While some types of tropical agriculture are believed by many writers to be limiting factors to development, other types receive wide support as the rational basis for agricultural development policy. The present chapter makes a brief assessment of a number of the most significant of these agricultural types from the point of view of the part they can play in the general processes of agricultural improvement.

Shifting-field cultivation. Perhaps the most widely condemned of all agricultural types in the tropics is shifting-field cultivation; and attempts to effect a change over from shifting-field to permanent-field cultivation loom large in several agricultural development plans. It is widely assumed that shifting-field cultivation constitutes an important restriction to development, especially in Africa, where it is most common, though it is also widespread in parts of tropical America and to a lesser extent in the more lightly populated parts of tropical Asia.

Much has been written on the question of shifting-field, or 'swidden' cultivation (Pelzer, 1957; Conklin, 1961; Watters, 1960), and a certain amount of controversy has arisen over terminology. As defined by Pelzer (1957) it is an agricultural system which is characterized by a rotation of fields rather than crops, by preliminary clearing by 'slash and burn', and by short periods of cropping alternating with long fallow periods. Only human labour is used – there are usually no draught animals – manuring is not practised, and the chief tool is the hoe. Other writers, however, feel it necessary to distinguish between shifting-field cultivation and rotational bush fallowing, the latter involving no movement of settlement; it is pointed out that rotational bush fallowing has often developed out of shifting-field cultivation as a result of a trend towards fixed settlement. And Brookfield (1960: 237), discussing the case of New Guinea, argues for distinguishing between swidden cultivation, long-fallow cultivation, and semi-permanent cultivation – the latter occurring only when the period of fallow is so short that the actual field boundaries are preserved from one period of cultivation to the next. For the purposes of the present study, however, the term shifting-field cultivation is taken to refer to all types of agriculture that are not strictly permanent-field.

There is irrefutable evidence of the dangers and limitations of this type of agriculture. Clearly the whole system depends on sufficient land being available so that adequate fallowing can take place. Especially where population density is high or where custom restricts the cultivable area, the system can lead to soil exhaustion, loss of fertility (especially by destruction of humus in the upper layers of the soil) and soil erosion. Shifting-field cultivation may also be responsible for the disappearance and degradation of forests. In southern Ivory Coast, for instance, it has been estimated that 12·5 million acres (5 million ha) of forest have been reduced to secondary jungle and bush as a result of shifting-field cultivation methods used by a million or so people living in the forest and needing a farming area ten times larger than that needed by the same number of people using permanent-field methods of cultivation. It will be obvious, too, that shifting-field cultivation is often largely responsible for the very low percentage of land under cultivation in parts of the tropics. Again, this type of cultivation has been held to constitute a major limitation to the spread of permanent tree crops; in Zandeland, de Schlippe (1956) has noted that shifting-field cultivation restricts the development of the oil palm, a crop which, he claims, could become a great asset to the agriculture and nutrition of the Azoroh if, as a crop, it was integrated into a system in which permanency of habitation and protection from bush fires would give it a chance. In many countries, indeed, shifting-field cultivation is now illegal (as in Malaya) or controlled (as in Ceylon).

On the other hand, shifting-field cultivation in some form or another must originally have been the practice of pioneer agriculturalists in most parts of the world and so may be regarded simply as an expression of a civilizational level – a stage through which most agricultural systems have at one time passed. Moreover, the destruction caused by shifting-field cultivation is often exaggerated. The removal of natural vegetation in tropical rain forests containing many large trees is an arduous undertaking, and usually the practice adopted is to remove only the smaller trees and undergrowth and leave the larger trees. These larger trees help in forest regeneration when the land is eventually abandoned, and the ash derived from the burning of the smaller trees and undergrowth helps to provide a soil rich in phosphorus and potash. Then there are a number of local variants, many of which have been empirically evolved to meet some of the limitations of the system. Thus in some forms of the *chitemene* system of Zambia the large trees are lopped and the loppings burnt together with the undergrowth, supplemented with loppings and undergrowth cut from adjoining uncultivated areas. The increase in the amount of ash allows land to be cultivated for longer periods than would otherwise be possible under ordinary methods of shifting-field cultivation.

One important advantage of shifting-field cultivation is that it provides a way of dealing with the very severe weed problem with which tropical cultivators are commonly faced. Burning destroys weeds and controls the growth of weed seeds for some time; and this point has been singled out by some writers as constituting the chief attraction of the whole system for the tropical cultivator. Certainly the imminence of weed invasion is a common indicator used by the farmer to ascertain when it is time to abandon his plot; and for this reason it has been suggested that one of the best

H

agricultural services which could be rendered in the tropics is to supply peasant cultivators with herbicides to control weed growth (Clark and Haswell, 1964).

Yet another advantage of shifting-field cultivation as an agricultural system is that it requires less labour to produce a specified amount of food than does the system of permanent-field agriculture. This is an important issue, for many writers have assumed the opposite: '*per se* it is no more difficult for an African family to cultivate a piece of land on the lines indicated for permanent cultivation, than to follow its ancient customs of shifting-field agriculture' (Pim, 1946: 21). Yet it is often pointed out that the preference shown by tropical farmers for shifting-field rather than permanent-field cultivation is really one of preference for leisure. Shifting-field techniques of production are more economical from the point of view of labour; 'in spite of the high initial input of labour, overall labour requirements of shifting agriculture are low and discontinuous' (Clark and Haswell, 1964: 71). Present evidence suggests strongly that shifting-field cultivation yields better returns in terms of labour input than does permanent-field cultivation. It is hardly surprising then to find that a tropical peasant may choose the former rather than the latter as long as conditions of population density allow him this choice. There are many examples of the truth of this assertion. Thus the Cabrais farmer of northern Togo, moving southwards to colonize part of the empty 'middle belt', quickly adopts shifting-field cultivation methods instead of perpetuating in his new surroundings the sophisticated system of intensive permanent-field cultivation which has characterized his densely populated homeland for centuries. Again, as Geddes (1954) points out for the Sarawak Land Dyaks, although sedentary swamp rice cultivation gives higher yields of about 1,700 lb per acre (1,903 kg per ha), preference is invariably given to the production of dry/hill rice in the hills where yields are only 1,400 lb per acre (1,578 kg per ha), using shifting-field cultivation methods; for whereas yield per man-hour on the swamp is 0·87 kg (giving a total input of 2,165 hours per ha), in the hill areas yield per man-hour worked is 0·95 kg (giving a total input of 1,663 hours per ha). In areas of low population density absolute yields per unit area are, of course, of very much less importance to the farmer than are yields per unit of labour.

It is possible, then, to defend the system of shifting-field cultivation within limits. The system is by no means to be condemned out of hand. It is not an unsuitable method of agriculture 'where population density is low enough to permit sufficiently long fallow periods so that soil fertility can be maintained by means of a grass ley in those parts of the tropics where shifting-field cultivators work grasslands and by means of a second-growth forest in forest areas' (Pelzer, 1957: 73). On balance it would seem that shifting-field cultivation, or some modification of it, need not necessarily restrict agricultural development and may, in fact, be the best form of land use in the early stages of settlement where population density is low. Pelzer is surely justified in concluding that the least imaginative approach to the problem of shifting-field agriculture in development is that of outlawing the practice, without showing the cultivators an alternative, without showing them how to develop a more intensive type of land use, and without making certain that shifting-field cultivation is not, in fact, sound in the social and natural environmental conditions under which the cultivators live.

The critical factor in any assessment of the unsuitability or otherwise of shifting-field cultivation is the density of population or, to put it in another way, the amount of cultivable land available *per capita*. What exactly the critical density is at which shifting-field cultivation becomes undesirable it is impossible to generalize about, estimates varying from 5 persons to the square mile (2 per km^2) in Zambia to over 310 persons to the square mile (120 per km^2) in Guatemala. In this connexion specific mention must be made of the work of Allan (1965) who developed in Zambia a method of calculating the carrying capacities, in terms of population, of various indigenous and changing agricultural practices on different types of soil; he also formulated a way of working out for different systems the critical population density beyond which the land would begin to deteriorate. This critical density figure must depend very much on a combination of local circumstances. Within the context of any one specific area, however, there seems to be a strong and natural causal connexion between an increasing density of population and the need to change over from shifting-field to permanent-field cultivation. Once the density of population reaches a point at which adequate fallowing is impossible, then the system of shifting-field cultivation breaks down; it must then be replaced by one in which at least the same amount of food can be produced from a smaller area of land continuously cropped. This relationship between population density and agriculture has been demonstrated by a number of writers, including Grove (1957) for northern Nigeria. In such a change over, however, certain techniques and practices such as manuring and crop rotation are usually essential features. These will be discussed later; but it may be noted here that there are many instances of quite indigenous adaptations or changes along these lines, so that where the need has arisen the shifting-field cultivator has always been able to change over to permanent-field cultivation, with all the refinements of techniques this implies. Apart from the innumerable examples of indigenous intensive permanent-field cultivation in such large areas as the Kano close-settled zone of northern Nigeria and the Boukombe area of north-western Dahomey, there is in almost all parts of the tropics some development of compound-land farming – *kampong* land in South-east Asia – around even the smallest rural settlements.

Presumably, however, large-scale empirical adaptations and changes of this kind occur under natural conditions only very slowly and lag behind the need to change as expressed in a rising density of population and falling levels of living. The central question today is not whether shifting-field cultivation is desirable or undesirable but how to encourage in any specific case a more rapid change over from shifting-field to permanent-field cultivation than that brought about through the stimulus of an increasing density of population. Here is an important though as yet almost untouched field of applied research.

Wet-rice cultivation. Wet-rice cultivation would seem to merit special though necessarily very brief consideration in this study of types of tropical agriculture because it is widely believed to be an ideal towards which many parts of the African and American tropics should aspire. It is often pointed out that wet-rice cultivation is associated with some of the most densely populated and long-settled parts of Asia and with the homes of a number of civilizations. Wet-rice cultivation is also permanent-field cultivation *par excellence*. Rice also has the highest nutritive value per unit area of all the tropical cereals, can grow largely irrespective of the fertility of the soil, and is not normally associated with problems of soil erosion. According to several writers, indeed, the absence of wet-rice cultivation in a tropical country is generally speaking a mark of economic backwardness. And it is certainly true that some of the most remarkable innovations in indigenous agriculture are provided by wet-rice cultivators like the Ifugao people of the Philippines, who cultivate terraces constructed some 4,000 years ago.

The cultivation of wet rice is now being encouraged in many parts of both the equatorial and savanna areas of the American and African tropics. In the Amazon Basin rice is being extended into the tidal and seasonal flood plains; and in the Sokoto region of northern Nigeria the *fadamas* (swamplands) – formerly dry-season grazing grounds for Fulani cattle – are being utilized for wet-rice cultivation on an increasing scale.

The development of land for wet-rice cultivation, however, faces a number of difficulties. Topographical conditions are not always suitable: in tropical Africa, in particular, there are few large flood plains. It is possible to create the necessary topographical conditions by terracing, as is shown so clearly in the Philippines, but unless labour is plentiful such works may be impracticable. As Pelzer has emphasized, 'land that can be kept inundated for all or part of the year is more valuable than high land from the cultivation point of view. This reflects the amount of labour that has to be invested in order to alter the topography, so that water can be held at a desired level and drained off when necessary' (Pelzer, 1957: 12). Climatically, too, the Asian sector of the tropics is favoured by the monsoonal conditions which give sufficient water but also guarantee substantial periods of dry, sunny conditions: truly equatorial conditions are by no means ideal for rice growing in that the cloud cover is too sustained and rain is always likely. The tropical savanna climate is also not ideal in that the total amount of rainfall is usually inadequate by itself.

Perhaps the greatest limitation to the extension of wet-rice cultivation in the tropical sectors of America and Africa, however, is cultural. It is difficult, for instance, to see the Yoruba of West Africa changing over quickly or easily from a yam-cassava to a rice culture. To most Africans, indeed, yams, cassava, maize, millets, sorghums, and plantains are their traditional basic foodstuffs; and most agricultural efforts to increase food production will probably continue to be directed chiefly at the production of these crops. Only in certain specially restricted areas are there real hopes for extending the production of rice. It is certainly misleading and unrealistic to suggest that rice, any more than any other single crop, should form the keystone of tropical agricultural development policy.

Subsistence and cash agriculture. Only rarely is it possible to make a clear distinction between subsistence and cash agriculture. To some extent this is a semantic problem. Some writers refer to 'subsistence crops', meaning thereby cereals and roots, and others talk of 'subsistence crop farming' to mean shifting-field cultivation or equivalent 'primitive' forms of agriculture. Yet another use of the term subsistence is to refer to 'subsistence economies' which clearly include the consideration of manufacturing as well as agricultural activities.

More important, however, the difficulty of distinguishing clearly between subsistence and cash farming is due to the fact that pure subsistence agriculture, in which no crops are produced for cash exchange at all, is now a very rare phenomenon indeed. In practice, a clear distinction can only be made between subsistence farming and cash or commercial farming at the extreme ends of the range – between a farmer who grows nothing at all for cash at one end and the farmer who grows everything for cash and nothing for local consumption at the other end. More commonly, tropical farmers practise a system which may involve a considerable degree of subsistence agriculture, varying perhaps from year to year and from season to season, yet always involving too an element – sometimes a substantial element – of cash cropping (McMaster, 1962). Subsistence agriculture today may perhaps most usefully be defined as an agricultural type which is devoted mainly to the production of food for local consumption but includes also a varying proportion of cash cropping. The very imprecision of this definition, however, is significant. One of the critical factors, clearly, is the intention of the farmer. If the farmer merely sells his surplus or sells some of it when he needs a bit of extra cash, then he is still a subsistence farmer; whereas if he cultivates with the intention of selling most of it he is a cash or commercial farmer. Yet this intention is itself a highly variable factor. Whether a Yoruba farmer, for instance, keeps all his yams, sells some of them or sells all of them, depends on his own particular food requirements in that year, the price of yams, his assessment of future price changes, and a host of other variables, many of them non-economic. Finally, it is not always clear whether to participate in local as distinct from more distant or external exchange for the disposal of agricultural produce implies a departure from subsistence agriculture.

Almost any tropical country is full of examples of how this difficulty of distinguishing between subsistence and cash agriculture operates in practice. For Malaya it has been shown how a Malay will, 'with the help of his wife, cultivate enough rice for himself and family, grow vegetables after the rice harvest to supplement the family diet and sell in the local market, and have a small area of rubber trees which he taps to sell the produce to a Chinese dealer for export. This mingling of activities has its advantages, by spreading the risks . . . His subsistence agriculture, then, serves as a kind of backlog for his economic system, and concentration on the export crop alone would result in an unbalanced system of production' (Firth, 1946: 22). This kind of situation is nowadays very much the rule rather than the exception.

It is clear, then, that the whole concept of subsistence agriculture is essentially a dynamic one, and is perhaps best thought of as being but part of a continuum or succession of stages. Thus for Africa, indigenous agricultural resources have been divided in United Nations reports into crops mainly for local consumption; crops partly for consumption and partly for export; and crops

mainly for export. Another classification refers to different economies – 'commercial', 'commercial-subsistence', and 'subsistence
with some commercial' – using the criterion of reducing propensity
to exchange. Winter (1956) has outlined the stages of agricultural
development from the point of view of an administrator imposing
taxation (Clark and Haswell, 1964):

(i) pure subsistence (no cash crops, no taxes, no import or
export of labour);
(ii) subsistence with taxes (some cash crops, labour going to
seek employment primarily to pay taxes);
(iii) subsistence and cash crops (cash crops grown primarily
for own cash needs, not primarily for taxes. No labour export);
(iv) subsistence and cash (cash crops grown primarily for own
cash needs, not primarily for taxes. Labour export important);
(v) agricultural plantations (most agricultural labour working
for wages);
(vi) industrial economy.

Winter's scheme is of particular value here in that it sketches the
normal trend of subsistence farming through commercial agriculture towards 'industrialized agriculture' and an industrially
oriented economy. In spite of its limitations, this scheme does
provide a conceptual framework within which to examine the
highly variable and discrete data about tropical cultivators and
their place in the general processes of economic development.

The importance to tropical development studies of this notion
of a continuum between purely subsistence farming at one end
and commercial farming at the other is emphasized by the common
assumption that successful economic development involves a decrease in the proportion of subsistence farming and an increase in
cash cropping. Some economists, indeed, do not regard subsistence
agriculture as an economic activity at all. Yet while most tropical
countries are rightly concerned to extend their non-subsistence
sector, the fact remains that still the larger proportion of food consumed by many, probably most tropical peoples, is still grown on a
subsistence basis. Consequently, far from trying to push subsistence farming farther into the background in development planning,

an immediate need is to try by all possible means to improve the efficiency of the subsistence sector. One of the limitations of subsistence farming is that little attention has been paid to scientific research into the staple food crops with which subsistence farmers are most closely concerned. Agricultural research in the tropics has concentrated upon the commercial crops which are exported to industrial countries (sugar, rubber, tea, and cocoa) and has almost entirely neglected what is produced for home consumption (yams, cassava, and sorghums). Only over the last decade or so has the picture begun to change. This is an important issue. It is not a question of trying artificially to bolster up subsistence farming with the intention of delaying any natural transition to commercial farming on the part of tropical cultivators; for apart from any other considerations, the crops involved are not exclusively 'subsistence crops' at all but crops which play an important part in cash farming as well. The transition from subsistence to cash farming does not imply a complete change of crops on the farm.

Without here questioning the need for a transition from subsistence to cash farming on the part of many tropical cultivators, a few of the implications of this transition may usefully be pointed out (Upton, 1966). One of the economic implications of the introduction of cash cropping is that land requirements per man tend to increase. There are two reasons for this: each man is willing to devote an increasing proportion of his working year to agriculture, assuming the effectiveness of the incentives for him to do so; and technical improvements increase the area which a man can handle (Clark and Haswell, 1964). There are difficulties, then, to be encountered in trying to encourage a greater proportion of cash farming in densely populated rural areas, although as a subsistence economy develops it is able to direct a gradually increasing proportion of its labour force to non-agricultural tasks. Furthermore, while in the normal course of events we should expect agricultural growth beyond the subsistence level to be in livestock products or crops other than staple food crops such as cereals and roots, in practice a country may continue to expand its production of these crops beyond its own requirements and export some of them. Another consideration to bear in mind is that as a subsistence farming community becomes more of a commercial farming community it tends at first to consume more of its own food: in other words, with the increase in cash farming the demands on subsistence crop farming increase. Here is further support for the view that subsistence farming must not be viewed simply as an anachronistic if picturesque survival from the past.

In spite of these reservations, however, there can be little doubt that the development of cash farming is a vital element in economic development and is a necessary prerequisite for and concomitant of industrialization and urbanization. But this accepted, the question arises – how is this development to be brought about? To a very large extent the effective extension of political, social, and economic control within the boundaries of most countries in the tropics has introduced taxation and so, inevitably, at least some element of cash farming; indeed, European administrations in colonial times frequently introduced taxes with the deliberate objective of promoting a transition from a purely subsistence agriculture to a cash economy. But as Winter points out, the tax incentive is generally left behind in subsequent stages in the trend towards purely commercial farming.

Once a community has discovered the opportunity of earning and spending cash, it does not automatically seek to work longer hours in order to earn more money. Numerous instances of this point have been described and the reasons for it discussed. One reason why the purely economic incentive does not always work is related to differing attitudes to work and material rewards on the part of the tropical cultivator. Thus in Indonesia it has been noted that 'preference for periods of idleness among Indonesians is to some extent derived from a philosophical outlook, backed up by bitter experience, which has taught that a life of ceaseless toil is hardly human, because it allows little opportunity for development of the spirit' (Indonesian Govt., 1951). In their non-agricultural hours, too, tropical peasants may have to make clothes, build and repair houses, or perform religious and similar duties. To some extent it is true that the opportunity to earn more may itself bring about the desired change in attitudes on the part of the tropical cultivator. But, again as Clark and Haswell (1964) have pointed out, an examination of the economics of subsistence agriculture commonly reveals a falling off of marginal returns to further labour inputs in any given area.

This whole question of incentives is clearly crucial in any consideration of specific measures to encourage cash farming. Much emphasis is often given to technological developments of one kind or another, but to the farmer concerned with the problem of whether or not to increase his cash crop participation perhaps the most critical factor is market opportunity. Most immediately the peasant is concerned with his own local market opportunities and organization for handling his cash crops, though on a wider scale this may be a matter of world markets. As one writer has noted, 'production for the world market has been an essential element in providing a large part of the peasant's cash income and raising his standard of living. But until a system has been evolved of effectively controlling the prices of raw materials (or food) on world markets so as to ensure a reasonable long-term security for the producer, the peasant has a serious problem in deciding what time and energy he should put into export production as against subsistence production' (Firth, 1946: 2). Another most important and closely related factor is transport. Both these factors will be examined in more detail in later chapters.

Smallholdings and plantations. Though the development of the production of cash crops may be accepted as a necessary element in economic development, there is some controversy over the relative merits of the two main methods of achieving such development — by the plantation or by the smallholding system. Historically, it is true, the production of cash crops for export on a large scale has been most closely associated with the plantation, especially for bananas, cocoa, coconut products, coffee, oil-palm products, rubber, sugar and tea, though the relative share of plantation and smallholding cultivation has always been subject to violent changes. Yet in West Africa, for instance, the cocoa industry has been built up almost entirely by native smallholders; and in Malaya smallholders are responsible for some two-thirds of the rubber production. The importance of the smallholder in tropical agricultural production is widely underestimated, especially in such exporting countries as Burma and Thailand (for rice), Colombia, Ivory Coast, and Togo (for coffee), East Pakistan (for rice and jute), Ghana and Nigeria (for cocoa), and Uganda (for cotton). Small-holdings – using the term in its widest sense to cover small shifting-field cultivators as well as the most sophisticated forms of peasant permanent-field cultivation – have always been responsible for the bulk of agricultural production, if not of large-scale export production, in the tropics. There are, in fact, few if any exclusively plantation crops; cocoa and oil palm, for instance, are peasant smallholding products in West Africa, but are plantation products in Brazil, Indonesia, and Malaya.

The plantation usually refers to a large-scale combined agri-cultural and industrial enterprise that is both labour-intensive and capital-intensive; it also raises, and usually processes industrially, agricultural commodities for the world market. Size and processing equipment are often important criteria. But the definition varies from country to country and from crop to crop: in Malaya, for in-stance, the rubber plantation is defined simply in terms of size, 100 acres (40 ha) or more constituting a plantation. In general the size of plantations tends to increase, except where they are indi-genous, as in parts of West Africa, or sold to indigenous peoples. On the other hand, recent studies on the smallholder in tropical agriculture indicate that the smallholder percentage in total pro-duction is increasing.

Most cash crops affected by plantation activities are tree crops, and in this fact lies much of the significance to tropical develop-ment of the relative advantages of the smallholding and plantation systems. For as many writers have pointed out, the development of tree crops is one of the keystones of tropical agricultural develop-ment. Pelzer (1957) notes that after the forest is cleared the soil may produce one good annual crop, but a second crop is greatly reduced in yield after the wood ash has been used up; thereafter it hardly pays to continue cultivation for the production of annuals. On the other hand, it may well pay to plant less demanding tree crops, such as rubber, on relatively infertile soil, especially where the woody matter is not burned but is broken down more gradually by the micro-fauna and micro-flora inhabiting the soil. Again, from the ecological point of view the cultivation of deep-rooting perennials, such as trees, is a highly desirable form of land use in the tropics, especially where land cannot be brought under ley-field cultivation or when soils are of medium or low fertility and therefore not suited to continuous cropping with shallow-rooting annuals.

There is little agreement about the relative long-term prospects of plantations and smallholdings in plans for economic development. Wickizer (1960) thinks that plantations can assume risks better, are better informed – they are certainly much more likely to apply the results of modern research than are smallholders – and are better able to judge future requirements. Bauer (1957), on the other hand, says that rises in wages and salaries have substantially weakened the competitive position of estates against smallholdings, and may well weaken the world's demands for tropical plantation products and stimulate the production of synthetics; he regards as a weakness of plantations their heavy overhead costs and the reliance of plantations on large numbers of hired workers, many of whom may leave when prices are higher elsewhere. Pelzer (1957) agrees that peasant holdings can certainly compete with plantations in the labour market. Reference is also commonly made to the arguments advanced against the establishment of the plantation system in West Africa, where the British authorities supported peasant smallholding agriculture as having in the West African context the advantages of firmer roots, lower costs, and greater adaptability to rapid expansion or change. As McPhee (1926) has noted, the value of the peasant method in West Africa was that it could be easily grafted on to the traditional economy.

A further argument against the plantation system rests upon the historical association of plantations with monocultural economies. Early European pioneers saw potential profit in developing the almost unlimited virgin lands of the tropics. Towards this end they imposed agricultural methods which were based on the practices of peoples of the temperate regions. Not infrequently these practices resulted in the establishment of monocultural systems of production, with consequent ill-effects on fertility. Moreover, monocultural systems of agriculture may leave a country wide open to world price fluctuations and crop failure. Thus Brazilian economic development has been held to be restricted, not by want of land or natural wealth but by want of labour and capital, 'and the fact that for 400 years the economy of the country was dominated by a series of monocultures': sugar-cane, cacao, tobacco, cotton, rubber, and coffee (Humphreys, 1946: 112–13). Again, the monocultural system is particularly susceptible to the onslaught of diseases. This holds true in temperate climates to some extent, but under tropical conditions infestations can easily become widespread epidemics; blights which have affected the cotton, cocoa, rubber, and banana industries in the past may face the monocultures of the future.

It seems that in certain circumstances and for certain crops – notably tea – the plantation may well be the best system for tropical countries, and in many countries plantations are now being introduced or reintroduced. Many new political leaders in the developing countries, however, still view the plantation with suspicion as an institution created by and for colonialism, though they recognize that in certain circumstances the plantation system has important advantages over the peasant smallholding system of cultivation. On the other hand, it is equally clear that smallholdings have a number of advantages over plantations in that they are usually more diversified in their crop structure and may include an element, perhaps an important element, of subsistence food agriculture; in this sense the smallholding system can provide greater security. Most of the available data suggest the invalidity of many of the comparisons commonly made between the two systems. To some extent they are not comparable because the criteria of judgement are different: to the smallholder interest focuses around maximum production per man-hour and per unit area, whereas in plantations maximum yield per tree and per tapper are normally the more important criteria. Furthermore, the smallholder's interests are more diffuse, for he often has other crops – including subsistence crops – which take some of his interest. This is clearly an important point in development planning, since policies aimed at improving smallholder cultivation are not necessarily relevant to the improvement of plantations.

In one of the most important analyses of the role of the smallholder in tropical export-crop production, Wickizer (1960) examines the relative significance of the smallholding and plantation systems for specific tropical crops. He comes to a conclusion that fits in with trends in tropical export-crop production since his work was published: the role of the smallholder in commercial agriculture in the tropics is gradually gaining in stature, but without completely displacing the plantation system or its equivalents.

Livestock farming. The need for introducing livestock into the agricultural systems of many parts of the tropics has already been indicated on a number of occasions. Apart from dietetic considerations – in particular the provision of animal protein elements in diet – there are many agricultural and industrial products associated with livestock rearing, notably hides, skins, wool, and dairy produce. It is especially desirable where there is a short rainy season and farming operations have to be concentrated into very short time periods. Finally, and perhaps most important, by providing manure, livestock farming constitutes an important element in attempts to effect that change over from shifting-field to permanent-field systems of cultivation discussed earlier in this chapter.

The generally small amount and poor quality of tropical livestock farming is due to a number of factors. In the first place, the average quality of the indigenous livestock – buffaloes, zebu cattle, swine, goats, sheep, and poultry – is low. As Tempany and Grist (1958) have noted, the chief methods of improving animals in the tropics are by selection within the native type, by grading up with improved types or breeds from other countries, and by the development of new types from animals that are partly graded towards the improved type. Increasing attention is being paid to the reaction of animals to climatic factors, a subject of particular importance because the upbreeding of indigenous tropical livestock frequently entails introducing animals from temperate regions. Disease is also responsible for the absence or poor quality of livestock in many parts of the tropics. Especially in tsetse-infected areas, the extension of livestock management must depend either upon controlling the fly distribution or upon the successful rearing of further disease-resistant strains.

At least of equal importance to the quality of the stock, however, is the quality of the pasture. Fodder grass is more abundant than good pasture grass in most tropical countries. Elephant grass (*Pennisetum purpurem*) has been found to be one of the most satisfactory fodder grasses, though it is unsuitable for pasture – except in its early stages – because it grows up to as high as 15 feet (4·6 m). Guinea grass (*Panicum maximum*) is another good fodder grass, though again it does not seem to be a satisfactory pasture grass. Generally speaking, tropical grasses are lacking in nutritive value, even where they are abundant, and result in a slow growth of animals and in the need to allow large areas of grazing per animal. At present, research on tropical grassland agronomy is only in its infancy and the potentialities of the tropics in this respect are not fully known. Sufficient experiments have not yet been made on the extent to which efficient grassland management and improved animal husbandry can influence the production of different plant associations under the wide range of conditions of soil and climate which occur in tropical latitudes. Nevertheless, it does seem that the grass resources of the tropics have not yet been tapped to any extent and that substantial increases in yield can be obtained from certain natural grass associations or cultivated grasses by the use of such simple measures as improved grazing management or the application of fertilizers. In parts of Central America experiments seem to have been generally successful in the growing of *Pangola* grass (*Digitaria decumbens*), used as paddocked, fertilized, and irrigated pasture. In conditions of good soil (or with fertilizers) and with adequate rainfall (or irrigation water), production levels have been as high as one ton of beef (live weight) per hectare per annum. This is twice the current yield from the best meadows in France (Dumont, 1966: 73).

The need to control and improve grazing management is strikingly illustrated by the damage which has already been done to tropical grasslands by overgrazing. The ecological balance on rolling tropical grasslands is sensitive: once disturbed its restoration may be impossibly expensive. As already noted in Chapter 3, overstocking and overgrazing have been responsible for serious soil erosion and soil exhaustion, notably in eastern and southern Africa, in Malagasy and in India. Not only is damage done by the stripping of the vegetation and by the hooves of animals, but burning is also an essential part of a pastoral economy in many parts of the tropics. It is believed that in some areas this has been a much more important cause of soil exhaustion and soil erosion than has agriculture or hunting: 'the cultivators' clearings and the desire to track down game easily when it has been frightened by fire or to get honey and wax are far less effective causes of the burning. They must burn to destroy the old hard grasses and encourage the new young grass' (ibid.: 291). However, burning for livestock rearing is probably inevitable in a tropical country with long grass and a well-marked dry season, though the whole question has aroused some controversy. But burning is desirable, under certain conditions, in removing old dried vegetation of little or no nutritive value and in facilitating the growth of new grass at the onset of the rains. It is also claimed that burning helps to keep bush encroachment in check. However, to the peasant cultivator the labour and time involved in cutting down the bush during the dry season is so great that it is safe to say that he would not cultivate or graze the area he does without burning. From the point of view of pasture improvement the effect of burning varies very much with the pasture. Certainly in Brazil, controlled burning is practised with the object of improving the composition and quality of herbage. And in Africa the dominance of certain desirable species of red cat grass (*Themeda triunda*) is favoured by burning, while certain undesirable species are suppressed.

Finally, the humid tropical climate tends to limit livestock and dairying industries because of the difficulty and expense of processing, storing, and preserving the products – especially milk, butter, meat, and cheese. Yet all these problems are clearly capable of solution, given time, continued applied research, and – particularly in the processing, storing, and preserving stages – large-scale injections of capital.

Mixed farming. By analogy with developed agricultural systems in temperate countries and indeed by the example of a number of indigenous economies within the tropics, it seems true to say that

I

the ideal system of husbandry is one in which crop and animal production are combined to form systems of mixed farming and alternate husbandry, producing both crops and livestock simultaneously or alternately from the same land (Stamp, 1964). Such systems of mixed farming, however, are little developed in tropical countries except, perhaps, in India. In most parts of the tropics there is little connexion between pastoralists and cultivators, though in certain parts of West Africa nomadic tribes may for short periods pasture their herds on the resting lands of the cultivators – a practice which helps to maintain fertility and may assist the cultivators to shorten the fallow period.

Mixed farming, however, should go far beyond a system in which animals simply supply manure, energy for pulling farm implements, and milk or meat. True mixed farming implies the integration of crop and animal farming in which the mutual benefits of the system are maximized; in particular, cultivation must provide the livestock with feed that is both regular and of a quality able to raise substantially the productivity of the livestock. It is possible to argue, however, that full integration of livestock and crop farming should be reached only in the middle and later stages of an animal's life. Dumont (ibid.: 108) has referred to the practice in which young animals are reared and brought up in non-cultivated areas – nursery grounds – from which they are sent eventually to the cultivated zones to provide draught labour, manure, milk, and meat. Upon reaching maturity the animals are fattened and moved on towards the chief exporting or consuming areas. Dumont cites the case of Brazil, where the land around San Salvador de Bahia is laid out so that the inner belt around the city is reserved for horticultural and dairy produce; the second belt beyond consists of rich fattening pastures; while the third belt provides livestock-rearing grounds for the first three years of an animal's life. The most distant areas – the *sertao* – thus produce the young calves and constitute the nursery country (ibid.; 108).

It is sometimes suggested that in the tropics better results are to be obtained from the use of artificial manures than from attempts to develop animal husbandry. One must also recognise the possibilities of a transition from hand to mechanical power taking place without the intervening stage of animal traction. But from the point of view of nutrition and diversification of agriculture, advantages attend the successful incorporation of animals into existing farming systems.

Several writers, however, emphasize the difficulties of extending mixed farming to the tropics. Some authorities find such a system more suited to drier areas where inherent fertility of the soil is greater and pasturage is richer. And it is suggested that mixed farming is perhaps 'more readily organized in countries that experience sub-humid or semi-arid conditions than in super-humid and humid regions' (Tempany and Grist, 1958: 52–3). Yet another authority is cautious about applying the system to the tropics, though finding it the best answer in the world as a whole. He concludes, however, that in due course and suitably modified through research and experimentation it may be extended to the tropics (Stamp, 1964).

The problems of mixed farming include peasant resistance to the introduction of draught animals into a hand hoe economy. This has been well illustrated by Haswell (1963) who discusses unsuccessful attempts to introduce draught oxen into Gambia. The peasant cultivators there objected that they could not feed both themselves and their oxen; and measurements of agricultural output and human and animal consumption showed this to be true. In milled rice equivalents the level of agricultural productivity did not exceed 438 kg per person per year, and averaged only 270 kg; whereas the ration recommended for draught oxen included 365 kg per beast per year. The local oxen there are a mixture of Ndama and Zebu and are fairly resistant to trypanosomiases except when underfed or overworked. This appears to be a common finding, and it is unlikely that draught animals will easily be introduced into areas where productivity is still too low to make their use economically feasible. There is, as Clark and Haswell show (1964: 48–68), an economic equilibrium between the ox plough and the hand hoe; and not until production reaches an average figure of 500 units kg grain equivalent per year is it worthwhile employing animal rather than human labour. In Indonesia, De Vries (1954) shows that the cost of keeping a buffalo only doubtfully balances the additional output obtained through its labour, and that the use of draught animals leads to further substantial increases in production only if sufficient land is available for the extra cultivation: Grove (1957: 11) makes the same point for parts of Katsina Province in northern Nigeria. On the other hand, it must be noted that there are certain parts of the monsoon tropics with a short but very wet season where the use of draught animals is a necessary condition without which agriculture would hardly be possible at all.

However, there are grounds for some optimism regarding the future of mixed farming in tropical countries. There are, after all, examples of indigenous developments of this type of farming. Among the Cabrais of northern Togo, for instance, a careful and intensive terraced agriculture is carried on, incorporating not only crop rotation but also the application of human and animal manure, the use of leys and the keeping of animals. Among the Chagga of Mt Kilimanjaro and the Ukara of Lake Victoria, too, similar developments may be seen where cattle are fed on cultivated fodder, kept in sheds, and the manure composted and spread on the fields. While it is true, therefore, that mixed farming calls for more knowledge and skill on the part of the farmer, he has, where necessity has demanded, been able to develop the necessary experience and skills. With indigenous mixed farming, as with other indigenous systems of tropical agriculture, no attempt at improvement can afford to ignore the ready fund of empirical knowledge already enshrined within the existing systems and types of agriculture.

CHAPTER 7

The Increase of Agricultural Production

Some remarks about the relevance of agriculture to economic development have already been made. That it constitutes an important means – in some countries the most promising single means – of dealing with the demographic–economic problem and so of raising the level of real income per head, cannot be doubted. But there are a number of difficulties about increasing agricultural production in tropical countries, many of which arise out of two features of tropical agriculture: low agricultural productivity *per capita* and per unit of land; and a low percentage of land under cultivation. The present chapter concentrates attention on these two characteristics and examines some of the related problems of development.

I. Intensification of Agricultural Production
Low agricultural productivity *per capita* and per unit area is one of the characteristic features of tropical developing countries. Whereas in North America the average annual agricultural output per person is 2·5 tons, in Asia it is less than 0·25 tons and in Africa less than 0·125 tons. Crop yields in tropical countries are almost invariably very low indeed. In Pakistan the average yield of rice is 828 lb per acre (930 kg per ha), compared with 2,334 lb in the United States, 3,360 in Japan, 4,582 in Italy, and 4,450 in Spain. As one report on African agriculture puts it, 'the increase in agricultural production has fallen behind the growth of population, and earnings from agricultural exports have steadily declined. On a *per caput* basis, production was lower in 1962–3 than five years before . . . and food production *per caput* was estimated to have declined by about 4 per cent . . . and may in fact have gone below the pre-war level' (F.A.O., 1966: 5–7).

Much has been written on the whole question of the intensification of agricultural production in the tropics, and success is clearly to be related to the whole field of agricultural improvement, including those issues already discussed in previous chapters – water supply and irrigation, soils, human resources, and the change of shifting-field to some forms of mixed farming and permanent-field cultivation. Similarly, issues to be discussed later – mechanization, technological improvements, marketing, and trade – are equally relevant to this question of how to intensify agricultural production in the tropics. It seems convenient, however, to concentrate here on five issues: land tenure; crop improvement; fertilizers and manuring; crop protection (pests, diseases, and weed control); and crop succession, plant populations, and plant spacing.

Land tenure. A great deal of discussion has centred around problems of land tenure in tropical lands, and it is now generally recognized that agricultural productivity may be dependent as much on the evolution of sound systems of land tenure as upon the development of improved agricultural practices. The relevance of the land tenure problem to the intensification of agricultural production is made explicit in most current economic development plans. In Pakistan's Second Five-Year Plan, for instance, particular attention is drawn to the small and uneconomic size of land holdings and to the excessive fragmentation of holdings as being among the chief causes of low crop yields; plans to increase crop yields, therefore, include the consolidation of holdings and the elimination of excessive fragmentation. Similar policies are to be found in the Fourth Five-Year Plan for India, where considerable progress has already been made in the Punjab, Uttar Pradesh, Maharashtra Gujarat, Madhya Pradesh; but elsewhere in India much remains to be done, especially in the Travancore-Cochin (Kerala) area where 95 per cent of all holdings are still under 5 acres (2 ha) in size. The splitting up of land into small, often widely separated fragments is commonly the result of laws of inheritance. But however it comes about it is undesirable for a number of reasons: it wastes time in the need to supervise; it makes capital duplication necessary; the small plots are difficult to work with ploughs;

weed and pest control is made difficult; and it limits experimentation.

Another common element of the land-tenure problem is the form of land ownership. Communal land ownership tends to give way to individual tenure as agriculture develops; but in many contemporary communities, especially in Africa, there is still a general absence of the concept of land as a negotiable possession. Such a system may conceivably operate satisfactorily as long as land is plentiful and as long as annual crops and nomadic grazing constitute the agricultural system; but difficulties arise where there is much demand for land. Even more important, the capital needs associated with the intensification of agricultural production have emphasized the need for a system of land tenure based on titles which can be sustained in law and so used as security for loans for development. Without such provision, many of the measures for increased production noted later on cannot be applied, and farmers are not so likely to take a long-term interest in their lands. In Trinidad and Tobago this problem was recognized in the 1961 Agricultural Smallholdings' Tenure Ordinance which provides for better security of farmers' holdings and allows farmers to obtain loans to develop their smallholdings; this measure is believed to be already affecting productivity and performance. Moreover, soil erosion difficulties are likely to be reduced, 'for farmers will know that to ensure a continuous stream of income from the soil he will have to take measures to care for it' (Trin. and Tob. Govt., 1963: 72). In Tanganyika, the oft-quoted report of the Royal Commission stated the need for new local land-tenure legislation and set out a number of basic requirements, the most important being to 'establish grounds for confidence that existing property rights will not be arbitrarily disturbed' (International Bank, 1961: 72). Without such confidence, it was argued, farmers could not be expected to show adequate interest in their lands.

Systems of land tenure in tropical countries are so varied and often so little understood that they cannot easily be subjected to general description or analysis. According to Meek (1948), however, the importance of land tenure cannot be exaggerated in former colonial countries where land is, for the most part, the only form of capital and its exploitation the only means of livelihood a farmer has. A number of writers argue that land reform can release energy for increased production in agriculture and can stimulate education, road construction, labour organization, entrepreneurial initiative, and industrialization (Kindleberger, 1966: 220). In Latin America, Carroll has called land reform a 'catalyst of a large chain of complex socio-economic movements' (1961: 175); and for India Krishna (1959) has demonstrated the great importance of land-reform measures. According to these viewpoints, no successful attempt at social and economic change can be made without appropriate land-reform measures; and this applies not only to indigenous small-scale land units but also to those large European alienated lands still to be found in parts of eastern and southern Africa (Floyd, 1962). The 1965 famine in Kenya, for instance, seems to have been due in part to a too rapid, perhaps too politically motivated change over from former large European farms – usually over 3,500 acres each in size – to small African smallholdings, most of which are under 24 acres in extent. Furthermore, this land reform measure was accompanied by little success in bringing the African out of a subsistence into a market-oriented economy. The result was a dramatic and catastrophic fall in maize production.

A contrary opinion about the significance of land-tenure systems is expressed by Lewis (1955) who contends that it is easy to place too much emphasis on such institutional matters as land tenure and too little upon other means of increasing agricultural efficiency, especially through improving water supplies, seed farms for improved seeds, fertilizers, and agricultural extension services. The present institutional framework, Lewis argues, is in most developing countries quite adequate for an important advance in productivity by means of the introduction of improved technology. Land reform is certainly by no means the only or even the most important precondition of improved agricultural efficiency. Bauer and Yamey (1957) note that such means as the transfer of land to small-scale tenant cultivators or the scaling down of rents or debt charges are unlikely to bring about any significant improvement in agricultural productivity. Moreover, while legal arrangements preventing a holding below a certain size from being divided up can admittedly prevent further fragmentation of holdings, they can do nothing to improve the ratio of land to population. Similarly the measures taken in India to consolidate (by exchange among small-holders) holdings formerly divided into several tiny plots, often widely separated from one another, are a needed reform, but cannot solve the fundamental problem of too little land (Lewis, 1955).

Crop improvement. The increase of agricultural productivity by crop improvements is very much a matter of applied research and covers a very wide range of adaptations to environment or to something which results in more being harvested. The primary aim of the plant breeder is to produce more uniform high-yielding populations. But he may also breed for disease-resistant or pest-resistant strains; attempt to improve the look or quality of a product; increase its oil content or fibre strength; or improve a crop's storage properties. The plant breeder may also attempt to produce more convenient sizes or shapes of plants: in Congo Kinshasa, West Africa, and Malaya, for instance, some attention has been given to the breeding of oil-palm varieties which do not grow to great heights and so save expense and energy in the reaping of the crop.

Perhaps the most striking point to make about crop improvement in the tropics is that until recently attention was directed at improving a few of the more important commercial export crops, such as cotton, rubber, oil palm, and coffee. Relatively little so far has been done about detailed research into methods and problems of improving many of the basic food crops – maize, millets, and sorghums, dry or wet rice, yams, sweet potatoes, bananas, or plantains. But as a perusal of journals like the *Empire Journal of Experimental Agriculture* or *Agronomie Tropicale* reveals, this picture has been changing rapidly over the last decade or so. Research into the improvement of tropical staple food crops is now being energetically pursued.

Most economic development plans already have a good deal to say about the needs and possibilities of applied research into plant improvement. In India, seed farms are being established in all development blocks to meet the requirements of foundation seed of improved varieties, the aim being for every village to produce its own requirements of improved seed. Apart from rice, on which a good deal has now been done, much work has also gone into evolving high-yielding hybrids of maize, and it has been found that with moderate amounts of nitrogenous fertilizers the yield of maize hybrids increases to over twice that of local varieties: 25 per cent of the maize area is now being sown under hybrid varieties. Similar work is also going on in evolving hybrid jowar seeds. In Costa Rica good results have been obtained with work into the black bean and coffee, while in Trinidad sugar research has already led to significant increases in yields through improved varieties. In Trinidad, too, cocoa planters have been able to draw on the results of applied research which has developed very high-yielding and disease-resistant varieties: clonal and hybrid seedlings are now available for distribution to planters.

But in spite of the obvious value of developing new crop varieties for particular purposes – all aimed fundamentally at increasing production – the limitations to crop improvements along these lines cannot be ignored. Potentially high-yielding varieties of crops can prove successful only if their cultivation requirements are adequately met. Higher crop yields also mean increased demands on soil fertility which must be satisfied by manuring, fertilizing, and more careful cultivation. Improved varieties of crops also usually require good soil structure, adequate water supply, and disease and pest protection.

Some of the difficulties of introducing improved crop varieties into an existing farming system have been well illustrated in the Abakaliki district of eastern Nigeria (Blanckenburg, 1962). Here the variety of rice recommended by the extension service is BG 79, a variety developed at the rice station at Badeggi. The bulk of the Abakaliki farmers, however, still use a mixture of this variety with inferior indigenous strains. These different strains have a number of different characteristics so that the material is very unequal, especially with respect to maturity date and the size and quality of grain. This makes harvesting and processing difficult. Another problem here is that many farmers do not use fully developed seeds at all, but use winnowings with yields of something less than the yields to be obtained from the BG 79. The reason for this practice is simply that the winnowings are very cheap, whereas the BG 79 seeds are expensive. Although the returns from the improved seeds are better, lack of initial capital forces the farmer to plant inferior seeds.

Again, in India, hopes of increasing food production are now resting very largely on greatly extending the use of high-yielding varieties of cereals. Under the 'new strategy' in India, 35·5 million acres (13·2 million ha) of the best existing land – that is, about 8 per cent of the total arable land in India – are being put under new varieties of wheat, maize and rice by 1970–1. Research stations and farmers have already shown that when properly used the new varieties can increase yields by between 50 and 200 per cent. But these new varieties demand different techniques precisely applied; they need good water control; and their vulnerability to pests and diseases is high. Moreover, these new varieties demand the application of large amounts of the appropriate fertilizer – 200 lb per acre (222 kg per ha) – compared with 40 lb per acre (45 kg per ha) – for the old breeds.

Fertilizers. In discussing fertilizers in tropical agriculture it must be emphasized that much still remains to be done in utilizing natural manures, and to point out once again that many indigenous developments of permanent-field cultivation have been accompanied by the careful use of human and animal manures. In some areas animal manure is wasted on a dramatic scale, notably in India where nearly 400 million tons of cowdung (wet weight) – equivalent to 60 million tons of firewood – are burnt every year instead of being put on the land as manure. Some authorities question the role of natural manures in tropical agriculture, and this controversy is really part of the wider question of the function and importance of organic matter in tropical soils already referred to (p. 35). As the rate of disappearance of organic matter in the tropics is so rapid that it is doubtful whether humus (as it is defined in temperate countries) is ever formed, it has been questioned whether organic manuring really has any beneficial effects on tropical soils. The bulk of the available evidence, however, suggests that in some cases organic manure is generally effective and is occasionally even better at maintaining fertility than is inorganic manure or fertilizers: 'apart from any possible effect on direct fixation of nitrogen, organic matter is needed to supply energy for the processes of the nitrogen cycle and for the production of carbon dioxide which assists liberation of mineral plant food. An appropriate balance between carbon and nitrogen seems to be essential, and as the rate of disappearance of organic matter in tropical soils is more rapid than under temperate conditions, the aim must be to maintain this balance' (Tempany and Grist, 1958: 3).

The need for fertilizers – either by manuring or by artificial fertilizers – is now widely accepted, and some authorities give this much prominence in their analyses of how to increase agricultural production in the tropics. The F.A.O. suggests that if modest levels of nutrition are to be attained by 1980 the less-developed regions of the world must increase fertilizer consumption to about 30 million tons of plant nutrients by that date. Certainly as far as artificial fertilizers are concerned, tropical soils are now thought to be much more amenable to improvement than many earlier writers believed possible. The critical factor is structure; for if a soil has adequate structure then the use of fertilizers is likely to be practicable, as long as the right kind of fertilizer is known for any particular soil and the appropriate amounts of application have been determined for any particular crop.

Only three types of fertilizer can be mentioned here: nitrogenous fertilizers, phosphates, and lime. In the tropics, where losses and gains of nitrogen take place rapidly, adequate supplies of nitrogen in forms capable of assimilation when the crop needs it are of great importance. The most popular form is sulphate of ammonia, which is highly nitrogenous, relatively cheap, easy to apply, and easy to transport. Examples of its use are for sugar-cane (in the West Indies, Mauritius, and Hawaii), tea (in Ceylon and India), cotton (in the Sudan), rice (in a great many countries), and rubber (in Malaya). Another, though generally less satisfactory inorganic nitrogenous fertilizer, is nitrite of soda. As for phosphorus deficiency, this occurs extensively throughout the tropics, especially in tropical Africa, where it frequently forms a major limiting factor to plant growth. It is important in connexion with root growth, fruiting, and seeding of tropical plants. In Nigeria, field trials on the fertilizer requirements of groundnuts have shown that soil deficiencies of phosphates or sulphur are limiting factors, and nitrogen as a fertilizer confers no benefit because provided that sulphur is not limiting, then the groundnuts appear to be capable of fixing all the nitrogen they require. In these conditions, superphosphates have been found to produce the best results. Finally, the approach to liming under tropical conditions is quite different from what it is in temperate latitudes. In the tropics, where many crops tolerate or prefer acid soils and where lime is expensive, it should be looked upon more as a fertilizer than as a soil amendment or conditioner.

Largely as the result of experimental work, knowledge about the response of tropical crops to fertilizers has increased immeasurably over the last century. For obvious economic reasons the application of artificial fertilizers was first and most vigorously directed at plantation crops – notably to sugar-cane in the West Indies, Mauritius, Java, and Hawaii in the latter half of the nineteenth century. In more recent years, however, the use of fertilizers in smallholdings for staple food crops has also been studied, and an extensive literature now exists on, for instance, the effect of fertilizers on rice crops in Asia, groundnuts in West Africa, and maize and millets in East Africa. Nevertheless, a great deal remains to be done; and differences in climate and soil conditions have in some cases resulted in widely divergent conclusions.

As with crop improvement, however, there is some danger of exaggerating the importance of fertilizers in increasing agricultural production in the tropics. Hardy (1951) has emphasized that unless the three prime factors of crop production – water, air, and root room – are present in satisfactory quantities, any attempt to augment nutrient supply by the use of fertilizers will be ineffective and wasteful. Furthermore, whether or not it is economic to use fertilizers must depend on the cost of fertilizers, the resulting increase in yield, and the cash value of the crop. Lack of capital or credit facilities may also inhibit the use of fertilizers. Certainly there can be no question of looking upon fertilizers as the panacea for tropical agriculture. Yet they can clearly make very real contributions to increasing agricultural production, levels of nutrition, and standards of living.

The consensus of opinion in F.A.O., indeed, is that the use of fertilizers should be looked upon as the spearhead of agricultural development (U.N., 1963). The Freedom From Hunger Campaign (F.F.H.C.) Fertilizer Programme, begun in 1961, has been working in a number of countries, especially in West Africa (Hauck, 1966) and northern Latin America, and has shown convincingly that fertilizers can be used successfully by small peasant farmers using their traditional methods. Small peasant farmers can increase their crop yields by an average of over 50 per cent by using fertilizers alone; and it is difficult to set a limit to the possibilities when fertilizers are combined with other improved methods of farming. The Fertilizer Programme has shown the governments of the participating countries how to persuade small farmers to use fertilizers, and how to organize fertilizer distribution and credit systems where necessary. The need is primarily good advice and instructions about what fertilizers to use and how to use them in any particular area. Once the farmers have convinced themselves of the value of fertilizers, they will be all the more willing to try other modern methods of farming – better varieties, crop protection, improved cultivation, and mechanization (Richardson, 1966).

Pests, plant diseases, and weed control. Pests and plant diseases are perhaps especially serious problems in tropical agriculture because of the favourable climatic conditions of continuous high temperatures and high humidities; another factor has been the introduction of crops into different environments, a procedure which frequently encourages pests and diseases of plants. The history of tropical agriculture abounds with examples of destruction or damage by pests and diseases: the 1727 Trinidad cocoa 'blast', the stem-root disease in sugar-cane in the West Indies in 1890, the swollen-shoot disease of cocoa in West Africa, the 'sudden death' disease among Zanzibar cloves, and the 'wither tip' disease of Dominican limes. More recently the virus disease of groundnuts (rosette disease) caused havoc in the early years of the East African Groundnut Scheme, and in West Africa there was a serious development of maize rust from 1949–53. This was introduced from America into the ideal conditions for spore germination and infection along the Guinea coastlands and resulted in a loss of maize yields of up to 40 per cent.

The importance of plant protection is now fully recognized and receives explicit mention in most development plans. In India an area of 50 million acres (20·23 million ha) is now under protection against damage to crops from insects, rodent and other animal pests, diseases, weeds and parasitic flowering plants. While it is difficult to assess the precise extent of damage caused by such pests and diseases, 'there can be no doubt of its serious dimensions . . . big losses are (also) caused by deterioration of food grains and other agricultural commodities through insects, rats, mice' (Indian Government, 1961: 39).

Crop protection clearly embraces some of the points already made in connexion with crop improvement, especially as regards the breeding of disease-resistant strains. During the 1953–6 period the maize-rust disease in Africa was largely controlled by breeding disease-resistant varieties, most of which were developed by utilizing varieties of Central American and South American origin. Considerable natural selection, however, also took place during this period. As for insect pests, methods of controlling these include mechanized devices, trapping, the use of insecticides, close seasons, the control of alternative hosts, and the protection of stored produce. In some cases, too, biological control is appropriate, as with the control of the leafhopper by the introduction into Africa of a capsid bug from Australia and Fiji.

Other ways in which crop protection can be achieved include environmental selection in which crops are grown only under the climatic conditions most suited to them. Outside of these conditions crops are likely to be very much more susceptible to diseases. The classic example of this is the Hemileia leaf disease of arabica coffee. As Masefield (1962) has shown, below 5,000 feet (1,520 m) in East Africa the coffee becomes heavily infected with Hemileia and other diseases and pests, and must be replaced by robusta coffee. Furthermore, a great deal can be done by the very act of cultivation. Since over 90 per cent of insects spend at least part of their lives in the soil, cultivation is itself an important method of control, killing some insects by crushing, some by burying, and some by exposing them to the sun, birds, and other enemies. A good deal can also be done by appropriate methods of cultivation. Thus in West Africa the maize-rust disease can be reduced by early planting. And in Zambia it has been found that early planting gives maximum yields of high-quality groundnuts and minimizes the effects of rosette and leaf-spot disease.

Finally, the control of weeds – which tend to grow very rapidly in the tropics during the wet seasons – is an important factor in plant protection and in the intensification of agricultural production. Many of these weeds can be controlled or removed simply by hand-weeding or hoeing. But many areas also have their own special weed problems arising from a combination of climatic and cultural practices. For instance 'couch grass' (*Digitaria scalarum*) is the most serious weed in cotton, coffee, tea, sisal, and plantain crops in East Africa and in Congo Kinshasa. This particular weed has roots which run laterally beneath the surface, and repeated cultivations are necessary to eliminate it. In Malayan rubber estates 'lalang' (*Imperator cylindrica*) is a similar menace. Elsewhere *Eleusine africana* is an annual grass which rapidly colonizes maize fields and seriously affects the nitrogen supply to the crop. Some grasses or sedges have underground storage organs and a rapid rate of regrowth; and these characteristics make control particularly difficult.

There is no doubt that weeds seriously reduce crop yields in many tropical countries. Ashby and Pfeiffer (1956) estimate that such losses are two to three times as great as in temperate zones; a loss of 50 per cent in cotton yield due to *Digitaria*, with a greater loss of the bean crop, has been quoted; and several writers stress the crucial nature of weed control in the early stages of the East African Groundnut Scheme.

The reason why weeds are generally restrictive on agricultural production, especially in attaining high yields, is that weeds compete with crop plants for oxygen and plant food, moisture and light; some weeds are also alternative hosts for fungus diseases and insect pests; while other weeds are parasitic on crops. Another argument against weeds is that they limit the area of land culti-vated by a farmer. According to some authorities one of the reasons for the relatively small dimensions of many tropical farms is the battle the farmers anticipate they will have to wage against weeds.

It is no doubt true that probably the most important means of weed control is cultivation: weeding, in fact, is often considered to be the most important function of cultivation. This is perhaps especially true in the tropics where selective weed killers are not only expensive and often difficult to apply, but where they also have one important limitation: whereas the selective weed killers so far available are most effective against broad-leaved weeds among cereal crops, some of the worst tropical weeds are grass weeds in broad-leaved crops. Chemical weed control is both rare and difficult in the tropics, for not only are grass weeds there more important than broad-leaved weeds, but most smallholder crops have a relatively low value, the plots are capable of being hand-weeded, and widely differing responses to existing chemical weed killers have so far been noted for different crops.

Weeding is clearly an important factor in the intensification of agricultural production in the tropics. It has been recognized, however, that indiscriminate weeding can create more problems than it solves. It is now known, for instance, that the *Oxalis* weed in the tea estates of Ceylon has no detrimental effect on tea pro-duction but in fact helps to guard the soil against erosion and is a useful indicator that the soil *ph* is sufficiently low. In Malaya it was soon found that clean weeding in rubber estates encourages soil erosion and that it can lead to loss of soil moisture, although this depends very much upon local climatic and edaphic conditions. In West Africa the very low atmospheric humidities during the dry *harmattan* wind season favour evaporation from the soil surface; but this evaporation is believed to be less than losses occurring from weed growth. Under such conditions, therefore, and in spite of the dangers of soil erosion, clean weeding of fallow land is often adopted to conserve moisture, while mulching is practised with the same object in view. Similarly, certain crops like maize are particu-larly susceptible to damage by weeds owing to the fact that they are slow starters and planted in widely spaced rows. While under

K

wet tropical conditions clean weeding does obviously entail a serious risk of erosion, weeding is nevertheless advocated, at least while the plants are young. Wet rice, too, is adversely affected by weed growth, largely because of the effect weeds have on reducing light. But in areas where draught power is lacking, adequate weed control in wet rice fields is very difficult indeed to achieve.

Crop succession, plant populations and spacing. If land is cleared and continuously cultivated with annual crops, ultimate failure almost invariably results. This occurred in Malaya as the result of the continuous cultivation of cassava and pineapples on upland soils without manuring and without adequate protection against soil erosion; the situation there was made worse by the invasion of the cleared land by *lalang* (*Imperator cylindrica*) which, by reason of its rank growth and liability to catch fire during the dry weather, prevents re-establishment of normal vegetational succession and so hinders regeneration. A similar situation arose in parts of Sierra Leone where continuous peasant food production of one crop – upland rice – led to the abandonment of large tracts of land.

A well-chosen succession of crops is clearly of great importance in maintaining fertility, for different crops have varying food requirements. Furthermore, depth of rooting varies, and a deep-rooting crop will utilize food which cannot be reached by those with shallow-rooting systems. A resting period, too, is desirable, so that fallow of one kind or another is often advantageously included in the succession. Examples of successful successions are, in northern Nigeria, guinea corn, cotton, groundnuts, and bush fallow; and, in eastern Java, rice, beans, and sugar-cane.

Frequently included in the rotation are leguminous plants, the value of which as a means of enriching soil has been recognized since ancient times. Today they enter into many successions in tropical countries: 'when their roots and stubbles are turned into the land, and . . . consumed on the land by livestock, they greatly increase nitrogen in the soil. Moreover, because they are deep-rooting, they help to bring mineral plant food from the sub-soil to the surface of the soil' (Tempany and Grist, 1958: 105–6). However, the use of crop successions is often limited by lack of labour;

and unless it produces unmistakable improvements in subsequent crops and includes only crops which are needed, either by the farmer or by some accessible market, a new, unfamiliar crop succession is unlikely to be accepted by peasant cultivators.

As for plant populations and spacing, not a great deal of information exists on this aspect of tropical crop production; but the work already completed indicates that yields can be very substantially increased in this way. Fayemi (1963) has shown that plant populations and spacing can have striking effects on the yield of maize in the tropics, finding in Nigeria a progressive increase in grain yield for populations up to an optimal figure of 14,500 plants per acre (36,000 per ha), above which a decline sets in, though drill planting methods can raise the optimal figure to as much as 19,630 plants to the acre (48,000 per ha).

. . . . . .

A final point emphasizes perhaps the most important practical issue in attempts to intensify agricultural production by any of the means discussed above: how to propagate the knowledge and techniques and to ensure their acceptance by tropical cultivators. Here is an almost untouched field of research; and it is to be hoped that some of the existing concepts and techniques of studying and directing the diffusion of innovations will be applied to tropical field studies by geographers. There are numerous attempts – some more successful than others – to bring about required types of agricultural change. The experimental case study at Uboma in eastern Nigeria (Upton, 1966: 7) is one of the more promising attempts. This is sponsored and managed by the Shell Company of Nigeria in collaboration with the Eastern Nigeria Ministry of Agriculture and was begun with a careful local socio-economic survey, followed by measures to induce the kind of technological and attitudinal changes required. Clearly there are no grounds for the kind of pessimism about the transformation and improvement of tropical agriculture such as is revealed, for instance, in the writings of Dumont (1962; 1966). Various forms of agricultural extension work, however, are essential features of any attempt to encourage farmers to learn how to use the more successful disease-resistant strains or higher yielding varieties of crops, or if the farmers are to be reached by those capable of performing bud-grafting and similar specialist services. It is not enough simply to provide the results of applied agricultural research in the form of new technologies – fertilizers, improved seeds, insecticides, irrigation, or machines; nor is it enough simply to tell the farmer what these techniques are, to demonstrate them and exhort him to change. It is equally important that the farmer be provided with the social, psychological, and economic environment in which his land tenure system, co-operative farming, credit facilities, and access to markets provide him with the necessary inducements to change. There is a close connexion between agricultural development on the one hand and, on the other, the general processes of social and economic development. Community development, education, schools, dispensaries: all are really part of the attack on low agricultural productivity in tropical lands.

2. The Extension of Agricultural Land

The generally low proportion of land under cultivation has led a number of writers to see the extension of the cultivated area as an important means of increasing agricultural production in the tropics. The proportion of land area actively under cultivation is certainly very small. Many tropical countries still have the bulk of their surface covered with forest, woodland, and wasteland (Table 6), even a relatively well-developed country like Malaya still having some 70 per cent of its surface classed as tropical rain forest. In Brazil only 2 per cent and in Congo Kinshasa only 1 per cent of the total land area is cultivated (excluding fallow); and in Sarawak only 11 per cent of the total area is cultivated, even including fallow. In spite of the many limitations to such data, the low proportion of land said to be used for agricultural purposes in most tropical countries indicates that land resources in the purely quantitative sense are ample. This is, of course, less true of the densely populated countries of parts of tropical Asia: in India, for instance, the percentage of total land area under cultivation is as high as 30 per cent.

But in practice the extension of cultivation is rarely an easy or practicable proposition. It is certainly misleading to suggest that there are vast open spaces – in Borneo, Africa, and in Brazil, for instance – just waiting for colonists. Apart from the demographic objections to large-scale migration and colonization already noted (pp. 92–3), the extent of the use of land is never a measure of economic efficiency in the use of land resources. Moreover, the qualitative

Table 6. *Land use in selected countries* (Percentage of total land area, 1964)

	Arable and orchard	Permanent meadow and pasture	Forest and woodland	Waste, city area, etc.
Guyana	5	—	95	—
Brazil	2	16	46	36
Brit. Honduras	9	—	79	12
Rhodesia	4	10	59	27
Kenya	3	20	3	74
Uganda	12	—	—	80
Nigeria	7	—	44	49
Burma	22	1	65	12
India	52	5	18	25
Malaya	18	—	69	13

Source: F.A.O., *Yearbook of Agriculture*, 1965

aspects of land resources are in this context at least as important as the amount of land available and still unexploited. Uninhabited is not the same thing as habitable. For the Dry Zone of Ceylon, it has been shown that 'an examination of rainfall and water-supply problems drives home the fact that the "empty lands" of the Dry Zone most certainly do not provide unlimited opportunities for settlement' (Farmer, 1957: 39); and this conclusion, significantly, conflicts with the view of Ceylon's Dry Zone as 'the granary for the future and as a home for the rapidly growing population of the island' (International Bank, 1962: 72). Soil conditions and a whole complex of economic and social considerations – communications, capital availability, essential skills, markets: these are but a few of the factors that may inhibit successful colonization in an area. Others include the difficulty of clearing operations in many tropical countries, while land tenure and health hazards in the receiving areas, too, are frequently discouraging to prospective migrants. Colonists today demand high standards of economic and social security from the moment they arrive in the area to be opened up. Almost any instance of modern standards in agricultural colonization includes model labour contracts conforming to governmental requirements and often also to the requirements of the International Labour Organization. Furthermore it is often very difficult to find sufficient numbers of colonists, for in few areas is population pressure on land already so critically severe as to make people want to move away from their traditional homes. In many countries, too – notably in Africa and tropical America – the human resources are so limited in size that intensification of production by increasing yields and by fighting pests and diseases is clearly the only possible agricultural policy, even though the country may contain large uninhabited and apparently cultivable lands.

It will be recognized that the extension of cultivation must normally involve an expansion into areas of often unproven quality, lying beyond the present settled limits, and farther from or less accessible to markets. The unknown variables and so the risks are therefore greater. As Farmer (1964) has emphasized, the decision about the relative value of extending the cultivated area and intensifying production in areas already cultivated requires difficult benefit – cost analyses, and in any case the whole problem is frequently crucially affected by non-economic considerations. Indeed, it is perhaps legitimate to question two assumptions: that these two complementary means of increasing agricultural production – by extension and by intensification – are normally available in most developing countries of the tropics; and that an extension of the cultivated area must necessarily be useful so long as cultivable land remains uncultivated.

On the other hand, it would be misleading to dismiss altogether the extension of cultivated land as a means of increasing total agricultural production within a country. Some writers give this point a great deal of attention. Lord (1963) argues that however much industrialization and intensification of agriculture are preferred as measures to meet the expanding needs and demands of

Africa's populations, the next decade or so will undoubtedly see an extension of agriculture into the largely empty lands. As will be shown later, a large number of schemes for extending agricultural land have already been undertaken. But in relating such schemes to the central demographic–economic problem as it has been posed in these pages and, more specifically, in relating these schemes to the need to increase total agricultural production, it will be realized that in fact the motivation of many of these schemes has often been highly complex. The extension of agricultural settlement may take place largely for political reasons, or in an attempt simply to relieve so-called population pressure elsewhere. If this is so, then the scheme has fairly to be judged by criteria other than the total agricultural production within a country.

3. The Large-scale Scheme

The large-scale scheme has played an important, sometimes dominant role in recent attempts to extend agricultural land; only rarely has it been applied to existing agricultural land. Yet while the difficulty of obtaining colonists has commonly made this the only practicable means of extending the agricultural land, a good deal of controversy nevertheless surrounds the whole concept of the large-scale scheme for agricultural development. On a number of economic and social grounds some writers prefer the small-scale peasant farm as an instrument for agricultural change. Lewis (1955) argues that peasant farms encourage more intensive, less wasteful cultivation; that a peasant farmer works harder and more carefully than the hired estate worker; that a family-size farm makes few demands upon supervisory staff; and that peasant farms have less serious repercussions upon the social life of indigenous communities. Certainly the assumption that the large-scale operation must necessarily be more efficient than the small-scale peasant farm has been shown to be untrue in many tropical countries. Not only is the large-scale scheme costly in terms of management and capital outlay, but it also often makes the maintenance of soil fertility and the avoidance of soil erosion very difficult to achieve, especially where the local physical environmental conditions are but little understood.

In most tropical countries today, indeed, increasing emphasis seems to be being placed upon the peasant farm or some rationalization of it rather than upon the large-scale scheme for agricultural development. The reasons for this change of emphasis include the dramatic failure of so many post-war attempts to increase agricultural production through large-scale schemes.

The East African Groundnut Scheme at Kongwa is perhaps the classic instance of how a large-scale scheme for agricultural development can run into all kinds of difficult and often unforeseen problems. This scheme was heralded as 'a kind of crusade for the betterment of African and Briton alike; the vision of swords being turned into ploughshares was to become a reality, and at a cost equivalent to that of only 2–3 days fighting' (Kimble, 1960: 271). Yet it failed for a number of reasons. In the first place, the main purpose of the scheme was to increase the supply of oils and fats for consumption in western markets – in other words, the motive was basically exploitative. Secondly, before work was begun no time was spared for 'satisfactory and sustained primary reconnaissance and survey, for preliminary photographic work, for topographic soil conservation and soil maps, or for adequate investigation of meteorological information bearing on rainfall' (Frankel, 1953: 146). Rainfall and soil data that did exist were sometimes interpreted as if Tanganyika were a temperate country, ignoring the fact that such data as the intensity and effectiveness of rainfall, and the relative functions of rainfall, soil, and temperature in agriculture are not only different but require different interpretation in a tropical context. There was also a tendency to assume a much greater uniformity in the natural environment and resources than does in fact exist: the amount and reliability of rainfall and the details of soil–crop relationships were found in practice to differ widely over surprisingly short distances. Thirdly, there were serious miscalculations about the cost and so the economic feasibility of the whole project. Soils were found to be especially difficult and costly to work for part of the year; the wear and tear on machines and equipment was much greater than had been expected; and the cost of keeping the machines maintained by European technicians proved to be prohibitive. Finally there were several serious problems relating to road and railway construction and the adequacy of port facilities at Dar-es-Salaam.

Another scheme – the Mokwa Scheme (Niger Agricultural Project) in Nigeria – failed for a number of somewhat similar reasons. Here again the motivation for the scheme and the whole general approach have been criticized. Great efforts were made to ensure that it bore no resemblance to a European-type enterprise at any stage. Large-scale initial planning, in particular, was virtually eliminated, and little information was available on the choice of crops, varieties of crops, planting dates, the use of fertilizers, weed control, practicable sizes of holdings, suitable types of tractors, the cost of mechanized operations, the marketing of produce, and the supply of labour. This lack of prior knowledge is particularly difficult to understand in the case of Mokwa because there was already some agricultural settlement there. Very little if any of the local knowledge was utilized, the African farmer's fund of empirical knowledge being largely ignored. For political reasons only immigrants from Bida and Kontagora emirates were accepted as settlers at Mokwa; yet these were the very people who could in no way be said to be suffering from population pressure on land resources in their own homelands. Furthermore, the new villages and facilities provided for the immigrants were not adapted to local customs (Baldwin, 1957).

Both the Kongwa and Mokwa experiments point to three main lessons. First, any successful agricultural extension scheme based on large-scale, highly capitalized methods, depends initially on adequate knowledge about the characteristics and significance of tropical conditions, about the theory of this kind of development, and about the complex of conditions existing in the actual area in which the development is contemplated. Secondly, any kind of agricultural innovation should proceed slowly and carefully, for the object of rural development should be simply to graft on to indigenous life the things that it lacks. Finally, these two schemes have emphasized the common fallacy that agricultural operations easily lend themselves to economies of scale. In fact, this idea runs counter to the accepted principle that 'agriculture is the least likely form of economic enterprise to yield considerable large-scale economies: its factors of production cannot be readily centred or supervised, nor in general are they sufficiently homogeneous to allow easily organized repetitive processes of production' (Frankel, 1953: 149).

With the large-scale scheme, as with the small peasant farm, many of the applied problems of agricultural development are essentially local ones. Research findings must be tested under operational conditions in experimental and pilot projects before committing them to larger-scale undertakings.

4. Mechanization

Over the last two decades or so a considerable amount of experience has been built up on the value of mechanization as a means of increasing agricultural production in tropical lands. This applies not only to the extension of agriculture but also to the intensification of production in existing areas of agricultural land. The chief advantages of mechanization are believed to be (i) the saving of labour; (ii) the gaining of time – in particular, land that could not otherwise be cultivated (as in areas where the soil is too heavy or where weather conditions allow too little time for hand methods to cope) can be brought under cultivation; and (iii) mechanization economizes because it releases for human use land which has otherwise to be used only for feeding draught animals, as in India.

Yet while the potential contribution of mechanization to tropical agriculture cannot be doubted, a number of difficulties have been shown to exist. In the first place, it will already be apparent from what has been said that tropical countries do not in general have any need to save either labour or time. As far as the saving of labour is concerned, the problem can most simply be stated as one of output per worker versus output per man; while mechanized production is usually more productive per worker, it is usually less productive per acre, hand labour usually being carried out with more care and the land utilized more intensively. In a heavily populated country like India the objective of agricultural policy might be to maximize output per acre, not output per worker; and in such a situation, clearly, mechanization is not necessarily logical. In areas of much lower population densities, as in much of tropical Africa or tropical South America, however, the chief aim of agricultural policy is perhaps more commonly aimed at maximizing production per unit of labour; and in such circumstances mechanization of agricultural production is clearly desirable. As far as the saving of time is concerned, it has already been shown that this is not normally a problem in tropical developing countries where, indeed, underemployment is a characteristic, even endemic, feature. Only in areas where there is a short rainy season – as in parts of India – is the saving of time an important factor.

Secondly, the feasibility or desirability of mechanical cultivation depends upon a number of conditions related to land. Mechanization is clearly best suited to areas where land is relatively flat, where the size of farms is not too small, and where holdings are not too fragmented or scattered. Then the difficulties of using wheeled machines in soft, sticky clay are well known; simple manual methods may often be the only feasible ones. In the Mokwa Scheme, too, it was found possible only to make use of machines for ploughing and ridging the land, for no machines capable of doing the other necessary operations could be found. The Mokwa Scheme also showed that while mechanization may speed the clearance between rows, it cannot help with weeding in between plants in the same row. In the early days of the scheme, land was cleared rapidly, but the rapid restoration of the undergrowth and small trees showed that the clearing, which was almost entirely by hand, had to be more thorough and therefore slower. Even then the prolific root system just below the surface of the ground caused severe losses from breakages of agricultural implements; the costs of repairing and replacing were very high. The desirability of mechanization also depends to a large extent on the crop. A low annual crop, such as groundnuts, is very much more suited to mechanical cultivation than are the taller perennial crops. Other problems are the poor quality of tractor drivers and the spreading of the working season of the tractors. This last point was again well illustrated in the Mokwa Scheme.

Thirdly, there is a whole group of problems related to the economic feasibility of mechanization; and many of these are related to initial capital availability, the cost and quality of supervisory and technical labour, and the seasonal flow of demand for mechanized processes in farming. As Clayton (1963) has shown in Kenya, this is one of the main reasons why mechanization is not always an effective capital substitute for labour in a physical sense. The use of tractors in the farms Clayton studied economizes labour only during the seed-bed preparation periods of the long and short rainy seasons; if restricting seasonal labour peaks do not coincide with these periods, then mechanization is unlikely to be effective or economic. This gives rise to the apparent contradiction of situations where labour, though underemployed, is nevertheless restricting but which cannot be ameliorated by factor substitution, that is by mechanization. Clayton finds that increased production on family farms is limited by labour and not by land, but that mechanization brings substantial gains (20 per cent or more) only on farms which can grow a high-value cash crop, such as pyrethrum, and which have land–labour ratios of not less than 2·9 acres (1·17 ha) to one man on farms with two cash crops and not less than 2·5 acres (1·01 ha) to one man on farms with only one cash crop (ibid.).

Mechanization of agriculture, in fact, is likely to be effective and fully economic only if applied simultaneously with all other appropriate measures to increase crop yields and farm returns. Initially, too, it is perhaps best applied to the 'bottle-necks' of farming operations rather than indiscriminately to all activities on the farms. Moreover, 'it is of the utmost importance that efforts to introduce mechanization of peasant farming in the tropics should not be attempted until its implications on the social habits of the people have been completely appraised, and not before practical trials of machines and organizations have been made on a sufficiently large scale to provide the necessary technical and economic and social experience' (Tempany and Grist, 1958: 136).

CHAPTER 8

Agricultural Development in Trinidad and Tobago, Uganda, and Malaya

To conclude this brief and necessarily highly selective discussion on agricultural development it seems appropriate to devote one chapter to a summary of current agricultural development problems and policies in three countries – Trinidad and Tobago, Uganda, and Malaya.

Trinidad and Tobago. Any analysis of agricultural development in Trinidad and Tobago must first of all take account of the fact that this is a small country with a population of now rather over one million, giving an average density of about 430 to the square mile (165 per km²). The pattern of land use reveals that of the total land area of 1,267,300 acres (506,920 ha) only about one-quarter is crop or pasture land, about one-half is covered with forest or secondary forest growth (*lastro*), and the rest is swamp land or is built up. Agricultural development planning here has also to take account of the fact that the economy as a whole depends very largely upon the petroleum industry and so upon the private sector and inflow of foreign capital: in development planning in Trinidad and Tobago, therefore, the decisions made by private producers assume overwhelming importance. Furthermore, Trinidad and Tobago's economy is exceptionally dependent on exports: in 1961 the ratio of total exports of goods to the gross national product was one of the highest in the world – nearly 60 per cent.

It is clear, then, that economic planning, and certainly the role of agriculture in development, must be very different in Trinidad and Tobago from what it is in a country like India which has a relatively low ratio of foreign trade, a relatively large public sector and a relatively small reliance on private foreign investment. Here in Trinidad and Tobago it is accepted that oil must continue for some time to be the basis of the country's economic viability, though it is accepted that economic development must also be based on the strengthening of other sectors, principally manufacturing and agriculture, and on 'the abandonment of the mercantilist philosophy' (Trin. and Tob. Govt., 1963). Agriculture, therefore, occupies a rather peripheral position in economic development thinking and planning in Trinidad and Tobago. Over the whole 1964–8 Second Five-Year Plan period, agriculture, forests, and fisheries together have been allocated only 12 per cent of the total proposed development outlay in the public sector. By 1968 agriculture will be taking only 7·5 per cent of the annual public sector outlay.

Within the field of agricultural planning in Trinidad and Tobago there are two main and quite explicit aims. The first of these is to raise the efficiency of productivity in agriculture at least to the level of other sectors of the economy. According to the 1960 Census, agriculture then employed some 55,400 – about 21 per cent of the working population – but contributed only about 7 per cent of the gross domestic product, suggesting that productivity per person employed in agriculture is only about one-third of the average for the whole economy. This kind of calculation is, of course, only very crude, ignoring, for instance, the fact that there is still a substantial amount of shifting-field cultivation, known locally as 'recent cultivation'; but it is nevertheless true that earnings in agriculture, especially outside the sugar industry, are substantially lower than in most sectors of the economy and that this is one reason for the rapid drift of population to the towns. A second aim is to achieve a greater degree of self-sufficiency in food supplies and so to protect the balance of payments situation.

Both these aims clearly emphasize the promotion of agricultural production for the domestic market. More specifically, attention is being concentrated on the production of livestock, fruit, pulses, green vegetables, and root crops: 'the aim over the plan period is . . . to establish the basis for a productive small and medium farm system geared to produce increasing quantities of milk, eggs, poultry, green vegetables, root crops, and pulses for the local market and in some instances for export in processed form' (ibid.:

27). In Trinidad and Tobago it is accepted that markets for the traditional export crops are strictly limited. Increased production in export agriculture, while not being discouraged, is being directed more at increasing yields over existing acreages, whereas increased production in domestic agriculture is to come both from the intensification of agriculture and from extending the cultivated area.

This last point emphasizes what has been described as the fundamental problem of dualism in Trinidad and Tobago's agriculture: on the one hand, the large-scale commercial and highly capitalized plantation agriculture (notably for sugar); and on the other, the small-scale, under-capitalized, and low-yielding peasant agriculture. It is against this background that the agricultural sections of the present development plan were formulated. The plan is designed to bring about sustained increases in agricultural production and a retreat from the dualistic nature of the traditional system. It is hoped to develop a more broadly based pattern of agriculture with a progressive reduction in the existing lines of demarcation between these two major agricultural types, and to ensure that organized scientific research is directed equally to the domestic and to the export agricultural sectors.

With the emphasis on food production for the domestic and increasingly urban markets, and upon participation by the small and medium farmer rather than by the large-scale 'colonial-type' plantation farmer, it is perhaps not surprising that in terms of the size of the plan allocation within the field of agricultural development, by far the largest single sum is for agricultural credit (Table 7). Credit has been accepted as the key factor in the country's agricultural development. The Agricultural Credit Bank, with an allocation of 17 million dollars over the five-year period, has been reorganized so as to be able to cope more effectively with the needs of the small and medium-sized farmers of the country. There has been a relaxation of the regulations concerning the provision of collateral for credit. Previously, only large well-established agriculturalists were able to obtain loans for development, but these facilities are now enjoyed much more widely.

The next largest allocation of public sector funds under the current agricultural development plan is 10,420,000 dollars for the improvement of marketing facilities and the provision of access roads to farms. A Central Marketing Agency (replacing the former Marketing Boards) has functions which include the setting of guaranteed minimum wholesale prices; trading and dealing in feeding stuffs for livestock needs, fertilizer, insecticides, and other agricultural supplies; collecting and distributing information on commodity prices; and encouraging research into local foods. The

Table 7. *Trinidad and Tobago. Expenditure on agriculture under the 1964–8 plan (public sector)*

	$ million
Agricultural credit facilities	17·0
Marketing facilities	5·3
Farm access roads	5·2
Forestry	3·5
Fisheries	2·5
Dairy and beef development	2·0
Land acquisition, settlement, etc.	2·0
Fertilizer subsidies	1·0
Others	2·4
	40·9
Total expenditure on plan	302·6

Source: Government of Trinidad and Tobago, *Second Five-Year Plan, 1964–68*, Port of Spain, 1963.

provision of additional access roads is seen to be an essential element of the policy of improving and widening marketing facilities and opportunities in the country.

Forestry and fishing have together been allocated some 6 million dollars in this country of islands and large areas of forests, and a further 2 million is to be spent on dairying and beef development – again aimed chiefly at domestic consumption and local processing. The 2 million dollars allocated for the extension of agricultural land is also meant for domestic crop production rather than for export crops.

Though the public sector funds allocated to it are small, there is a good deal of research into soils and soil conservation, land use, crops, livestock, costs and prices, production and farm management, and in the collection of statistics of all kinds. By tropical standards, the research programme in agriculture is already well advanced in Trinidad and Tobago, and a great deal of agricultural research has been directed from the former Imperial College of Tropical Agriculture in Trinidad, now the Faculty of Agriculture in the University of the West Indies. One of the best-known series of experiments conducted by this institution was concerned with the economics of peasant farming. There is also a related institution known as the Regional Research Centre (R.R.C.) which arose from an amalgamation of three separate schemes for research on soils, cocoa, and bananas. With the population increase and high food import bill for Trinidad and the other islands of the West Indies, increasing emphasis is now being placed on food-crop breeding and the control of pests, diseases, and weeds. As might be expected, perhaps the greatest amount of research here has been concerned with sugar, but research into food crops, citrus fruits, and cocoa has already produced several improved and higher-yielding varieties. Most recently, emphasis has been laid on research into ways of improving and expanding the livestock industry, and some remarkable experiments on the establishment of pasture grasses (notably *Pangola*) on cleared forest land seem to be meeting with success. Soil research is now fairly well advanced in Trinidad, especially in the central areas, and soil conservation measures are being encouraged in northern Trinidad and in Tobago. A land capability map is being prepared. Finally, in order to assist in the field of food processing and to improve the nutritional levels of the population, a Food Service Laboratory is being set up to produce technical guidance and information for farmers, food-processing industries, and Government personnel.

Agricultural development planning in Trinidad and Tobago is unusual among tropical developing countries in concentrating at developing production for the home market, both for direct consumption and for local processing industries. In the public sector fund allocation, greatest weight is given to the provision of funds for agricultural credit (especially for the small and medium farmer)

L

and for improving marketing facilities and access roads to the farms. In other words, the emphasis in the plan is not so much on the actual production side as on the provision of capital and better distribution and marketing facilities for the farmer.

Uganda. In its agricultural development Uganda is in almost every respect the antithesis of Trinidad and Tobago. It is a much larger – 91,134 square miles (236,000 km²) – entirely landlocked and high plateau country with an average altitude of about 4,000 feet (1,220 m). With a population of over 7 million it has an average density of population of only 86 per square mile (33 per km²). Unlike Trinidad and Tobago, Uganda's prosperity is derived largely from farming: two-thirds of its gross domestic product is derived from agriculture, and over 90 per cent of the value of all exports are produced from the land. Whereas petroleum dominates the export economy of Trinidad and Tobago, agricultural products – cotton and coffee – are the major determinants of the size of the national income in Uganda: about 77 per cent of Uganda's export earnings come from these two crops alone. It is not surprising therefore that the most recent Uganda development plan (1961) accords pride of place to agriculture. It is assumed that investment in agriculture here will bring greater returns in terms of agricultural output and incomes than comparable investments in almost any other sector. The proportion of the proposed capital and development expenditure in the public sector allocated to agriculture is currently 23 per cent as against 7·5 per cent in Trinidad and Tobago (Table 8).

Uganda, too, provides excellent material for a case study of Africa's agriculture, for in many ways Uganda represents the norm. 'Not exceptionally rich or poor, not remarkably backward or advanced' (Masefield, 1962: 27), her economy displays a classic dependence on export crops, but still includes a good deal of subsistence farming. Non-African plantations were a factor in her economy, but were not sufficiently large to distort the natural development of African agriculture (ibid.: 87). Furthermore, Uganda has distinct climatic contrasts which are reflected in agricultural types: the high rainfall areas are characterized by planted crops, such as plantains, sweet potatoes, or cassava, and contain the major export crops of coffee, cotton, sugar, and tea; whereas the low rainfall areas more commonly grow sown crops like finger millet, maize, or pulses as well as being the major livestock areas of Uganda.

Table 8. *Uganda. Expenditure on agriculture under the 1962–66 development plan (public sector)*

	£ million
Agriculture and co-operatives	11·9
Crops marketing	0·2
Livestock and animal industry	2·4
Fisheries and forestry	0·5
Agricultural credit	1·5
Total	16·5
Total expenditure (all sectors)	71·7

Source: Government of Uganda, *Development Plan, 1962–1966*, Entebbe, 1961.

The four main measures taken under the current development plan to increase agricultural production in Uganda are, first, to extend the cultivated area. This policy continues trends begun in Uganda during the 1950s, when spontaneous movements for agricultural pioneering greatly outweighed any sponsored settlement schemes (McMaster, 1966: 73). Belshaw (1964) estimated that some 75,000 people were resettled officially in the 1946–62 period, but this figure was certainly far exceeded by spontaneous agricultural settlement during the same period in just one county – Bugerere. In discussing this spontaneous areal extension of agricultural land, McMaster also emphasizes the significance, not only of transport improvements but also of insect control. The control since 1952 of the fly *Simulium damnosum* has been a vital factor in opening up Bugerere and the contiguous area of Butembe-Bunya.

Certainly there are large areas of fertile, well-watered lands in Uganda which can be brought under cultivation with no more capital outlay than is required for initial clearance and breaking. For this reason, and because capital is scarce, the main emphasis of the Government's policy for small-scale agriculture is on encouraging and assisting individual farmers to bring more of this land under cultivation. It is recognized, however, that there are also extensive areas which, with modest capital outlays on irrigation or drainage, offer higher yields and the possibility of inducing farmers to work under the direction of scientific management without making them wage-earning labourers. Measures are therefore being taken to explore the economic, technological, and sociological problems involved in this kind of development. In order to induce farmers to adopt new techniques which will enable them to expand acreages, the programme provides for a scheme whereby progressive farmers may obtain certain items of equipment at subsidized prices; the programme also provides for a considerable expansion of the tractor-hire service. Connected with these schemes are the Progressive Farmers and Co-operative Credit Schemes and, as regards tractor hire, a scheme to encourage group farming. Furthermore, an experimental bush-clearing unit has been established for clearing land in connexion with settlement schemes, especially those associated particularly with tsetse control. Special emphasis has been placed on the Kigezi swamp reclamation scheme; and a substantial part of the feeder roads programme consists of the construction or improvement of roads likely to open up new areas of production.

Secondly, the policy plan for agriculture emphasizes livestock development, especially the integration of livestock into crop farming. Internal demand for meat is growing, as is the demand for dairy products which are at present being met largely from outside Uganda. There is as yet very little in the way of a commercial attitude towards livestock in the country, and the social restraints to be overcome in bringing livestock into the market economy in the various tribal areas are considerable. The aim, however, is to increase the livestock population in those areas suitable for the purpose which are not already overstocked, and to develop for livestock those areas where tsetse infestation has previously been the limiting factor. It is also hoped to increase the offtake of cattle to the market in all these areas as well as in those districts, like Karamoja, where there is already serious livestock overpopulation.

Measures to improve disease control and management are clearly important elements in this policy, and these include tsetse control, the provision of veterinary dispensaries and a mobile disease investigation unit, equipment subsidies, schemes to eradicate ticks in areas where exotic cattle have been introduced for dairying purposes, and special measures to control and eradicate rinderpest and contagious bovine pluro-pneumonia.

Thirdly, the current development plan emphasizes the need to intensify crop production by applied research into higher yielding and pest-resistant varieties of crops. A tea research station at Toro and an arabica coffee research centre at Bugisu are centres for this kind of work. Finally, there is a policy of diversification of agricultural production, the aim here being to lessen the country's dependence on coffee and cotton and to give the farmer greater cash stability and an improved dietary. In pursuance of this policy of diversification, the planning programme provides for the further development of tea on an outgrower basis; for measures to bring the quality of fire-cured tobacco up to export standard; for a pilot project to improve the quality of groundnuts for export; and for measures to establish cocoa production in suitable areas. In this connexion some support is being given to the development of large-scale plantation agriculture, and a number of schemes have been initiated by the Government through Agricultural Enterprises Limited and other subsidiaries of the Uganda Development Corporation. But the main emphasis in the agricultural policy is certainly on small-scale farming rather than on the large-scale plantation; and this emphasis dates back to a political decision made in the early 1920s when the failure of coffee prices led to many European plantations in Uganda being ruined. Since then the coffee industry in Uganda has been almost entirely built up on the basis of African small farming; and cotton is an exclusively African peasant farm crop. Asians, however, have introduced sugar estates into the Ugandan agricultural economy, and this raises a difficult issue for Uganda's agricultural policy today. As the 1962 International Bank Report pointed out, the racial barriers to owning land in Uganda restrict the output of sugar – now the main plantation crop in the country – and tea.

Against the background of some of the comments made in earlier chapters, especially on pp. 119–42, it is possible to question the emphasis and priorities in the current Ugandan development plan, at least in so far as they refer to agriculture. In particular, it is perhaps legitimate to question the pride of place given to the extension of agricultural land in Uganda. It is true that Uganda has a number of advantages for agriculture over many of her neighbours – her moisture and soil resources are generally believed to be superior to those of Kenya and Tanzania, for instance – and vast areas of Uganda are almost without agricultural settlement at all. Furthermore, it can be argued that by encouraging the extension of cultivated land, the plan is simply following a trend in settlement that had already begun quite spontaneously in the 1950s (McMaster, 1966). On the other hand, neither the Agricultural Productivity Committee of 1954 nor the International Bank Report of 1962 recommended encouraging the extension of cultivation on any scale: the Agricultural Productivity Committee, in fact, made specific recommendations against any large-scale extension of agriculture in Uganda, using arguments similar to those advanced earlier in this book. The Ugandan development plan, indeed, is clearly motivated in part by a desire to maximize the use of land as a factor of production; believes that the extent of the utilization of available resources is a criterion of economic growth; and is affected by the severe practical problems – physical, social, and political, as well as economic – of intensifying agricultural production in the existing agricultural lands of Uganda. The two chief measures suggested by the International Bank Report as the basis for agricultural development in Uganda – to encourage agricultural diversification and to improve dramatically the livestock industry in the country – have not been completely ignored in the current development plan. But it is unlikely that great success in these fields will ever be achieved while the extension of cultivated land remains the keystone of agricultural development policy.

Malaya. The peninsula of Malaya, with an area of about 51,000 square miles (132,000 km²) and a population of some 9 million, has a difficult physical environment in many ways. Here is a hilly peninsula with often poor soils, an equatorial climate and three-quarters of its surface still covered with tropical rain forest and swamp jungle. On the other hand, Malaya's environment contains great possibilities. The peninsula's favourable geographical position, the occurrence of rich tin deposits, and a climate well suited to the growing of rubber have already made possible the growth of one of the most prosperous countries in Asia (Hodder, 1959). Tin, rubber, and padi form the three pillars of the economic prosperity of Malaya, and 'with its Malay population primarily engaged in subsistence production, the Chinese and Indians of the tin and rubber belt concentrated on production for export, and the inhabitants of Singapore and Penang maintaining a far-ranging entrepôt trade, Malaya's economy is hardly less plural than its society' (Fisher, 1964: 602).

From the point of view of export earnings, rubber production is the most important activity – agricultural or non-agricultural – in the country. In 1955 the International Bank Report accepted that this dominant position of rubber would continue for some time to come. The Bank Report recommended that 'within the agricultural sector the highest development priority should be given to maintaining the position of the rubber industry in its present outstanding place in the Malayan economy' (p. 33); and this recommendation was made chiefly because no other crop or combination of crops seemed then to promise possibilities for expansion on a scale and at a rate which could compensate for a major decline in rubber production. The Report recommended giving priority to the replanting of estates and smallholdings with new high-yielding strains.

This recommendation was accepted by the Malayan Government. Of the allocation of public investment for the Second Five-Year Plan (1961–5), agriculture took about 21 per cent, of which rubber planting alone took over one-quarter. This continues to be logical in that rubber is still far and away the leading product of Malaya, and her economic life still depends heavily on this one commodity. Rubber still accounts for about one-quarter of the gross domestic product, the bulk of export earnings, and a substantial portion of government revenue. Rubber covers about 3·75 million acres (1·52 million ha), or over four times the area covered by the next most important crop, rice.

It should be emphasized here that the uncertainties and instability of the rubber industry in Malaya have not led to a decline in the emphasis on rubber in the country's agricultural planning. This seems at first sight rather surprising, because price and demand fluctuations have often been very severe: the average price for the first six months of 1963, for instance, was 30 per cent below that for the year 1960. On the other hand, there has been and continues to be a change in the structure of the industry, especially as regards the relative decline of estates as against smallholdings. If the pressure for higher wages in the rubber industry continues, 'the estates may lose some of their at present considerable competitive advantage. Moreover, socio-political considerations similar to those in other parts of South-east Asia may ultimately favour the predominance of the smallholder in rubber production' (Fisher, 1964: 613).

The current development plan – the First Malaysian Plan (1966–70) – continues the policy of maintaining the position of rubber in Malaya's economy, though whether this is wise in view of the long-term prospects for rubber and the growth of the synthetic rubber industry in many of the consuming countries is a matter of opinion; it also continues the policy of diversification begun under the last Malayan plan (Table 9). As a result of a report published in 1963, five measures are now being undertaken with agricultural diversification in view: a soil survey of Malaya, which has already resulted in the publication of a detailed soil map; a land capability classification map, designed to assist the selection of new areas for agricultural development; an accelerated rate of determining forest resources and their utilization; a vigorous programme of agricultural research and education; and an increased flow of agriculturally trained people. In terms of crops a great deal of emphasis is being placed upon the oil palm, cocoa, coconuts, pineapples, tobacco, groundnuts, cashew nuts and tea.

As far as oil palm is concerned the acreage has increased from some 100,000 acres (42,000 ha) in 1957 to over 250,000 acres (104,000 ha) today, and is expected to reach 400,000 acres (168,000 ha) by 1970. It has been calculated that even assuming a price fall of 25 per cent over the next decade, the rate of return on investment for 6,000 acres (2,500 ha) of palm oil is 16·9 per cent while that on the same acreage of new land in natural rubber is only 10·9 per cent (*Times*, 17 November 1967).

Table 9. *Malaya. Expenditure on agriculture under the development plan, 1961–5 (public sector)*

	$ million
Rubber replanting	140·8
Drainage and irrigation	124·3
Land development	156·9
Co-operative credit	0·1
Coconuts	3·7
Research and Extension	23·2
Animal husbandry	13·4
Forestry	5·0
Fisheries	3·5
Survey	5·6
Other	73·3
Total	549·8
Total plan expenditure	2,606·3

Source: Government of Malaya, *Interim Review of Development in Malaya under the Second Five-Year Plan*, Kuala Lumpur, 1963.

It is also recognized that research and experimentation into local food production, especially rice, cassava, and maize, has been greatly neglected in the past. The current development plan emphasizes the need to increase the proportion of domestic food produced in Malaya. Rice yields in the peninsula are already well ahead of the average for South-east Asia, but a good deal can still be done by applied scientific research and mechanization. Intensification of production receives the greatest emphasis, but the extension of padi lands has also been encouraged in a number of schemes such as the Tanjong Karang and Trans-Perak River Irrigation Schemes. Land development, drainage, and irrigation, in fact, took over half the total public fund allocation to agriculture during the last Five-Year Plan. In Malaya there remain large areas of unused land appropriate for agriculture, though some authorities put the amount of cultivable land not yet being utilized as low as only 50 per cent of the present cultivated area. Settling this new land provides employment for farmers who may have no land, or who have insufficient land to meet their needs. The first step in developing unused lands is for the government holding the title to release or alienate the land for approved uses. Land alienation has already taken place under three schemes: the Federal Land Development Authority (F.L.D.A.), Fringe Alienation, and Controlled Alienation. Altogether, and within its limits, the extension of agricultural land is having some significant success in Malaya. During the first half of the Second Five-Year Plan 37,000 families were settled on 179,000 acres (72,000 ha) of new land.

Malaya is by tropical standards a thriving and prosperous country, and this prosperity has long been and still is very much dependent on one agricultural product – rubber. The dilemma facing Malaya today is that it must continue for some time to come to depend upon rubber in this way, while at the same time trying to give more stability to the country's economy by diversifying agricultural production and by industrializing. But above all, the agricultural development of Malaya cannot easily be separated from the political and social problems which exist here in a particularly virulent form.

Apart from the Malay–Chinese dichotomy in social, economic, and political life, Malaya now has to consider her development within the larger framework of Malaysia. Contemporary events, notably the secession of Singapore from the Malaysian Federation and the conflict between Malaya and the Borneo territories of East Malaysia, give an air of unreality and frustration to agricultural development planning where it emphasizes Malaysian as distinct from Malayan interests.

.   .   .   .   .

The above three case studies have been selected because they help to illustrate some of the principles and generalizations made in the preceding chapters; they indicate the relevance to agricultural development of many issues not yet considered or only referred to indirectly in these pages; and finally, these three case studies illustrate the wide differences in characteristics and problems between the various countries of the developing world. While it is both useful and valid to formulate certain theoretical and descriptive generalizations about tropical countries, any applied situation in agricultural development is at least partly a regional or local problem, the understanding and solution of which must take account of a wide range and unique combination of resources, opportunities, and limitations.

CHAPTER 9

Agriculture or Industry?

Three points of view. One of the central issues confronting tropical countries is sectoral balance, and in particular concerns the relative significance of agriculture and industry in development planning. While decisions on this issue sometimes reflect differences in natural, human, and financial resources between countries, they perhaps more commonly reflect an adherence to one of three widely divergent viewpoints. First, there is the view that increased agricultural production is the only sure foundation for successful industrialization at a subsequent stage in the development of an economy. A second point of view is that only a rapid increase in industrialization can ever enable a developing country's economy to break out into something approaching that of a developed country. Finally, and somewhere in between the two other standpoints, is the view that agricultural and industrial development planning cannot usefully be considered separately, and that in development planning they are equally important. It seems necessary at this stage in the discussion to look a little more closely at these three very different points of view.

The view that agricultural development must be given greatest weight in economic development planning in tropical countries usually finds more support in actual development plans than in the theoretical literature. The International Bank Mission Reports to Uganda and Malaya discussed in the previous chapter, for instance, recommended emphasizing agricultural development for the very simple reason that these countries are still very largely agricultural. This pragmatic argument varies in its applicability from country to country, and the case of Trinidad, also discussed earlier, is just one example of a tropical country whose present level of prosperity is largely dependent on non-agricultural production. However, it is generally true that rather over 50 per cent of the national income of tropical countries comes from agricultural sources, and in few tropical countries is less than 70 per cent of the working population in the agricultural sector: in these two senses, certainly, agriculture is easily the most important economic activity in the tropical world, and economic development there must largely imply rural development (Balogh, 1966).

Another argument in favour of emphasizing agriculture rather than industry is that while in the past a great deal of attention has been given to export cash crops, relatively little research, capital, or expenditure has gone into improving the domestic food situation in the tropics. Yet in terms of diet and health the need to increase domestic food production is very urgent and should perhaps be given priority over any other form of economic development planning. The potential domestic market for increased food supplies is clearly immense, and the redistribution of surplus rice, maize, or other food production between the various countries of the tropical world could also form a useful basis for the growth of inter-tropical trade.

Again, it can be argued that an agricultural revolution should perhaps always precede an industrial revolution, and in particular that the advantages of technological change in the first instance are most appropriately channelled into agriculture – notably by the mechanization of agriculture – and not into manufacturing industry; for large-scale modern industrialization, with its emphasis on labour-saving devices, is illogical in tropical countries where underemployment is a widespread, even endemic feature of economic life. Furthermore, industrialization is usually capital-intensive and so, again, is not wholly appropriate in those parts of the world where supplies of capital and domestic savings are so short. Then the demands on an educated and more particularly on a technologically educated élite are very great in industrialization, and it seems unwise to encourage industrialization on any scale before the basic needs in terms of human resources have been provided. Finally, social changes of many kinds are rapidly helping to bring about increased urbanization; and this implies a need for greater efficiency in the production of surplus food for the growing non-agriculturally productive sections of the community. For several of these reasons, Benham and Holley (1960) have advised Latin American countries to choose agricultural and mineral development rather than industrialization.

A contrary viewpoint is expressed by the school of development economics that assigns to agriculture a relatively minor role and argues that pride of place should be given to industrialization, together with all associated lines of development except agriculture (Rosenstein-Rodan, 1961). According to this viewpoint, only industrialization can break the vicious cycle of underdevelopment and create the necessary preconditions for economic 'take-off'. Some economists go farther than this and regard economic development and industrialization as roughly synonymous terms.

Of the many arguments put forward by the proponents of this school, the first is to suggest that industrialization is demonstrably responsible for the higher material standards of living in the developed countries. It is pointed out that the value of output per man is greater and is growing more rapidly in industry than in agriculture, and that the proportion of the population engaged in industry is normally higher in wealthy countries than in poor countries. The success of Russia and Japan as rapidly developing industrial states is often quoted to support this viewpoint.

Secondly, it is argued that industrialization is the best way of bringing about greater economic diversification and stability – something which all tropical countries are seen to need. At present they depend in their external trade upon the export of a comparatively restricted range of agricultural and mineral raw materials. In this sense most tropical economies are non-diversified and so liable to instability, making development planning difficult. Industrialization can also add value to existing raw material exports by processing before export and can further help the balance of payments situation by the final processing or assembly of imports. Furthermore, industrial growth is cumulative and can stimulate progress in other sectors of the economy, particularly in ventures which meet its requirements for engineering, repairing, transport, fuel, electricity, finance, and distributive services.

Thirdly, industrialization may be advocated as a more important need than agricultural development in tropical countries in that it can absorb workers who are at present 'underemployed' in agriculture or petty trading; the value of their work to the community and so their own incomes will thereby be increased, the marginal value product of labour being in these circumstances higher in industry than in agriculture. The advantages of specialization of labour are also much more easily achieved in industrialization.

In the fourth place, it is possible to question the view, implicit in the argument of those who give priority to agricultural development, that the agricultural sector in a tropical country is sufficiently commercialized to respond to the usual economic incentives. The view that agriculture is more important than industrialization depends entirely on this initial assumption, which is perhaps not valid where subsistence agriculture is dominant. In most tropical countries the key to development 'is provided by an increase in industrial productivity . . . Policies aimed at lifting production in the agricultural sector are in this setting unlikely to foster self-sustaining growth and may even frustrate it' (Gutman, 1957: 291). A requirement for economic take-off is a class of farmers willing and able to respond to the possibilities opened up for them by new techniques, land-holding arrangements, transport facilities, and forms of market and credit organizations. Without such a class of farmers no substantial leap forward in economic development is possible through agriculture.

Again, in supporting the 'industrial' school a number of writers point to the greater flexibility and adaptability of industrialization. The demand for agricultural products is relatively inelastic. Furthermore, the proportion of fixed to operating costs is much smaller in industry than in agriculture, so that industrial activity can be more easily cut down or expanded than can agricultural production. Industrial production can more easily be controlled in relation to costs, prices, and demand. Control and flexibility are also easier in a situation where production is so little dependent upon the vagaries of nature. The fundamental disadvantage under which agriculture labours, in fact, is that the farmer has little control over the natural forces of his environment, and any kind of change in crops or techniques is commonly inhibited by the way in which the agricultural way of life is so clearly woven into the fabric of tropical society.

It is also pointed out that industrialization has a powerful, indeed irresistible, psychological attraction. Most tropical countries equate civilization and power with industrialization and are determined upon the rapid development of the industrial sectors of their economies. Whatever theorists may say, industrialization, at a pace and to an extent which many would call too ambitious, is certain to take place; and if this is so, then it is only practical policy to try to facilitate and direct the processes of industrial development.

A final argument for emphasizing industrialization is related to the demographic–economic problem referred to earlier (pp. 85–96). According to available comparative data, industrialization seems to lead inevitably to urbanization. Particularly in its early stages, manufacturing industry is related to the urban centres where markets, labour, and a range of public utilities are available; and it can be argued that this urbanization, resulting from industrialization, will eventually help to reduce the rate of population growth.

The third school of thought includes a wide spectrum of viewpoints, but in general embraces all those who recognize the essential interdependence of agriculture and industry. Lewis (1953) and Nurkse (1959) are perhaps the best-known exponents of this school, but over the last few years it has received a good deal of theoretical expression, especially by Jorgensen (1961), Ranis and Fei (1961), and by Johnston and Mellor (1961). All argue that agriculture and industry are equally necessary to economic development. Either explicitly or implicitly, most geographical writings support this third school of thought.

According to this viewpoint there are no inherent advantages of manufacturing industry over agriculture or for that matter of agriculture over industry (Viner, 1953). Spate has illustrated this for India where 'without a great increase – and a better distribution – of rural income, industry cannot develop to the full, since agrarian poverty severely restricts the effective demand of the numerically huge internal market, and continually maintain, or at least augment, the immense pool of landless or underemployed rural labour and thus keeps the worker's wages low, his living conditions often unspeakably bad, and his efficiency as a natural consequence poor. Conversely, the vital significance of the industrialization contribution to agricultural reconstruction is patent: fertilizers, cheap machinery, and a market. Field and factory, then, are symbiotes' (Spate, 1967: 257). India, indeed, provides a good example of the need for the 'feedback' of industry into agriculture, not only in mechanization but perhaps even more immediately important in the field of fertilizer and pesticide manufacture. In extending the use of the new varieties of wheat, maize and rice in India, one of the chief difficulties has been the supply of fertilizers and pesticides upon which the successful cultivation of these new varieties depends. In 1966 the domestic production of fertilizer was only about 40 per cent of requirements at that time, the remainder, together with most pesticides, being imported at high cost in foreign exchange. Present strategy demands a great increase in fertilizer and pesticide production, which can be achieved only if foreign capital can be induced to invest heavily and quickly.

Again, a need has been noted for the mutual self-support between agriculture and industry, whereby the surplus agricultural population is siphoned off into industry as agriculture, under the stimulus of greater demand, becomes more efficient and as industry in turn raises the market for agricultural produce (Mountjoy, 1963: 85). As another writer has summed it up 'industrialization is dependent upon agricultural improvement: it is not profitable to produce a growing volume of manufactures unless agricultural production is growing simultaneously. This is also why industrial and agricultural revolutions always go together, and why economies in which agriculture is stagnant do not show industrial development' (Lewis, 1955: 433). According to a number of well-known historical analogies, too, the connexion between agricultural improvement and industrial development is very close. In Britain, for instance, the Industrial Revolution was made possible by the mid-eighteenth-century introduction of scientific farming, better crops, the stall-feeding of animals and a new rotation of crops which included the turnip, as well as by subsequent improvements in drainage techniques and ploughing (Ernle, 1937).

The need to try to achieve a balance between the two forms of

M

development – agricultural and industrial – can be argued on three further grounds. In the first place, the diversion of labour from rural to urban occupations implicit in industrialization requires that the depleted ranks of rural labour should provide the rapidly expanding urban food demands. If agriculture fails to provide food for the growing industrial and urban populations, then much-needed capital will have to be spent on importing foodstuffs and development will be retarded (Mountjoy, 1963: 79). This is a particularly important issue because of the high elasticities of demand in food in the early stages of economic development. There is always a real danger that increased incomes will be spent chiefly on food to the extent that 'demand for food will expand more than the supply, while the supply of industrial products increases more than the demand' (Kindleberger, 1966: 215). Important data on this whole question have been presented by Kaneda and Johnston (1961) in their study of urban food expenditure patterns in tropical Africa. According to their findings, normally between 50 and 68 per cent of total household expenditures are devoted to food, and urban income elasticities of demand for food are normally very high (0·6–0·9) compared with relatively low figures (0·2–0·3) in developed countries. Total expenditure on food in African urban areas, then, tends to rise very substantially as income rises.

Secondly, the movement of resources from agriculture to industry is advantageous to the total economy only if the resources left in agriculture are employed so as to produce, at reasonably low costs, certain of the raw material requirements of industry. And finally, an enlarged and diversified agricultural sector may be necessary to produce exports with which to obtain the foreign exchange needed for industrial development.

The validity of the hypothesis that sustained industrial growth is closely linked with the expansion and improvement of agriculture must vary considerably from country to country. In Ceylon, export agriculture still earns good net returns whereas in Burma and Thailand the chief agricultural export – rice – is now highly depressed. By and large, however, the market situation as well as psychological and political needs seem already to demand a moderate and selective development of industries in most tropical countries.

Agriculture must still be expanded wherever it has better scope; but this expansion will itself necessitate and permit industrialization. Higher agricultural productivity will provide capital and markets for new industries, while the industries will absorb the surplus labour which agriculture must release in its process of improvement. Thus industrial and agricultural development are complementary.

· · · · ·

Any review of the existing empirical evidence seems at first sight to give general support to the third 'balanced growth' viewpoint. Industrialization must be accompanied by increased efficiency in food production; but this increased efficiency in food production cannot be brought about without a feedback from industry into agriculture, making it possible to apply to agriculture what has been called 'the tricks of manufacture'. Two important qualifications, however, need to be made. In the first place, the examination of specific case studies can lead one to diametrically opposed conclusions about the relative roles of industry and agriculture in the economic development of different countries. While some theoretical or conceptual framework is necessary to any informed analysis of a specific case study, the details of the local situation make any indiscriminate blanket model or theory quite impossible; as Martin (1961) has noted, for instance, Lewis's prescriptions for Ghana and the West Indies are quite different as far as emphasizing agriculture or industry is concerned. Secondly, the viewpoint that agriculture and industry should be given equal weight in development planning must clearly accept the fact that in terms of employment, agriculture should become relatively less and less important, while secondary and especially tertiary production should become relatively more important. Rising income levels have to be accompanied by a corresponding change in employment structure involving a relative shrinkage of the agricultural sector (A. Fisher, 1935; 1939; Clark, 1957). If a 70:30 ratio of agricultural to non-agricultural labour is typical of developing countries, then something like a 30:70 ratio is typical of countries at a high level of economic development. A convenient assumption for an economy in a fairly rapid process of economic development is that the agricultural population will remain constant in absolute numbers and that changes in structure will be brought about by a concentration of the natural increase of population in the non-agricultural sector (Singer, 1964: 385; and Fig. 3). The aim is thus to increase agricultural production with the constant numbers of people employed in agriculture, yet to provide sufficient food for the increased population in the non-agricultural sector, and to provide for such increases in consumption as are part of the development programme.

The development continuum. It seems appropriate here to point out that the dichotomy between agriculture and industry implied in much of the discussion outlined above is to some extent false. It is always difficult and sometimes quite impossible to make a clear distinction between them, except in the earliest stages of economic development; and it is only quite arbitrarily, in fact, that the line dividing the two forms of economic activity can be drawn. Quite a large part of the industrial sector in tropical developing countries both depends upon agriculture for its raw materials and is itself aimed at feeding back into agriculture the products and techniques of industry. After a certain critical stage in the development of agricultural systems, the feedback of technology from industry into agriculture is crucial.

Fig. 3 indicates in broad terms this line of thought about the agricultural–industrial continuum and relates it to different stages or systems of agriculture as well as to population density. The two extremities of the continuum are represented by shifting-field cultivation and what has been termed 'industrial agriculture' respectively. Somewhere in between lies the stage of permanent-field cultivation, the spontaneous or indigenous development of which was earlier shown to be related to critical population densities (p. 101). In the first half of the continuum the chief agent of change in agricultural systems is a rising population density; but in the second half of the continuum the technological feedback from industry (whether in the same country or originating from outside) is the main agent of change and results in a relative decrease in the agricultural population as population density and urbanization increase. The actual timing of the indigenous permanent-field cultivation stage depends on a great number of unknown variables, making precise generalizations impossible; and the exact shape of the population growth curve will similarly vary. But it is contended

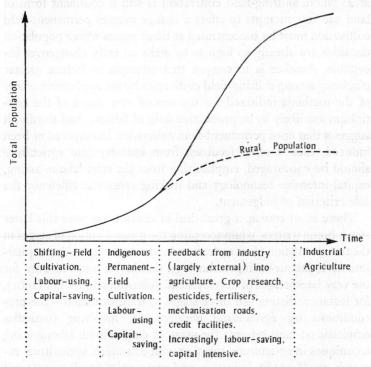

Fig. 3. The development continuum from agriculture to industry.

that one of the overriding aims of economic development planning in tropical developing countries must be to proceed along this continuum as quickly as possible – though without attempting to jump any of the intervening stages – and that the feedback from industry into agriculture cannot usefully be attempted until at least the stage of indigenous, simple permanent-field cultivation has been reached. In this sense, there are obvious weaknesses in trying to apply to most African agricultural economies the kind of measures to improve agricultural production that appear to be appropriate in, for instance, the heavily populated, wet-rice cultivated areas of the Asian tropics.

This notion, if valid, has a number of practical implications for agricultural development planning, one of which is that in those areas where shifting-field cultivation is still a dominant form of land use any attempts to effect a change over to permanent-field cultivation must be concentrated at those points where population densities are already so high as to make an early changeover inevitable. Another is to suggest that attempts to induce greater efficiency among shifting-field cultivators by the application of any of the methods indicated for the second two stages of the continuum are likely to be productive only of failure. And thirdly, it suggests that once permanent-field cultivation has evolved or been induced, then a rapid feedback from industry into agriculture should be encouraged, emphasizing from the start labour-saving, capital-intensive technology and making economic efficiency the sole criterion of judgement.

There is, of course, a great deal of controversy over this latter stage. Some writers, while accepting the general notion of stages in the transformation of an agricultural economy, suggest that capital-intensive, labour-saving technology should be reserved only for the very latest stages of development. Johnston and Mellor (1961), for instance, distinguish three stages of transformation – the pre-conditions for agricultural development, involving particular emphasis on land reform; the stage of emphasis on labour-using techniques in agriculture, together with education, agricultural research, roads, credit, irrigation, and community development; and finally, the stage of labour-saving technology in agriculture, emphasizing mechanization and capital-intensive methods generally. In this work the authors are in effect suggesting a compromise between capital-intensive and labour-intensive technology, reserving the former until a fairly high level of productivity has been achieved. As will be noted later, however, this argument seems to be restrictive on development in that it helps to perpetuate existing land–labour ratios and so encourages stagnation and inhibits self-generating change. But the emphasis in the earlier stages of permanent-field cultivation on such measures as agricultural research, education, transport facilities, and the provision of credit facilities seems entirely logical.

While this idea, expressed diagrammatically in Fig. 3, is necessarily very tentative and generalized, it does suggest a framework for thinking about the whole very complicated and diffuse issue of the transition from primitive to advanced forms of agricultural activity. It also summarizes, however crudely, many of the points made in these pages; it supports the belief that all economies, whether tropical or non-tropical, are at some stage along the same development continuum; and it rejects any rigid concept of 'developed' and 'developing' economies as mutually exclusive categories.

CHAPTER 10
Industrialization

Labour-intensive or capital-intensive technology? Some of the remarks made in the previous chapter imply a point of view about
the relative importance to tropical developing countries of labour-
intensive and capital-intensive technology, either in agriculture or
in industry.

The main conflicting viewpoints on this matter can be put very
briefly. Those writers, like Hayek (1955), who support concentrating on labour-intensive technology, are concerned with the implications of existing factor proportions, especially capital/labour
ratios. Where labour is abundant and capital is scarce the only
appropriate technology, so it is argued, is one that is labour-
intensive; in much of India, therefore, labour-intensive technology
is always to be preferred. Against this point of view it can be argued
that the labour-intensive approach is essentially static, negative,
and, in the long run, inhibiting to economic advance. Furthermore,
much of the argument for emphasizing labour-intensive technology
rests on strictly non-economic grounds – on, for instance, the need
to maximize employment rather than output (Eckaus, 1966). As
Kindleberger (1966) argues, however, the decision whether to
maximize employment or output is not a matter for an economist
to decide upon. It is also important to point out that many, perhaps
most, tropical countries do not have abundant labour and that
densities are not nearly so high as is commonly believed; the
'endemic underemployment' characteristic, in fact, is often exaggerated.

The case for emphasizing capital-intensive technology wherever
possible rests not only upon theoretical arguments but also upon
empirical and historical evidence. Leibenstein (1960) argues that
capital-intensive techniques should be preferred to labour-intensive
techniques both because of their immediate productivity and be-

cause of their greater contribution to savings and hence future growth. He suggests, furthermore, that in most developing countries capital can be substituted for labour in capital-intensive production methods, but not in labour-intensive methods. Gerschenkron (1962) uses historical analogies to support similar conclusions. The introduction of capital-intensive technologies into developing societies seems to him essential for economic development, for historically 'borrowed technology was one of the primary factors assuring a high speed of development in a backward country entering the stage of industrialization' (Gerschenkron, 1962: 8).

It must be admitted that any emphasis on capital-intensive technological change may have some unfortunate social, psychological, political, and even economic implications – such as those associated with what is sometimes called the dual economy, well analysed for Indonesia (Furnivall, 1948; Boeke, 1942; and Higgins, 1959). Moreover, it is once again unwise to generalize about the merits or demerits of particular lines of policy without specifying the actual country under consideration. Some tropical countries, like Malaya or Venezuela, are already well along the development line, while others, like many of the African countries, have hardly started; some have high population densities while others are very sparsely populated and suffer from a shortage rather than from a surplus of labour.

Yet the general arguments in favour of emphasizing capital-intensive technology – either in agriculture or in industry – seem convincing. Not only do these arguments fit in with the available empirical evidence but the emphasis on capital-intensive techniques gives further support to the development continuum expressed in Fig. 3. As long as the capital-intensive, up-to-date techniques are able to operate in situations where capital can earn sufficiently high returns, and as long as such technology is diffused throughout the economy through training and labour stimulation, then the transfer of modern technological innovations from the developed to the developing countries is not only to be encouraged: it is critical to the kind of rapid economic advance required.

The obstacles to industrialization. Three obstacles to the industrialization of tropical countries are given particular prominence in the literature. The first is the poor quality of industrial labour. Some reference to this point has already been made in discussing the qualitative aspects of human resources, and it was concluded that given time and proper training there is no reason to suppose that tropical peoples have any less innate capacity for industrial activity. This is not to suggest that difficult social, psychological, and economic problems do not arise in trying to create an industrial labour force in tropical countries. Some of these problems have been well described for growing industrial areas by a number of writers. But none of this work necessarily implies any basic incapacity for industrial operations on the part of indigenous workers. From a study of industrial operations in Nigeria it has been concluded that the African there does not possess any inherent incapacities or attitudes which are detrimental to efficient production in modern industry: 'in fact it can be argued that regarding continuous labour and repetitive operations he is peculiarly well-suited to modern production. Second, the African's willingness to work considerably exceeds that of labourers in developed economies. Third, with regard to machine technology, there are certain aspects of machine operation and maintenance to which the African, because of his environmental background, does not naturally adapt. Training, however, will rectify these shortcomings. Investment in human skills, the training of competent craftsmen and technicians, is of recent origin. Careful selection, training, marketing incentives, and surveillance from higher management will reduce supervisory weaknesses to negligible proportions. Thus one may say that the quality of African labour is adequate to meet the needs of developing economies' (Kilby, 1955: 22).

The problem of manpower for industrialization in tropical countries clearly resolves itself into a question of training and experience, not only for semi-skilled and skilled labour but also at the organizing and managerial levels. This may well form the most important single brake on the pace of industrial development; for investment in human resources is never a very speedy process, and some of the related problems of social change may involve opposition to the introduction of industrial processes. The reasons for and the nature of such opposition varies from place to place – often over very small distances – and may reflect the intensely practical but parochial interests of small individual social groups. In West Africa one writer has described the opposition to oil mills among the Mba-Ise people of Iboland. The reasons for this opposition include the fears that women would lose their rightful profit from the kernels, that oil mills would put out of business the small middlemen and middlewomen, and that widespread idleness would result. These reasons for opposing the mills show an intelligent self-interest on the part of the Mba-Ise people (Ardener, 1953).

A related aspect of the qualitative manpower problem is the entrepreneurial shortage. Little attention has been given to this in the literature on economic development, though it seems to be no less serious a handicap (Harbison and Myers, 1964). Capital cannot by itself produce anything – it must be harnessed for producing capital goods and the capital goods in turn harnessed for producing consumer goods; and this investment process requires the services of some agent or intermediary who initiates, organizes, makes decisions, takes risks, innovates, and sometimes also manages. According to Hirschman (1958), decision-making of this kind is 'the scarcest talent' in developing countries. In the developing economies of the tropics the necessary sponsors or entrepreneurs are very few in number, and this is probably an important reason why industrial development is slow to take place. On the other hand, some writers have argued that the entrepreneurial ability of many tropical societies is already very great, as in parts of India and in Guatemala (Bhagwati, 1966: 80).

A second major obstacle to industrialization in tropical countries is lack of capital. According to some writers, capital accumulation and industrialization are in practice virtually identical processes; and though some increase in industrial production is possible by improving industrial organization, methods, the quality of labour and factory management, the scope of such measures is limited. For a large advance in industrial production, particularly if it is to exceed the increase in population, capital formation on a large scale is indispensable. Yet the amount of capital required per worker in modern manufacturing industry is high, and this is one of the main reasons why the 'take-off' into self-sustained growth is such a difficult operation. Furthermore, capital requirements for industry are commonly higher in tropical than in non-tropical countries: in West Africa, for instance, the initial amounts of working capital and fixed capital required per worker have been estimated to be £13,150 for a cement factory, £3,000 for a vehicle assembly plant, and £2,800 for a plastics factory: the equivalent figures for about three-quarters of British industry all lie between £1,000 and £3,000 (U.A.C., 1957).

A third obstacle – the narrowness of market opportunities – is a distinctive feature of most tropical countries. The nature and causes of this condition vary from one country to another, but in general they can be said to include a lack of capital for storage, inadequate and costly transport, and, above all, the low purchasing power of the population. Market opportunities and economic prosperity are clearly closely linked and it is perhaps only an analytical convenience to distinguish between the supply and demand sides of the problem of increasing production.

Home market opportunities for industrial products, though automatically widening as economic development and population growth take place, can be widened still further by various means. As will be shown in a later chapter, one of the arguments for improving internal lines of communication is that they will help to increase the extent and intensity of market contacts within a territory. It is possible to advocate the enlargement of the home market by the simultaneous expansion of a large number of industries which buy one another's products; this kind of group advance will automatically create its own market and will also, if localized, increase the external economies enjoyed by each firm and so reduce costs (Nurske, 1953). Then there have been attempts to widen and diversify the domestic market by creating regional groupings of one kind or another, like the East African Common Market, the South-east Asian Common Market, or the Caribbean Economic Community. According to Prebisch's thesis, indeed, many nation states in the developing world are too small for effective industrialization. Where countries have only small populations, industrial costs are higher, so that highly protective tariffs are forced upon them and small uneconomic plants develop. Large-scale industrialization cannot be built upon fragmentation of this kind; and the need for regional groupings for industrial development among developing countries is therefore urgent (U.N., 1964). It has also been suggested that the home market may be enlarged for home products by capturing what is at present supplied by foreign producers – that is by creating import-substitution industries – and to this end the development plans of many countries include such incentives as duty drawbacks, investment allowances, and tax concessions. However, in relating the home market to industrial expansion, where market limitations are especially cramping, the pattern of spending among tropical peasants must not be ignored.

The narrowness of foreign markets is no less inhibiting to industrial development in tropical countries. More will be said on this point in a later chapter, but it can hardly be overemphasized. In the absence of adequate domestic market opportunities, industrialization in tropical countries must look for market opportunities in the developed world; yet it is difficult to envisage a situation in which the peoples of the developed world would be prepared to buy manufactured products from the developing countries when they can buy the same, probably better and cheaper, products from each other.

These three obstacles to industrialization – lack of skilled labour and any substantial managerial or entrepreneurial class, lack of capital, and the narrowness of domestic and foreign markets – are met with in varying degrees in all tropical countries and must deeply affect the extent and nature of economic planning.

Cottage and small-scale industry. There is a substantial body of opinion which holds that the main objective of industrial development policy in tropical countries should be the encouragement of a variety of cottage, small-scale industrial enterprises; it is argued that the concept of industrialization as necessarily involving large-scale, heavy industrial enterprises, is not relevant to the needs of countries in the tropical world.

An important reason for arguing in this way is that small-scale cottage industry can deal most effectively with the three obstacles to industrialization already discussed. Cottage industry is the kind of venture which depends upon traditional skills and so can help to build up the supply of manufacturing, managerial, and entrepreneurial experience which in turn can form the basis of a subsequent, more impressive, industrial expansion; it economizes with the scarce factor of capital and makes a fuller use of manpower, being labour-intensive rather than capital-intensive; and it is aimed at producing the kinds of consumer goods with which the domestic market is already acquainted and which it is more likely to be able to afford. Both from the population and employment angles, indeed, small-scale cottage technology would seem to be logical in tropical countries.

Another argument sometimes produced in support of small-scale or cottage industrial activity is that developing countries, especially tropical developing countries, are not well endowed with the natural resources essential for the development of heavy industries such as those of iron, steel, and motor vehicles. Yet if the remarks made in Chapter 1 – that the natural resource base must be assumed to be potentially as adequate in the tropics as anywhere else in the world – are indeed valid, then this argument can be dismissed out of hand.

Nevertheless there does seem to be particular scope for the encouragement of small-scale or cottage industry in the tropical world, especially in the production of such goods as textiles, footwear, domestic hardware, glassware, ceramics, umbrellas, soap, and biscuits. Japan has gone a long way in converting family industries into decentralized light industries, and her example may profitably be followed by the countries of the tropics. Where cotton is grown locally it should not be difficult to get the co-operation of overseas capital and expertise to make it up – as at the Kaduna Textiles factory – a joint venture between Northern Nigeria and Lancashire enterprises. In India some notable successes in small-scale industrialization have already been achieved, especially in the state of Punjab at Ludhiana.

On the other hand, it is only too easy to exaggerate the potential role of small-scale or cottage industrial enterprise in the industrial development of the tropics. It should perhaps be pointed out that the present differential in industrial activity between the developed and developing world is to some extent the result of European nineteenth-century colonialism which tended to inhibit industrialization in the tropical world. During the nineteenth century the western countries looked upon the tropical developing world largely as a source of raw materials; later on, 'as the internal market in Europe began to show signs of satiety, the western powers began to look overseas for markets as well. One consequence was to flood the Orient with cheap manufactures and ruin the handicraft industries of India and China which might otherwise have been growing points for industrialization' (B. Ward, 1964: 52). There are numerous examples of local cottage industrial activities being unable to compete with imported Western products; and the result has been that indigenous cottage industries in many areas are now stagnant or derelict and can hardly be expected to form the basis of any substantial increase in industrial production. Furthermore, whatever the theoretical or indeed the practical advantages of the small-scale or cottage industrial enterprise may be, there is no doubt that it is already irrevocably supplanted in the minds of most tropical peoples by the large industrial enterprise. The powerful psychological attraction and mystique of large-scale modern industry can only confirm the trend towards the large-scale industrial unit in development planning. And the United Nations Committee for Industrial Development (U.N., 1966) has supported the view that small-scale industry should only be developed within the total framework of industrialization programmes, and not instead of, or in preference to, large-scale or medium-sized industry.

CHAPTER 11

Industrialization: Venezuela, Nigeria, and India

The three cases examined very briefly in the present chapter have been chosen to illustrate some of the general ideas already put forward and to emphasize once again the widely differing problems and approaches which need to be taken into account in any realistic analysis of the industrial development problems of the very diverse countries of the tropical world.

Venezuela. Probably in no other tropical country has industrialization taken place so rapidly and in many ways so effectively as in Venezuela. This country has more than doubled its industrial output since 1950, and the industrial sector is currently expanding at about 11 per cent per annum. To a large extent this impressive development of industry in Venezuela has been due to the rapid growth of petroleum refining, which increased fourfold over the 1948–53 period alone and has provided a large part of the capital requirements for industrialization in the country. For some time now there has been a conscious and official policy of what is termed 'sowing the petroleum' – that is, reinvesting royalties from oil in capital assets. Venezuela is now the world's largest exporter of petroleum, depends on oil and its derivatives for 90 per cent of her export earnings, and receives about 60 per cent of her total revenue from oil royalties and taxes.

Structurally, Venezuelan industry has shown a number of important changes since the Second World War. In 1948 over half of all manufacturing originated in food, beer, and textiles – industries most characteristic of countries in their earliest stages of manufacturing industry; but by 1958 this proportion had dropped to one-third and is today only about one-quarter. Venezuelan industrial enterprise has already emerged from the initial stages of industrial development and some considerable heavy industry has been set up, especially in the shipyards and in the petrochemical works of Moron, near Puerto Cabello. This relatively sophisticated industrial structure helps to explain the fact that Venezuela has one of the highest *per capita* national incomes in the tropical world; and in this connexion it is worth pointing out that Venezuela also has one of the highest rates of natural increase – probably approaching 4 per cent per annum – in the world. Venezuela, in fact, is a classic instance of the point made by several writers: that rapid population growth need not necessarily act as a brake on economic development.

A number of other points can be made about Venezuelan industrialization. First, and in spite of the relative importance of industry in Venezuela compared with many other parts of the tropics, this is still very much a developing country, only 14 per cent of the national product originating in the industrial sector. Secondly, the relatively high *per capita* national income figure is particularly misleading here because the majority of the population lives at standards no higher than elsewhere in the tropical world. Thirdly, Venezuela is very much a high-cost producer. As the International Bank Mission concluded some years ago, 'depending on specific manufacturing characteristics and the type of product made, manufacturing costs in Venezuelan industry are almost always substantially higher than those elsewhere. Labour costs, capital costs, construction costs, costs of agricultural materials, and the costs of imported raw materials – all these are high; and the only low-cost items tend to be . . . the low cost of minerals, low transportation, and low electricity and power costs' (International Bank, 1960: 203). A good deal of protection, too, has occurred in Venezuela and has helped to keep costs high and reduce foreign market opportunities. Indeed, there is plenty of evidence that the high cost of Venezuelan manufactures has been a serious limitation to increasing manufactured production for export. Export manufactures have so far been largely confined to petroleum products, cement, and sisal rope. Manufacture is thus largely dependent on the home market which is small, not only because the total population barely exceeds 8 million but also because of the low purchasing power of

N

the majority of Venezuelans. A fourth and final point is that several Venezuelan industries, notably textiles and sugar manufacture, have developed at the expense of traditional craft industries.

Most industrialization in Venezuela has in the past been concentrated into the Caracas area and along the northern mountain slopes and coastal strip. Caracas itself has 24 per cent of the total population of Venezuela, but has 45 per cent of the total personal incomes and some 70 per cent of the total industrial production in the country. This kind of concentration is a common feature of many tropical countries and is logical in a situation where industrial location is still geared towards the supply of non-durable consumer goods and services.

One of the most remarkable industrial developments and experiments in the tropics, however, is now taking place, not in Caracas or in the coastal area of Venezuela at all, but in the east, in the Guayana region. The fact that the natural resource base is not entirely an irrelevance in decision-taking in development planning – a point made earlier in Chapter 1 – is clearly illustrated in the case of Guayana. For Guayana is immensely rich in a number of natural resources. The reserves of iron, now being exploited at a rate of about 15 million tons a year, have yet to be calculated, but are believed to be very great: local iron reserves at Cerro Bolivar alone are over 500 million tons, have a 64 per cent metal content, and already form the basis of an integrated steel mill at Matanzas on the Orinoco River. This mill was built by a group of Italian companies, including Fiat and Innocenti, and is concentrating on producing rails, bars, and tubes. Bauxite, manganese, and titanium are but a few of the many other minerals to be found in the Guayana area. The potential natural wealth of the region is not confined to its mineral resources, for it is also rich in timber for use in construction and cabinet work. But above all, Guayana has great reserves of hydro-electric power. The mean annual rainfall of the Guayana region is not less than 70 inches (1,778 mm). Heavy flow rivers, unfit for navigation, present incalculable advantages for the production of cheap power in almost unlimited amounts. Of all rivers in the region the Caroni River stands out, though other rivers such as the Paragua, the Caura, and the Cuyuni could also be utilized in the same way. The Caroni River Basin comprises 37,000 square miles (96,000 km²) and its water flow is some 15,000 cubic metres per second. The potential of the lower Caroni alone is estimated at 4 million kilowatts, and the Guri Dam on the Caroni will eventually be the largest single dam in the tropics.

The advantages of the Guayana region then, include vast resources of minerals and hydro-electric power. The region, too, has good potential facilities for cheap transport by water, especially with the dredging of the Orinoco, which will connect a deep-water port at Puerto Ordaz–San Felix to the mouth of the river.

An examination in the 1950s of Venezuela's needs, potentialities, and existing industries led to the conclusion that the country's industrial development should focus strongly on the production of metals, petrochemicals, and machinery. Existing Venezuelan industries – largely final-assembly activities – require these basic and intermediate products. Their production would not only fill gaps in the domestic economy but would also provide Venezuela with export goods for trade with other Latin American countries and the rest of the world. The studies suggested that the country should give high priority specifically to the production of iron and steel, sponge iron, aluminium, other metals and metal products, heavy machinery, electro-chemicals, and forest products such as pulp and paper.

Analysis of location, cost, and other factors indicated that if these activities were located in the Guayana region they would enjoy comparative advantage and could compete successfully in foreign markets. On the basis of the many factors involved, including projections of the future demand and markets for the various products, a comprehensive programme for investment in production facilities was worked out. Since Guayana is a food deficit area the programme included proposals for increasing the production of food, particularly in the area of the Orinoco Delta.

Venezuela incorporated this programme in its national plan. It projected a total investment of some $3·8 billion in the Guayana region over the ten-year period. Of this amount the Venezuelan Government itself is providing more than $500 million for the period 1965–8 and will contribute about $1·5 billion for the period

1969–75; together this amounts roughly to 10 per cent of the total Venezuelan public investment. The rest is expected to come from private capital (domestic and foreign) and from loans by international agencies. As a result of these investments it is hoped that by 1975 the Guayana region will provide about one-fifth of Venezuela's total of manufacturing and export products. By this date metals output should account for 14 per cent of the country's industrial production, with more than 90 per cent of this output occurring in the Guayana region. Production of machinery and transport equipment may make up 12 per cent of Venezuela's industrial output in that year, and 35 per cent of this, including most of the heavy machinery, will originate in Guayana.

The focal point of this industrial development is the new city of Ciudad Guayana, planned to contain a population of about two-thirds of a million by 1975. This city is more than just an urban settlement: it is the centre of an effort to establish the national economy of Venezuela on a broader and more stable basis. As recently as 1950 the population of the Guayana area was only about 4,000. Then two American-owned organizations – the Orinoco Mining Company and the Iron Mining Company – built plants in Guayana for iron-ore processing and created small settlements for their staffs. Later, the Venezuelan Government began the construction of a large steel plant on the Orinoco a few miles west of these centres. In 1959 a public corporation – the Corporacion Venezolana de Guayana (C.V.G.) – was set up to plan the development of the region, making the most of the great potential water-power, mineral resources, and good water transport. The corporation took over the steel plant and the Macagua Dam at the Caroni River Falls. It also took over the job of planning the growth of the city. Ciudad Guayana is now an outstanding example of the urban nucleus of a new and rapidly expanding industrial region in a developing country in the tropics. As such the city is perhaps one of the most ambitious and significant enterprises of its kind in the world today.

Nigeria. Before 1939 there was virtually no manufacturing industry in Nigeria. Cotton was partially processed, and cigarettes were manufactured at Ibadan; but there was very little else. In recent years, however, and particularly since 1948, there has been a rapid and important growth of factory industry. A major objective of the country's economic policy is 'to promote the growth of industry, both to increase the wealth of the country and also to provide new sources of employment. Industrialization will also help to make Nigeria less dependent on the relation between the world prices for primary products which she exports and manufactured goods, nearly all of which she at present imports' (Nigerian Govt., 1962: 72). Moreover, as the largest and most populous country in Africa, the newly independent nation of Nigeria is very conscious of the prestige value of large-scale industrialization.

In formulating a policy for industrial expansion, the government had to take into account certain factors militating against rapid expansion in this field. First, the Nigerian has little or no industrial labour experience and lacks knowledge of the managerial and technical skills required for industrial development. While a good deal is now being done in the way of more formal technical education, the government is also encouraging small-scale industry, partly with the same aim in view. To meet the demand for industrial research, and in accordance with a recommendation of the 1954 International Bank Mission, an Institute of Applied Industrial Research was set up in 1956 near Lagos. The institute has already been able to give advice to local entrepreneurs and overseas firms as well as to regional departments and the various corporations. Secondly, Nigeria suffers from a severe shortage of indigenous capital. This has been tackled by establishing a number of development boards to make loans and grants for industrial development. In 1953 the Aid the Pioneer Industries Ordinance was enacted. Any undertaking satisfying the provisions of the Ordinance – which are broadly that the industry is favourable to Nigeria and in its interests to assist – may be declared a pioneer industry and granted a Pioneer Industry Certificate; it is then relieved from paying income tax for a specified number of years.

All these measures are designed to attract both indigenous and overseas capital. In Nigeria the official view is that the country must for long continue to depend primarily upon foreign rather than indigenous capital to finance her industrialization. At present Nigerians tend to prefer to invest in trade; and 'though this pattern will improve, the pace of industrialization in Nigeria will depend very much for a long time on the volume of overseas investment' (ibid.: 29). To assist the flow of overseas capital the Investment Corporation of Nigeria Limited and two Development Companies have been set up. These bodies not only have capital of their own to invest but they also encourage the participation of overseas enterprises.

As for the home market in Nigeria, this is potentially very large in a country of some 55 millions, but at present the market opportunities are limited in many areas by poor communications and almost everywhere by the low purchasing power and the spending habits of the population. Admittedly, however, every increase in the national income increases Nigeria's attractiveness as a potential market for industrial goods; and an expansion in agricultural exports by raising the national income could probably do more in a short time to encourage industrialization than anything else.

Though large-scale factory production is being encouraged in Nigeria, this is not being done at the expense of small-scale industries. Small-scale industries constitute about 1·5 per cent of the national income and provide the primary occupation of over half a million people. They include the working of brass and silver ware, tin-smithing, carving, joinery, cabinet-making, calabash-carving, pottery-making, leather-work, hand-weaving, dyeing, textile manufacturing, and the making of baskets, straw and raffia mats and hats, glass beads, ornaments, rope, twine, and nets. Not only do these industries provide a living for a large number of people but if they did not exist, Nigeria would either have to import equivalent articles or do without.

The development of small-scale industries is being assisted in a number of ways, including the making of loans by statutory bodies and the giving of advice by qualified technical officers. In addition, small viable industries, for example cloth-weaving, have been set up, and school-leavers and others are trained in such crafts as broad-loom weaving, designing, and dyeing. Measures taken by the government include also the giving of advice on the use of indigenous raw materials by the Institute of Industrial Research and the renting of factory units at the Yaba Industrial Estate, which is also equipped with a mechanical workshop. Small industrialists also benefit from the Approved Manufactures Scheme. Finally, the Nigerian Government arranged with the International Co-operation Administration of the United States for two experts to visit Nigeria in 1959 and advise on how the Federal Government could improve on the assistance already being given to small industrialists.

Planned industrial communities in Nigeria now include: (i) an industrial *estate* at Yaba (near Lagos) for small-scale industries featuring standard factory buildings, common service facilities, and advisory services; and (ii) twelve industrial *areas* offering improved and unimproved plots for medium-sized and large-scale industries. Whereas the main purpose of the Yaba industrial estate is to provide a nursery for small-scale industries and technical training, the main purpose of the industrial areas is to attract foreign enterprises. The latter range in size from 60 acres at Gusau to 2,500 acres at Toms-Amadi, near Port Harcourt (U.N., 1966: 48–9).

An example of a rapidly developing industry in Nigeria is the textile industry. Although Nigeria has long possessed both the raw material and markets for a textile industry, not until 1958 was there any significant development. For nearness to market and raw materials are not overriding factors in determining the location of textile ventures in Nigeria; transport costs generally form only a small proportion of the delivered costs of textiles. Possession of sufficient capital and manufacturing skills are usually the decisive factors.

In the case of Kaduna Textiles Limited, established in 1955, the share capital was provided by the Northern Region Marketing Board, the Northern Region Development Corporation, and David Whitehead (Nigeria) Limited. The last is the subsidiary of an old-established Lancashire firm and able to draw on the expert advice of its parent. It acts as managing agent and has provided technical staff. Northern Nigeria offered the main market for the finished product and proximity to the cotton-growing areas and the ginneries which serve them. Within the region, however, the choice of site was determined by the availability of an abundant and guaranteed water supply. Kaduna was able to provide this together with electricity, land, and labour. Another essential was air-conditioning, 'not, as is usual in the wet tropics, in order to dry the atmosphere, but to simulate the damp conditions prevailing in Lancashire . . . unless the appropriate degree of humidity is provided by the factory, the cotton will spin and weave erratically' (U.A.C., 1957: 21). The mill has concentrated so far on spinning and weaving baft. This concentration on a single product, apart from conferring the normal advantages of an uninterrupted production flow, has also been invaluable in assisting the Nigerian workers new to factory employment of any kind to acquire proficiency and to adapt themselves to an industrial environment. Production costs are slightly higher than those of some overseas suppliers, but it is hoped that they will decrease as the Nigerian workers become more proficient. A separate training school has started with the object of attracting and training Nigerians who will be capable of supervising the various textile processes. Until these have been found, manufacturing costs will have to bear the expense of a relatively high proportion of expatriate staff (40 Europeans to 1,000 Nigerians). The Kaduna mill, however, is protected from the severest overseas competition by import duties.

In the African setting, Nigeria would seem to have a number of distinct advantages for industrial growth, including mineral and power resources and a large domestic market. Recent rapid developments in the production and processing of crude oil and the setting up of a basic iron and steel industry indicate that the immediate future of the Nigerian economy will depend increasingly on a substantial measure of industrialization. Political factors, however, may once again prove to be crucial. With her federal structure and uneven distribution of peoples, resources, and growth points of development, it is difficult to see how the necessary co-operation and integration for mutual economic development projects between regions of the country can for long continue.

India. India has experienced the most massive industrialization of all tropical developing countries since the end of the Second World War. During the decade of the industrial revolution in India (1951–61), organized industrial production almost doubled; and the Third and Fourth Five-Year Plans have been attempting, though with very much less success, to maintain as far as possible this rate of industrial growth.

The broad strategy of economic planning in India in relation to the relative roles of agriculture and industry has shown a number of interesting changes over the last few Five-Year Plan periods. Table 10 attempts to summarize the sectoral expenditures over the

Table 10. *India: Financial provisions in the four five-year plans*

Sector	1st plan (1951–6) %	2nd plan (1956–61) %	3rd plan (1961–6) %	4th plan (1966–71) %
Agricultural, community and village development	15	11	14	20
Irrigation	16	9	9	6
Power	13	10	13	13
Village and small-scale industries	2	4	4	2
Organized industry and minerals	4	20	20	20
Transport and communications	27	28	20	19
Social services	23	18	20	20
	100	100	100	100

four periods and shows how 'organized industry and minerals' has taken an increasingly large percentage of total plan expenditures. But this table, especially as regards any comparison between the third and fourth plans, gives a largely misleading impression. In sectors like industry, which uses large imported components, costs in terms of rupees went up suddenly and substantially with devaluation in 1966. In agriculture, however, costs have not gone up in the same way, and it is estimated that the total provision for agriculture in the fourth plan is, in real terms, over twice what it was for the third plan. In comparing agriculture and industry in any sectoral analysis, indeed, it is more accurate to conclude that greater emphasis is now being placed on agriculture. This change has been very much forced upon India by the series of food crop failures in 1965–6 and by the general deterioration of food supply conditions in the country.

Even within the field of industrial development itself, the food supply situation has had its effect. The 1964 Memorandum on the Fourth Five-Year Plan made proposals about industrialization which have not been carried forward into the plan itself. Within the industrial sector the emphasis is now quite explicitly on the kind of industry that can help to maximize agricultural production: 'production of such goods as fertilizers, insecticides, agricultural implements, including pumps, diesel engines, tractors . . . will be given the highest priority in the programmes for industrial development (Indian Govt., 1964: 16). Here is an interesting case of industrialization involving the feedback into agriculture of the kind implied in the development continuum (Fig. 3). Up to the middle 1950s, the emphasis on agricultural planning in India was on extending the cultivated area; and the emphasis in industry still lay with the traditional industries of cotton, jute, and sugar. But the emphasis is now on the intensification of new forms of agricultural production by the provision of Indian manufactured fertilizers, pesticides, irrigation tubewells, and fuel oil for pumping water and for irrigation schemes generally. By the end of the Fourth Five-Year Plan (1971) new fertilizer plants will have been constructed at Durgapur, Kotah, Goa, Cochin, Madras, Kanpur, Kathgodam, and Haldia; and the fertilizer production capacity will have more than doubled to some 1·8 million tons per annum, rising eventually to 2·4 million tons. Pesticide productive capacity will rise from 18,000 tons in 1965–6 to at least 100,000 tons in 1970–1.

The other major emphasis in current industrial development planning in India has also been forced upon the Government by events – the need to do something about the serious balance of payments situation. The foreign exchange problem has become one of the overriding considerations in determining Indian economic policy; and this exchange problem shows no sign of improving while India's chief exports – largely manufactured exports – give so little sign of growing in value. During the Third Five-Year Plan period India's exports grew in value less than did world exports, so that India's share in world exports fell from 1·2 per cent in 1960 to only 1 per cent in 1965: and this for a country with perhaps one-seventh of the world's population. A great deal of Indian industry depends upon imported foreign components. Current policy, therefore, has as one of its major aims the saving of foreign currency by encouraging the indigenous manufacture of these necessary components.

Apart from the current food supply and balance of payments situations, India's industrial development has also been deeply affected by the political factor, and in particular by the conflict between the Centre and States and, inevitably, between public and private investment. Indian economic planning, as stated explicitly in the Five-Year Plans, is aimed at creating a socialist state. This has meant encouraging public as against private investment in industry. Since the first plan, public investment in industry has gone up from only 55 to 3,926 Rs crores in the fourth plan; whereas private investment has risen from 235 to only 2,350 Rs crores in the current plan. According to a number of observers, however, this trend has had the effect of restricting industrial development. In particular, it has been pointed out that in the iron and steel industry in India the public sector is not doing nearly so well as the private sector.

By tropical standards the amount of heavy industry in India is very large indeed. The iron and steel industry has a number of difficulties to contend with, not the least of which is transportation; iron ore deposits are scattered all over the country, and the existing railway network seems to be inadequate to handle the tonnage to be moved. Nevertheless, by the end of the Fourth Five-Year Plan the iron and steel capacity should be of the order of 14·8 million tons of steel ingots and about 3 million tons of pig iron. To make this possible, the existing works at Bhilai, Durgapur, and Rourkela are being expanded and a new plant, built with Russian aid, constructed at Bokaro. About 4 million tons of the total 14·8 million tons of steel ingots will be produced by the private sector. It is accepted that this scale of iron and steel production is necessary if the foundations are to be laid for an expanded heavy electrical and machine tools, machine building, and other branches of heavy engineering; chemical (including fertilizers and pesticides) industries; and cement and paper manufacture.

At the other extreme some emphasis is being placed on small-scale industries. In the current (fourth) plan this form of industrial enterprise is being encouraged by providing direct financial assistance, by developing institutional credit, intermediate technology and training programmes, by decentralizing the manufacture of equipment, and by the organization of co-operatives. It is hoped both to increase total production and to widen the range and variety of goods produced by small-scale industries. But a particularly interesting feature of small-scale industry in India is the establishment of industrial estates. Many factory sheds in industrial estates equipped with power, water supply, roads, and other facilities have been established to encourage investment in small-scale manufacturing industries. During the first three Five-Year Plans, 107 industrial estates containing 3,787 factory sheds were established. It is interesting to note, however, that those estates set up nearest to towns have been the most successful; so that, in fact, the industrial estates have not so far been conspicuously effective in dispersing industry. Perhaps the most successful estates of all have been those located around large-scale industrial units to which they have supplied parts and components.

In spite of her impressive industrial sector, India faces a number of particularly difficult problems in her industrialization programme. Mention has already been made of the problems of food supply, balance of payments, markets, and politics. During the Third Five-Year Plan (1961–6) there was some encouraging progress in industrialization at first – continuing the work already begun during the first two Five-Year Plans. But this progress ceased during the latter part of the third plan period; and this resulted not only from the shortage of foreign exchange after the hostilities of 1962 and 1965, when certain foreign credits were suspended, but also from the shortage of hydro-electric power caused by the 1965–6 droughts. But behind all these problems lies the crucial question of scale. The sheer volume and scale of industrialization required in a country of some 500 million people would seem to be such that no normal sources of capital, organization or government can reasonably be expected to deal with them unaided.

CHAPTER 12

Transport

The role of transport. The urgent and now widely recognized need to improve and extend transport facilities in tropical countries is clear from the fact that transport and communications commonly take over 40 per cent of the total public outlay in development planning. Many aid funds have been selectively applied to this particular field of development; and the principle is now generally accepted that the improvement of transport forms perhaps the most valuable single contribution towards economic, social and political development. Certainly in the early stages of economic advance in communities where subsistence agriculture is still important, transport is probably the key to development: 'fertilizers, improved strains of seed, education and other objects are all of the greatest importance. But the need for transport is prior to all these' (Clark and Haswell, 1964: 216).

There are two major reasons for emphasizing the role of transport in economic development, more especially in tropical developing countries. First, transportation is seen as the *sine qua non* of colonization and so vital in the extension of settlement in a region. Humphreys (1946) has shown how important transport facilities are to the opening up of tropical South America. The eastern valleys of Bolivia and parts of Peru and Ecuador are potentially good areas for settlement, but they are inaccessible and too distant from markets and ports. Then there are great areas bordering the Amazon Basin now empty of people but which will prove suitable for settlement when such highways as the Lima–Tonjo Main Pacific Highway have been constructed. The Matto Grosso is hindered in its development by lack of communications, as is the open plain country at the foot of Bolivia near Santa Cruz de la Sierra. According to Humphreys, if transport were improved sufficiently Brazil could support a population of some 400 million people – well over four times the present population. The building of the new capital of Brasilia is one example of attempts to direct attention away from the coast towards Brazil's vast but thinly populated interior. Brasilia is located at the nodal point of a new and extensive road network from Brasilia to Rio de Janeiro, to the Pacific coast, and to Belem on the Amazon River.

Secondly, and more important, improved and extended transport facilities are necessary to the widening and fusion of the market in areas already settled, and in stimulating further production for internal or external trade in a country and so in encouraging the growth of a modern exchange economy: 'cheapening transport fuses markets, bringing additional buyers and sellers into contact with one another, increasing elasticities of demand and supply' (Kindleberger, 1966: 167). Furthermore, transport allows the free exchange of goods between rural areas and urban centres, 'whereby it becomes possible for the economic position of the cultivator to rise above subsistence level, consuming locally grown food and simple handicrafts produced in his own village, and practically nothing else; while in the absence of transport towns could not exist at all' (Clark and Haswell, 1964: 167). Transportation facilities also encourage and facilitate the geographical specialization of agricultural production. Finally, improved transport facilities may make possible the intensification of agricultural production, with all the improvements in techniques this implies: it is useless, for instance, to try to encourage the use of manures or cultivated fodder on fields far distant from the farmstead where 'the farmer or his wife has no means of transporting it other than by head porterage. Intensification calls first of all for continuing efforts aimed at reducing the costs of all the operations involved, starting with the production and transport costs of cultivated fodder and manure' (Dumont, 1966: 71).

Forms of transport. Over the larger part of the tropical world most transport services are still performed by the individual, often in the form of head, shoulder or back porterage, and without any capital equipment at all; and it has been suggested that the extent of human porterage – if it could be measured – might well provide one of the more illuminating indices of levels of economic development (Bauer and Yamey, 1957). Simple carts, wagons, or beasts of burden may also be used, and the bicycle is playing an increasingly significant role in the movement of goods where topographical conditions make this possible. All such elementary forms of moving goods must for long provide the bulk of transport services, even where they become merely tributary to major modern lines of transport.

The individually small-scale nature of all these simple, often primitive means of transport in tropical countries is not to be condemned and discouraged out of hand. In the majority of cases, indeed, the present means of transport may be said to be adequate in the prevailing physical, social, and economic conditions. Nevertheless, there are many areas where they can already be said to present a barrier to economic development. Certainly in economic terms the apparently 'cheap' method of transport – human porterage – is commonly prohibitively expensive. Human porterage has been said to be some nine or ten times as expensive as transport by water, motor vehicle, or rail; forms of transport at present available to the bulk of tropical peoples, in fact, are so costly that produce often 'only has to be carried a limited distance before most of its value, from the point of view of net returns from the sale, has gone' (Clark and Haswell, 1964: 156). This is partly because of the frequent repetition of transport movements demanded in a situation where only very limited amounts can be carried by the individual in each operation; but it is also partly due to the fact that distances covered by human porterage are necessarily severely limited. According to Gourou (1966) the average figure is 30 miles (50 km) a day at an average load of 88 lb (40 kg). The implications of this point for economic development are obvious, but include the important one that the choice of crop is often determined at least partly by reference to the costs of available transport facilities. In East Africa, for instance, it has been shown that Africans have chosen coffee because the value of the crop makes it one of the few crops which can support the existing burden of transport costs (Clark and Haswell, 1964: 156). Again, high transport costs have been shown to affect the price of land in Mindanao

(Philippines) where land prices drop markedly with distance from markets.

The other simplest form of transport – by water – is in economic terms perhaps the least costly of all forms of transport. The role of water transport in tropical countries is commonly underestimated and has received remarkably little treatment in the literature, perhaps because it commonly applies to areas with relatively low population densities and often with only vestigial forms of economic development. Yet water transport has played an important role in the early penetration and development of large parts of the tropics; and in many countries the river is still the real focus of economic life and commonly provides the only means of transport. This is particularly true of the lowland equatorial tropics: in Congo Kinshasa, Sarawak, and northern Brazil, for instance. But in many other areas throughout the tropics the potential for water transport and development is considerable. This is illustrated by the detailed report of NEDECO (1960) on the improvement of navigation on the Rivers Niger and Benue in Nigeria.

The present poverty of rail transport in most tropical countries is very striking and, especially where the final stages of the movement of export crops and minerals are concerned, this may certainly be restrictive on development. The economic history of most countries in the tropics abounds with examples of how crop and mineral production had to await the building of railways: cocoa in Ghana was stimulated by the Accra–Kumasi railway; the production of cotton in Uganda was made feasible by the construction of the Kenya–Uganda railway; and the mining of tin on the Jos Plateau of Nigeria and of copper in Katanga also had to await the arrival of the railway before any great development could take place. In particular, as the case of Nigeria shows, the correlation between export crops and railway building has sometimes been remarkably close. Groundnuts did not figure significantly in Lagos exports until after the completion of the Lagos–Kano railway in 1912; and the same is true of cotton and hides and skins, all of which originated in the northern savanna lands.

In recent years, however, the emphasis has shifted away from the role of the railway to the role of the road in economic development,

o

though the traditional role of the railway in development has by no means been destroyed. Controversy over the relative merits of railways and roads in stimulating economic advance is still common, and striking instances of this have occurred over the last decade or so. In Nigeria the International Bank Report of 1954 considered proposals to build a railway reaching into the north-eastern corner of the country and, on reviewing the evidence, rejected them; but it supported alternative proposals to extend the road network into the same area. Subsequent work and political considerations, however, led to a reversal of this decision, and the Bornu Extension Railway, as it is now called, was finally constructed between 1960 and 1964. The avowed purpose of this line was to bring to north-eastern Nigeria the same opportunities of agricultural expansion and cash crop production, based on cheap transport, that are already being enjoyed in Kano Province; and it was hoped and expected that as purchasing stations for groundnuts and cotton were established along the line in Bauchi and Bornu Provinces, the population would migrate towards the line and turn to the cultivation of substantial surpluses for sale through the apparatus of the Marketing Boards. This, it was hoped, would succeed because the region is thinly populated, so that land for commercial agriculture is readily available. The railway had turned the Kano close-settled zone into a major producing area of groundnuts for export, and it could do the same for Bornu, where rainfall and soils were no less favourable (Emerson, 1959). Already, however, it is becoming clear that the build-up of traffic on this line is unlikely to be fast enough to enable the railway to be run at a profit; certainly it will not enable Nigerian railways to undercut substantially the rates charged by lorry operators for carrying agricultural produce to the coast (Barbour, 1966).

There seems little doubt that the road will continue to capture an increasing share of internal traffic in most tropical countries. In Uganda, O'Connor (1966) has shown that road transport has continued to remain more important that the newly constructed railways, and that the latter have had remarkably little impact on local or regional trade. Not only is the road a much more flexible instrument for inducing economic development – it can proliferate more easily and can be tapped at any point for the purposes of distribution – but the road is also a much less capital-intensive method of providing transport facilities. It is not only that construction and maintenance costs are higher for railways than for roads, but also that railways are indivisible investments. These are normally built and owned by governments, simply because railways represent heavy investment based on future demand patterns. In a few cases, as in Costa Rica, private companies have built the main railways; but in general it is true that private enterprise could not be expected to be interested in such risky investments. Roads, however, represent divisible investments, and road transportation can be developed in relatively small divisible units. Government participation is required only in the construction of the basic road network itself, while the rest of the investment is commonly provided by private enterprise. As a number of writers have pointed out, indeed, this divisibility of investment in road transport, compared with investment in railways, may be crucial in the early stages of a country's economic development, when domestic markets are narrow and the volume of traffic is small. Furthermore, as another authority has emphasized, although the adverse effects of tropical climates upon surface structures make it costly to build roads and railways, the latter 'require to be kept in a much better state of repair in order to maintain services' (Hawkins, 1962: 29); and experience in Costa Rica has demonstrated very clearly the difficult and costly problem of railway maintenance in a tropical, mountainous environment. Yet there may be a danger that the wholesale and indiscriminate building of roads will become accepted as automatically beneficial – almost as the latest of a series of panaceas for the problems of developing countries.

The economics of transport. A great deal, certainly, needs to be known about the economics of transport, and the available evidence in almost any field of transportation studies in tropical countries is both scanty and fragmentary. Hawkins (1958) has suggested that when traffic reaches 300 vehicles a day on a road then bituminization becomes economically worthwhile in Nigeria. Sargent (1960) estimates that each kilometre of road built has the effect of opening some 60 hectares of new agricultural land in Sabah. In West African countries Pedler (1955) puts the savings from bitumenization at 18 per cent. But all such data can as yet do little more than enable us to ask our questions rather more precisely than before: the answers to most of the urgent practical problems of transport economics in developing countries of the tropics have still to be found and must await the kind of thorough descriptive analysis presented for the movement of export crops in Nigeria by White (1959).

Some of the difficulties in building roads in tropical countries are well illustrated in Sarawak where new roads are a costly undertaking, not only because of the difficult terrain but also because the climate and general unsuitability of local building materials make a high and expensive standard of construction essential if the road is to give reasonable service. Moreover, the sharp contrasts in population distribution, and the low average density of population in the country means that roads have to pass for long stretches through uninhabited country and so face large initial operating deficits. Again, in Nigeria, as in most countries of the tropics with a substantial and definite dry season, earth roads are likely to be usable only during the dry season. Nevertheless, so expensive are bitumenized roads that even today still only 4,000 miles (6,440 km) out of 37,000 miles (59,500 km) are bitumenized, the balance consisting of gravel and earth roads.

· · · · ·

Attention in this very brief summary has been concentrated on transport in relation to economic development in a tropical country as seen from inside that country. But equally, of course, transport facilities in relation to economic development must be considered at an international level: in fact, it is rather arbitrary to make any clear distinction between internal and external transport facilities in discussing economic development. Air transport improvements have their repercussions upon many sides of the complex process of economic development, as is well shown in West Africa and Latin America; and the importance of creating, maintaining, and improving port facilities is particularly obvious in countries whose prosperity continues to be so closely linked to the export of basic raw materials or commodities and whose economies depend so heavily upon imported manufactured goods (White, 1959). Both internally and externally, it is probably impossible to exaggerate the importance of transport to economic development in the developing countries of the tropical world. The theoretical and practical arguments for giving priority to such issues in the early stages of a country's economic planning are familiar and convincing. Whether at the national or at the individual level, increased production is always likely to be frustrated unless two requirements – good cheap transport and good market opportunities – are fulfilled. The next chapter concentrates on the second of these two requirements.

CHAPTER 13
Markets and Trade

Most of the literature on economic development and, indeed, perhaps the larger part of the present volume, is concerned with the problems of increasing production as seen from the supply point of view. The utilization and improvement of natural, human, and capital resources is viewed primarily in relation to the aim of increasing production. Both at the local level and at the level of national economic development, preoccupation seems commonly to be with the supply side of production in all its various manifestations. Quite clearly, however, this is a somewhat arbitrary and misleading emphasis, for it is little more than an analytical convenience to distinguish rigidly between the supply and demand sides of the problem of increasing production. The present chapter concentrates attention on the demand side as expressed by internal and external markets and trade.

Internal markets and trade. It has already been necessary on a number of occasions to refer to the narrowness of the home market in tropical developing countries. This narrowness is a characteristic of underdevelopment and is frequently held to constitute a formidable obstacle to agricultural and industrial development. The nature and causes of this condition vary from one country to another, but in general may be said to arise from the low purchasing power and restricted spending habits of consumers; from lack of capital for storage; and from inadequate and costly transport. Market opportunities and economic prosperity are here closely interdependent.

Home market opportunities, though automatically widening as economic development and population growth proceeds, can be widened still further by various means. As was shown in the previous chapter, indeed, one of the arguments for improving internal lines of transport is that they will help to increase the extent and intensity of market contacts within a territory and so lead to economies of scale. Another way in which the domestic market can be widened is by providing capital for storage and credit facilities to farmers. Again, Nurkse (1953) advocates the enlargement of the home market by the simultaneous expansion of a large number of industries which buy one another's products; this, he argues, will automatically create a market and will also, if localized, increase the external economies enjoyed by each firm and so reduce costs – which is one reason why industries tend to be gregarious. It has also been suggested that the home market may be enlarged for home products by capturing what is at present supplied for foreign producers. This may be possible in a few fields, particularly in small-scale industries. But in relating the home market to industrial expansion, where market limitations are especially limiting, the pattern of spending among tropical peasants cannot be ignored. In Ceylon, for instance, the average consumer spends 60 per cent of his total expenditure on food and only 2·5 per cent on clothing and 0·1 per cent on shoes. The level of income is so low that these percentages would not be likely to alter much even if incomes rose moderately. In many tropical countries, especially those that are heavily populated, the income elasticity of demand for food is close to unity: in other words, people would still continue to spend the bulk of their income on food until their income reaches a certain critical figure above which Engel's law applies and the consumption of food decreases as a percentage of income. Data for Greater Delhi seem to support this general principle (Table 11). In this situation, clearly, a producer will be reluctant to launch into any ambitious schemes for the production of manufactured goods. There are important differences in elasticities, both of demand and supply, between developing and developed countries; and some economists argue that in developing countries the price system is therefore ineffective and that the normal marginal analysis associated with the price system of advanced societies is inappropriate in the context of developing societies.

However it is accomplished, there can be little doubt that to widen the home market opportunities and to improve opportunities for trading and marketing are crucial in any attempt at inducing economic development. Some writers give this point pride of place in their analyses and prescriptions, arguing that unless the producer's incentives to change or increase his production are affected, then no technical or institutional improvements are likely to have

Table 11. *Household expenditure patterns in Greater Delhi* (*Average monthly figures*)

Expenditure Range (Rupees)	Total (Rupees)	Percentage of Total				
		Food	Cloth	Fuel	Rent	Other
<100	62·4	61	10	7	7	15
100–249	138·4	58	10	6	8	18
250–499	285·7	53	10	5	8	24
500–999	513·3	47	10	4	9	43
>1000	1169·5	38	8	3	8	43

Source: Rao and Desai (1965), p. 239

much success. And it is undoubtedly true that a tropical farmer is unlikely to increase his production unless an increased demand is there, is seen to be there, and is easily accessible. Improved seed, fertilizers, and better irrigation facilities: a tropical cultivator is unlikely to use these to increase his total production unless the market for his increased production is first seen to exist and is accessible. It is probably always true to say that there is no point in a farmer having a new crop variety or fertilizers, which will enable him to increase his food production very substantially and immediately, if at the same time his form of transport is so costly or the demand for the extra produce is so uncertain or so distant as to make such an increase worthless. From the point of view of the individual farmer who makes the increase, increased production implies increased sales. And increased sales implies an increased demand which the farmer is aware of, responds to in terms of his spending habits, and which he can easily and economically reach (Krishna, 1959). Only when these conditions are fulfilled is it logical to attempt to improve crop production by the application of scientific methods and research or to attempt any of the more complex agricultural or infrastructural changes increased agricultural production implies.

Unfortunately, however, our knowledge of the forms, mechanisms, and institutions of indigenous trading and marketing in most tropical countries is very scanty and uneven (Galbraith and Holton, 1955), and has to depend very much upon the attempt to draw analogies with early market institutions in Western Europe or upon contemporary work in non-tropical countries, notably in China (Skinner, 1964–5), where it is argued that the phenomena described are really characteristic of all 'peasant' or 'traditional' agrarian societies. As pointed out elsewhere (Hodder, 1961), the geographical analysis of the economies of tropical countries commonly concentrates either on the productive sector or on large-scale internal and external exchange sectors. Remarkably little attention has been paid to the local exchange sectors or to the functions and characteristics of local market institutions like the rural periodic markets of Africa or the water markets of parts of South-east Asia. Yet for the bulk of the population, both in rural and in urban areas, it is through some form of local market that most agricultural and cottage industrial products enter the exchange economy; and it is through these same market institutions that goods from abroad and elsewhere are absorbed. Clearly, then, it is at the level of local exchange that we must look in any attempt directly to affect the production and consumption of the majority of tropical peoples.

To take the case with which the writer is personally most familiar – West Africa – the lively system of local trade there has been shown to be of considerable economic significance. The general characteristics of some of the market institutions of West Africa have now been presented in a number of studies (Bohannan and Dalton, 1962; Hodder, 1961, 1965a, 1965b; Hill, 1966a, 1966b), and some of the facts about the periodic markets – their cyclical or periodic nature, their organization into market rings or circuits, their commodity structure and economic functions, for instance – and about the daily markets, especially their relevance to 'central-place' theory, are now beginning to be understood, though a great deal remains to be known about markets in the region. It is still impossible to generalize confidently about the processes and socio-economic significance of all West African market institutions.

The origins of traditional, pre-European, indigenous markets in West Africa have been examined elsewhere (Hodder, 1965b; Ukwu, 1965), it being suggested that political control of a kind able to guarantee the market peace, a sufficiently high density of population, and location on or near long-distance trade routes were necessary elements in the rise of indigenous market institutions in West Africa. This point about market origins is important to the present study, not so much because it helps to explain why West Africa has such a highly developed system of market institutions – the region having a number of powerful early political states, being threaded by long-distance trade routes of great antiquity, and having by African standards a high density of population – but because it may be relevant to contemporary attempts to induce self-generating change to a market economy among those peoples of the tropics who as yet lie largely outside modern economic influences. If this notion has any validity, it means in modern terms that only where there is an effective political administration, a sufficiently high density of population – probably not less than 50 persons to the square mile (20 per km^2) – and long-distance lines of transportation, especially good trunk roads, are efforts to induce rapid economic change likely to be effective. And where these conditions are not fulfilled, then their provision must be a precondition for any significant economic development.

How far local trade and its associated institutional mechanism of the market place is increasing or decreasing relative to other forms of trade is a controversial issue. As far as West Africa is concerned, it has been suggested by some writers that market institutions are declining in importance, for as economies become more sophisticated these institutions become less necessary: 'the more pervasive the market principle the less the economic importance of the market place' (Bohannan and Dalton, 1962: 25). Yet there are strong practical reasons, such as increased urbanization, improved transport, higher purchasing power, increased occupational specialization, for presuming that the total quantity of goods sold in West African markets is in fact increasing proportionately far more quickly than the size of the population (Hill, 1963). This is not the place to discuss the relative merits of these two opposing viewpoints, except perhaps to point out that the evidence from the few studies so far made is conflicting and that much more serious study of specific communities is indicated (Ukwu, 1965). What is beyond doubt, however, is the fact that the character of most West African markets is beginning to show signs of radical changes. Two of these changes are the shift from periodic to continuous trading and the shift to specialized wholesale markets. Though markets in West Africa today still largely take the place of shops in Western Europe, the tendency is for the balance to change – for indigenous shops to increase in number and importance, especially around the periphery of the larger daily markets in the main towns; and for periodic markets to take over most of the largely wholesale functions in distribution. This is a process quite independent of the existence and growth of introduced European retail and wholesale shopping nuclei which are still the dominant form of shops in almost all the larger towns of West Africa.

This point about the development of indigenous shops and the changing relative significance and functions of periodic and daily markets can be related to an hypothesis which sees all types and operations of markets in West Africa as intermediate stages on a single, albeit many-stranded continuum from the most primitive to the most complicated economies. Simply stated the argument can be expressed as follows:

Periodic Markets⟶ *Daily Markets* ⟶ *Retail Shops*
where the dominant   associated especially
interest is the   with urban life,
injection of local   where the dominant
foodstuffs and craft interest is the
products into the   buying of local and
exchange economy by   imported goods
wholesale selling and
buying

⟶ *Specialized Wholesale Markets*

This hypothesis, tracing the development of markets from the simplest periodic markets through to the retail shops and large specialized wholesale markets in the largest towns, appears to fit in with the facts so far available; and this notion is further strengthened by a number of analogies drawn between markets in West Africa and those of Europe from medieval times to the present day. Any attempt to widen this hypothesis to other regions of the tropics must await similar work elsewhere. But the immediate and practical importance of such considerations for urban and rural planning and for the processes of economic development needs taking into account in all such research.

As for internal market opportunities and trade within a country, material in this field is even more scarce than in the field of local markets and trade. Once again, West Africa is rather better served in this connexion than are most other parts of the tropics. For Dahomey, Tardits (1962) has described how the agricultural products of the south are exchanged between the different geographical units – plateau and valley, coasts and inland areas – and how goods are sent from the rural areas into the urban markets of Cotonou, Porto Novo, Ouidah, and Abomey; for Ghana, White (1956) has demonstrated the internal exchange of movements of staple food crops; and Tricart (1956) has described the nature and characteristics of internal trade in Togo. In East Africa, Ford (1956) has described the trade of Lake Victoria. In the context of a nation's economic development planning, clearly, internal trade of this kind is of great importance and is of particular interest to the geographer in that it expresses the geographical pattern of ecological regions with different agricultural and craft products and specialization of production.

This whole question of internal distribution and marketing is perhaps of particular importance in large countries like India where food-surplus areas and food-deficit areas are widely separated and where an ancient, unorganized but normally effective system carries surplus cereals from the village to the consumer centres. But this system works without any direction or plan. Its purpose here is not really distribution but profit, and the whole machinery operates on price variations. When there is local scarcity prices rise, bringing more food on to the local markets but reducing consumption: when prices go up sharply the poorest in the villages may begin to starve. The system works in the same way on the national level, cereals going from the food-surplus states (Andhra Pradesh, Madhya Pradesh, Maharashtra, Orissa, Punjab, and Madras) to those states which do not produce enough food for themselves. But at this level political interference begins. In times of relative or expected scarcity the governments of the food-surplus states may resist, openly or furtively, the export of food to the usual markets.

External markets and trade. It is widely held that the economic development of many tropical countries has been restricted by their existing patterns of foreign trade. This has a number of important implications for development, one of which is that apart from South-east Asia, where there is some considerable movement of rice from the surplus countries to deficit countries, trade between the various countries of the tropics is only very small. The reasons for this are well known, and include the important one that the range of raw materials available for export is generally so small and frequently so similar that tropical countries have very little to offer each other. A further implication is that most of the efforts to improve production within tropical countries have been controlled and financed by the metropolitan powers and have been directed almost exclusively at those crops and other raw materials most needed by the manufacturing nations of the developed world. As noted earlier in the present chapter, this concentration on foreign trade items and on foreign trade as a process has usually been at the expense of other exchange sectors. The resulting 'économie de traite' is vividly illustrated in the pattern of internal communications in tropical countries. Only in a few cases, such as the palm-oil export industry in West Africa, in Bombay or in Minas Geraes, did this kind of economic development lead to any rapid advance in local modernized farming or local industrialization.

Independent tropical countries have also been left with a legacy of external trading organization which many believe to restrict rapid economic advance. In particular, the association in the minds of tropical peoples between colonialism and export economies is emphasized by the concentration of the large-scale export and import trade in the hands of a few large, mostly European, concerns. This has been illustrated for West Africa where the external trade is still largely in non-African hands: in 1949 about 85 per cent of the import trade in Nigeria was handled by European firms, about 10 per cent by Levantine and Indian firms, and only about 5 per cent by African firms. It is true that attempts are now being made to reduce this concentration in the import–export trade of West Africa, more especially since independence. But so far there has been little success in this direction. The reasons why these firms continue to be few and large include the fact that capital requirements are very substantial in the export of such primary commodities as palm oil, groundnuts or cocoa. Storage and transit difficulties in the prevailing conditions of poor transportation, scattered populations and immense distances, too, favour large organizing units. And all these facts call for the kind of sophisticated supervisory and technical management only likely to be encountered in the large European, or at least European-type, firm.

But probably the central problem in this context of external markets and trade is the perpetuation of the nineteenth-century pattern of external trade whereby tropical territories export certain raw materials, in which they have a comparative advantage, to the developed countries, and import manufactured goods from the same sources. Primary, mainly agricultural products and some minerals, dominate in exports; and finished consumer goods – textiles, vehicles, bicycles, cement, building materials, and machinery – account for most of the imports (Table 12). Furthermore, in many tropical countries exports comprise only a very few items: Senegal and Gambia both have over 80 per cent of the value of their exports accounted for by groundnuts; Sierra Leone has over 80 per cent of her export earnings provided by mining; 95 per cent of Columbia's foreign earnings come from coffee, petroleum, and bananas; and 88 per cent of Ceylon's earnings come from tea, rubber, and coconut products.

Much has been written about this tendency to depend on a small number of export raw materials in tropical countries. Some of the problems it raises are related to the repercussions such a pattern of exports has upon the production side of the economy, on labour market policy, on soil fertility and conservation, on crop pests and diseases, and on the improvement of dietary standards among tropical peoples. Some writers contend that the relation of productivity to prices in tropical lands is such that the exchange by them of primary products for the manufactures of developed

Table 12. *Import–export structures in selected countries*

	Major Imports as % of total imports by value, 1964		Major Exports as % of total exports by value, 1964	
Venezuela	Machinery and transport materials	41	Crude petroleum	66
			Petroleum products	26
	Manufactured goods	23	Iron ore	5
Ghana	Manufactured goods	35	Cocoa	65
	Machinery and transport materials	22		
India	Machinery and transport materials	35	Textile yarn	41
			Tea	20
	Manufactured goods	19	Jute fabrics	16
	Food products	15		

Source: U.N., *Statistical Yearbook,* 1965

countries, while especially profitable for the latter, is almost inevitably injurious to the former (Viner, 1953). Other authorities, for example Myrdal (1956), do not accept this view. But it is on the economic instability caused by overdependence on one or two raw material export products that attention is normally concentrated. Certainly the purchasing power of exports may fluctuate quite dramatically. Between 1959 and 1961, for instance, the average price of Ghanaian cocoa dropped by 32·4 per cent; and such fluctuations are always likely to occur in a situation where the manufacture of synthetics or substitutes – notably fibres, resins, detergents, dyestuffs, and nitrites – is common and where demand patterns are continually changing. Then, too, many other technological developments are likely to work against the developing countries simply because they reduce the possibility of advance towards industrialization by transforming exhaustible natural assets into valuable man-made wealth; for the whole tendency of technological advance, as was pointed out in Chapter 1, is to make natural resources more homogeneous, both in quality and in their distribution, and to reduce the actual or potential value of high-quality natural resources that were once essential for industry (Barnett and Morse, 1963).

Again, increased agricultural productivity in the developed, industrial countries has usually been accompanied by measures to protect these producers from adverse price effects arising from competition from low-income tropical countries. Similarly, the protection of other domestic producers, such as oil and mineral producers in the United States, denies low-cost producers in the developing countries any ready access to existing industrial markets.

In whatever way and from whatever cause these fluctuations in world market prices and so in the value of exports arise, these fluctuations affect not only export earnings and so the balance of payments situations in developing countries but result also in changes in revenues to the governments in the form of customs duties. This is an important point in countries where export–import duties still make up over half the total government revenues.

The problem, then, is that the low-income countries of the tropics are today faced with a fluctuating and often generally declining world market for their traditional raw materials. It may be true that fluctuations in export earnings are really no greater in tropical developing countries than for advanced countries. Yet tropical countries have few alternative opportunities for international trading in other agricultural or industrial products. Present trends in the pattern of international trading would seem to favour increasingly the industrial countries at the expense of the low-income countries of the tropical developing world. It is now commonly argued, moreover, that the widening gap between rich and poor countries is caused by the fact that the consumption of primary commodities by the rich nations does not increase at the same rate as their economic expansion; new processes and new materials tend to reduce the consumption of industrial raw materials in relation to output; and with food products, higher incomes do not lead to a parallel increase in consumption in the rich countries (*The Times*, 1964: 27 October). The terms of trade seem in the long run to favour developed countries and turn against developing countries, illustrating the Prebisch effect – that primary production tends to increase beyond what is required by the relatively slow increase of demand. And it was partly the great interest in this fact that led to the setting up in 1964 of the United Nations Conference on Trade and Development (UNCTAD).

One way of dealing with this broad problem of external trade in tropical countries is to encourage diversification. This can be pursued in export crop production by introducing new export crops: in West Africa, for instance, ginger in Sierra Leone, beniseed in Nigeria, and Karite seeds in Upper Volta are being expanded. In this sense, changing land-use patterns are both caused by and are the cause of changing patterns in international trade. Then diversification of production for the home market is sometimes prescribed as the solution to the problem of economic instability arising from the dependence of export economies on a fluctuating market, though there is some controversy over this policy. It is true that diversified production for the home market as a substitute for specialized production for the export market might well involve loss of productivity and a deterioration in living standards; and it will be appreciated that a country like Malaya has been able to achieve a relatively high level of *per capita* income largely because of her specialization in the production of exports for the world markets. And some writers, indeed, argue strongly against diversification and point to the fact that a country like Malagasy, which has a wide spread of crops and products, has a weaker economy than many of its 'one-product' neighbours. But on the other hand – and quite apart from considerations of economic nationalism and the revolt against the 'colonial pattern of foreign trade legacy' – the tendency to change the emphasis from export industries in favour of diversified production for the home market has to varying extents been forced upon tropical countries by the changing nature of world markets. As already noted, the

P

demand for primary commodities in which tropical countries have traditionally specialized is becoming weak and uncertain where new sources of production, natural and synthetic, are being tapped; and the export outlook for manufactured goods is even less promising because of severe competition from highly industrialized countries and restrictive trade policies in most importing countries.

Industrialization represents yet another way of trying to deal with the problem of overdependence on a few raw materials in world markets. In this context industrialization has among its aims not only the desire to earn more foreign exchange by the further processing and therefore the increase in value of raw material exports, but also the desire to save foreign currency by substituting domestically produced items for manufactured goods at present imported from abroad. In West Africa some success has been achieved in this direction with the rapid increase over the past few years of such import-substitution industries as flour-milling, beer, tile, ceramic, and cheap textile industries; meat and fish canning; and car assembly plants, especially in Nigeria, Ghana, and Ivory Coast. On the whole, however, the effects of import-replacing industrialization on the foreign trade of West Africa has so far shown little sign of changing the traditional pattern of trade by reducing the imports of manufactured items. In Ghana, and in spite of such industrialization, agricultural raw materials continue to dominate Ghana's exports, and manufactures her imports. What has changed is the composition of imports from manufactured consumer goods to manufactured capital goods. Here again, perhaps the crucial issue is market opportunity. Industrialization, as we have seen earlier, is severely limited by the very characteristics of developing societies that it is intended to remedy. Yet it would be misleading to overemphasize this as a continuing problem. There are already clear examples of tropical countries diversifying their exports by industrialization and by finding the necessary markets within other countries of the tropics. One example is Kenya, where every effort is being made to widen the base of the exports to include a greater quantity of manufactured goods. Kenya is fast becoming a major supplier of neighbouring countries in Africa and the Indian Ocean. Including exports to

Uganda and Tanzania, over 43 per cent of Kenya's total exports by value are sold within Africa, for, in addition to manufactured goods, many African countries have to import the temperate climate's agricultural and dairy produce which Kenya is ideally suited to supply. During 1966 there was a sharp increase in exports to other African countries outside East Africa. This increase was in part due to the temporary problems facing Zambia, but more significant was the substantial increase in exports to Congo Kinshasa, Rwanda, Burundi, and the Sudan (*The Times*, 1966: 20 October).

Another means of lessening the ill-effects of existing trading patterns upon the economic development potential of many tropical countries has been the establishment of a number of centralized marketing institutions. These have been particularly important in West Africa, more especially for specific export crops. Known as Marketing Boards or, in some of the French-speaking territories, as *Caisses de Stabilisation*, they have monopoly powers for the purchase and sale of the principal export products. Attempts have also been made in a number of cases to eliminate or at least to reduce the problem of market competition between individual countries, as with the International Coffee Organization.

The arguments lying behind the formation of these boards and other organizations concern matters of efficiency, standardization, and stability. Certainly these marketing boards and their equivalents have had some effect in stabilizing incomes, if not prices, from year to year. On the other hand, their effect on forecasting and controlling surpluses has not been remarkable for, as several authorities have shown, the export surpluses of a number of West African countries were relatively about the same before the war as during the post-war period of statutory marketing schemes. A number of writers, indeed, have come out strongly against all such monopolistic and centralized schemes. Bauer (1963b), in particular, has attacked the whole concept of these boards, partly on the grounds that they choke normal competitive instincts and so limit individual experience in marketing.

A fourth way of dealing with the external trading problems of tropical countries is to encourage regional economic co-operation between groups of states in an area (Urquidi, 1962; Allen, 1961). A number of attempts at establishing preferential trade agreements between groups of countries can be cited: the Latin American Free Trade Association (LAFTA), Gran Colombia, the Caribbean Free Trade Area, the Benin–Sahel Entente, the Customs Union for Equatorial and Central Africa, the East African Common Services Organisation (EACSO), and the South-east Asian Free Trade Association. The international framework within which all these attempts have operated or continue to operate is the General Agreement on Tariffs and Trade (GATT), the successor of the International Trade Association (ITA). This agreement has laid down the two exceptions to the general rule prohibiting trade discrimination: that countries forming a customs union can eliminate tariffs between them and adopt a common tariff against the outside world; and the granting of 100 per cent mutual preference in specified commodities by developing countries. As Kindleberger (1966) has pointed out, all these customs unions, free-trade areas and 100 per cent preferences in specified commodities would appear to be a useful means of co-operation between developing countries. By widening their domestic markets the member countries are able to achieve the economies of scale necessary to any rapid industrialization programme; and if the developing countries are in foreign exchange difficulties, mutual exchanges even of high-cost products are a means of getting goods which they might otherwise have to do without.

In fact, however, there has been to date (1967) no really success-ful attempt at this kind of regional economic co-operation in trade. The difficulties are many. As pointed out earlier in this chapter, tropical countries trade very little with each other. Furthermore, in new goods which might be produced in the region, it is difficult to arrange who produces what. Tariff reductions are also difficult for countries with a weak balance of payments. Again, there is the problem of the gains and losses among the various countries: the richest of the member countries might believe itself to be suffering from having to make larger contributions than its neighbours while the poorest members might suffer from having to open their markets to the industries of the more prosperous states. Yet again,

differences in language, in currencies and in existing trading ties
can so easily frustrate successful co-operation. Finally, political
difficulties of many other kinds commonly arise; and it is possible
to argue that the basic obstacle to regional co-operation for
economic development is political rather than economic.

The interdependence and significance of markets and trade. Geographical, economic, and anthropological research in the tropics
has tended to ignore the many varied phenomena and processes
associated with trading activities. This is perhaps particularly unfortunate at a time when purely subsistence economies are a rarity,
and when all contemporary agricultural, industrial, and infrastructural change can be seen to imply mutual adjustment to the
limits and opportunities set by existing trading patterns. Assuming
an adequate understanding of the varied and complex forms and
processes, therefore, trade can clearly be a powerful instrument of
change.

Any real understanding of the implications of trade for economic
development generally in the tropics, however, is limited not only
by the scarcity of data and information but also by the tendency to
view trade as composed of a number of distinct 'types', each with
its own problems, characteristics, and opportunities. It is true that
a classification of trade into a number of types has obvious analytical convenience as a breakdown of the various distributive
streams between producer and consumer; yet it does tend seriously
to exaggerate the differences between them. More accurately, the
whole trading pattern in any tropical country should perhaps be
seen as a number of interwoven and interdependent types of trade.

To bring this whole question down to the level of the individual,
a farmer in Yorubaland may be involved either directly or indirectly in all types of trading. He may be growing cocoa, which
moves to the export port through the Marketing Board machinery.
He may also be growing kola, which goes to the local market place
where it is bulked up by a Hausa trader for transport to the
northern areas of Nigeria or beyond to the Niger Republic. He
may also grow food crops, some of which he will consume himself,
and some of which will go to the local market place, from where it

may reach the final consumer, be taken on to the urban retail markets, or move through the urban wholesale markets for dispatch to the Eastern Region. But almost every pattern reveals the very great significance of the periodic market place in the whole distribution network in this area. As a producer and consumer, much of the actual distribution takes place through the farmer's wife. At the local market place she may buy his imported tobacco, a shirt from Japan, or a new farm tool from Birmingham. At the same time she may buy high-value, low-bulk imported goods so that during the next few days she can operate as an itinerant trader travelling perhaps into Dahomey, down to Lagos, or just visiting other markets in her market circuit. The possibilities and variations are infinite, and it is one of the characteristics of trading life in many parts of the tropics that exclusive patterns of trade are the exception rather than the rule.

It is equally misleading to view trade out of the context of the whole production–distribution–consumption continuum. Thus the farmer referred to above cannot but be affected by fluctuations in world demand and prices for his main export crops – even though he may be cushioned against these by Marketing Boards – as well as by changes in inter-state, inter-regional, or local demand and prices. At the same time he is affected by his own production and marketing problems, soil erosion and fertility problems, pests and diseases, water supply conditions, transport facilities, and transport costs. To the farmer these are all urgent issues of which he is uniquely aware and which he must take account in all his efforts to increase agricultural production. Consequently, just as it is misleading to think of a number of quite distinct types of trade, so it is misleading to concentrate on one part of the production–trade continuum, for each affects and is affected by the other.

.   .   .   .   .

It has been implied in the above discussion that one of the crucial problems in tropical development is concerned with markets and trading – and in particular with the dependence of the tropical world upon the commercial attitudes and trading activities of the developed world. Present international trading policies still underpin the old traditional circuit of Western manufactures in return for raw materials. Western tariffs still discriminate against processed goods. It is clearly necessary to devise trading policies which have the opposite effect: 'that of stimulating local advance, stimulating local manufacture, building up export incomes, and in fact avoiding the situation . . . in which every penny of aid that has been given has been nullified by the collapse of raw material prices and by the unbroken increase in the cost of Western Manufactures' (Ward, 1964: 63). There seems indeed to be a strong case for arguing that the trading problems of the tropical world can only be solved within the wider context of changing trading policies in the developed world. Measures for bringing about trade innovations of the kind required are, admittedly, politically difficult, even when they seem economically simple. But most tropical developing countries argue with justification that the present international trading structure permanently inhibits rapid economic advance in their economies; that commodity stabilization schemes, largely financed by the developed countries, need to be put into operation; and that developed countries can do a great deal to improve and expand trading opportunities for developing countries by accepting simple manufactures among imports, and by reducing tariffs on such goods as coffee, cocoa, and bananas. In this sense the economic development of tropical countries rests as much with such international organizations as the United Nations Conference on Trade and Development as it does with the tropical countries themselves. The final chapter underlines this point within the wider context of economic development planning and international aid.

Economic Development Plans, Capital Resources, and International Aid

Economic development plans. While it may be true that economic development does not depend upon a plan, almost all tropical countries have development plans of one kind or another. Some of these are comprehensive, covering total national targets; detailed assessments of the natural, human and financial resources available, and of the investment required; an allocation of the public and private investment among major sectors together with policies to stimulate and direct private investment; and a detailed list of projects to be financed by the public sector (Galbraith, 1963). A comprehensive development plan is a valuable policy state- ment and an essential document for any geographical analysis of a country's economic life and problems. Such a plan is India's Fourth Five-Year Plan. Careful reading and consideration of this plan, together with the three earlier plans, provides a centralizing, focusing point for a series of otherwise discrete studies in the geo- graphical analysis of Indian economic development. And even a simple table showing the financial provisions for the different sectors of the Indian economy made by the four development plans suggests a number of ideas and questions which are of interest not only to Indian administrators and academic economists but also to geographers concerned with the regional study of contem- porary India (Table 10). The plans of many other tropical coun- tries, however, are of relatively little value, for they comprise little more than a list of projects – like Niger's First Three-Year Plan for 1961–3. In many countries, of course, there are not enough data available from surveys, maps, or statistics to make integrated development planning possible. In such cases, government plan- ning can mean little more than deciding how to resolve the most obvious problems in a few economic sectors (Eckaus, 1966).

Economic development plans also differ widely in their motivation. In general terms it may be true that the goal of economic development in all countries is to raise *per capita* incomes, but such a statement oversimplifies the issue for those countries where the decisive criteria of a successful plan are more social, political or strategic than economic. Thus whereas in one country the overriding objective is a high rate of growth of income, in another country it may be full employment, the development of backward regions, the creation of strategic industries, or the reduction of reliance on foreign trade (Bhagwati, 1966: 105). Furthermore, investment policies depend partly on a government's attitudes to public and private investment; for a conflict can easily arise between the interests of economic equality and economic growth. Again, plans differ in the emphasis they give to the various lines of development. Certainly one of the most important features of any plan is the making of decisions about the relative importance in development of agriculture, irrigation, land reform, industry, price stabilization, roads, health, and education. A choice has also to be made about the kind of balance to be reached between those projects likely to show a profit quickly and those projects – like roads, physical surveys, and social services – which can only be expected to bring long-term and indirect results. A good deal of thought, too, has to go into the 'matching and phasing of the various segments of the plan – into ensuring that kinds and amounts of steel being produced will match requirements for steel in kind and amount and that this balance between supply and requirements is maintained over time' (Galbraith, 1963: 29). The high priority given to transport and communications in most plans reflects the general consensus of opinion in economic development planning that most other aspects of development depend on good transport, which normally fails to attract substantial private investment, especially in the early stages of development, and so provides a particularly important field for large-scale public expenditure.

Economic development plans clearly represent an attempt to look at the various lines of development within a country, not as individual strands or projects but as part of the whole problem.

Plans direct, stimulate and control against a background of policy relating to priorities, and aid from outside is often contingent upon such planning. Integration and balance – these are normally important ingredients of any development plan; and this is why the examination of the plan and development problems of a particular state often provides the geographer with a useful focusing or integrating point in his analysis. A plan represents an attempt at analytical synthesis within the framework of a particular areal setting.

Some of the requirements of a 'good' plan are implicit in what has already been said. But it is perhaps worth emphasizing here three further and, according to Galbraith, often missing elements of an economic development plan. First, it should provide a strategy for economic advance without which the plan easily becomes only 'a bit of all the things that everyone would like to have done or that anyone believes ought to be done' (ibid.: 37). Those elements that are central or vital to economic development in any particular case must be emphasized and isolated from those elements that are merely useful or passive. At first sight this is similar to the point already made about the need to choose between different sectors of investment – between agriculture, industry, or transport, for instance. But Galbraith's point goes farther than that. His point here is that the various elements of each sector need to be subjected to a decision about the distinction between the vital and non-vital. Thus in agricultural development it might be decided for any particular country that water, fertilizers and improved seed are vital; and that land-tenure reorganization, mechanization, or credit facilities are merely useful. Secondly, a plan should emphasize both the visible and invisible dimensions of industrial achievement: 'like an iceberg, much of modern industrial society is out of sight. To get capital plant – steel mills, railway lines, coal mines, aeroplanes, oil rigs – into use is the visible achievement of developing planning. To ensure that this plant is efficiently used – that management is independent and sound, that in consequence material costs are low, product quality good, cost of production low, and earnings adequate for replacement and expansion of plant – is the much larger part of the task' (ibid.: 42). This brings us back to a point made earlier in this book: that the improvement in the qualitative aspects of human resources, in management, entrepreneurial activities, and the development of labour skills – what Schultz (1964) calls 'investment in human capital' – is as much an essential part of the processes of economic development as are the more obvious or visible dimensions of industrial progress. Finally, an economic development plan should have a theory of consumption which, as the previous chapter argued, is a much ignored aspect of the problem. Without a theory of consumption related to conditions in the particular country for which the plan is drawn up, consumption patterns of western developed countries or even of other developing countries will be accepted and followed as a matter of course. Each development plan, however, needs to keep clearly in mind the consumers for whom the planning is intended.

It will be noticed that these three requirements emphasize two issues: the need to consider the human context and human problems of social and economic change; and the need to consider each problem within a specific areal setting – normally the state area – rather than attempt to apply to each area and problem blanket solutions or theoretical prescriptions based on evidence drawn from often widely differing situations. The theoretical literature on economic development now abounds with planning models and analytical schemes; but, as Eckaus (1966: 393) has emphasized, there is no single best planning theory or model. Each country and each set of circumstances requires a 'tailor-made' procedure. To some extent, the same is true of regional economic planning within each state where the problems of locational specialization, especially in industry, may be crucial (Bhat, 1964; Learmonth, 1964; Grove and Huszar, 1964). Little work, however, has yet been carried out into the characteristics and implications for economic development of regional variations in industrial or any other kind of development in a tropical country, even where a federal structure confronts the planners with pressures for evening out regionally the benefits of their development programmes. Locational analysis and regional planning within the state framework has so far received remarkably little attention from those, including geographers, concerned with the study of tropical development.

The Ghana Development Plan (1963) is unusual in containing a substantial element of regional planning between different parts of the country and relies less than do most development plans upon sectoral analyses and recommendations. The question poses itself, however, as to whether a national development plan and a regional development plan within that same country may not have conflicting aims and interests. Certainly the chief criterion of a national development plan appears most commonly to be the maximizing of total production; whereas in regional planning within a state the aims are often more dominated by social, employment, and political considerations. If this is so, then internal regional development planning may in economic terms constitute a drag on national economic progress.

Rather more information is available about regional planning in the sense of co-operation between states. Some comment has already been made in the previous chapter about co-operation between states in forming free-trade areas, customs unions, and the like. Then there is co-operation for specific projects, such as the West African project for the building of one large international iron and steel mill to serve the whole region; this failed, again largely for political reasons, several of the member states – notably Nigeria, Ghana and Liberia – deciding to go ahead with their own iron and steel works. Then there are a number of attempts and proposals to create regional units for physical planning of one kind or another. River-basin and river-valley development, for instance, is seen to be desirable where rivers are international in character. There are many striking examples of this situation in the tropics – the Amazon and Orinoco in South America, the Niger, Congo, and Zambesi in Africa, and the Indus, Salween, and Mekong in Asia. But there are numerous other small though locally highly important schemes, like the Mono River Project for hydro-electric development between Dahomey and Togo in West Africa. Assuming political agreement, co-operation between states in all these cases must result in mutual benefits in the division of water, the division of costs, and the sharing of the joint benefits. The fact that it is still impossible to point to any wholly successful international river-basin development scheme in the tropics is further testimony to the political difficulties associated with such agreements.

Capital resources. It will already be clear that one of the fundamental practical problems in formulating economic development plans is to decide on the way in which available capital resources for investment are to be shared out. Economic development plans are in effect investment plans, and it is important to emphasize the relative roles of public and private investment.

Public investment has five main sources of money: budget surpluses – India aims to raise over one-fifth of her total current plan investment by this means, but in most tropical countries this is not yet a very significant source; profits from public enterprises, in which state ownership of profit-making enterprises contribute to the total public investment; public borrowing, which again is of small importance in most tropical countries, though it provides some 12 per cent of the total public investment in India; foreign assistance or aid, about which more will be said later – much of it, in fact, may be available not for development investment at all but for direct expenditure on imports of consumer goods, on imports to maintain and supply existing industries, and on repaying interest or principal on loans; and deficit financing, or drawing on reserves, or printing more money.

Private investment is significant only in the more advanced developing countries like India (39 per cent) and Venezuela (76 per cent) though, as pointed out earlier, political attitudes and action often affect the size and relative significance of private and public investment. Thus in India the current (fourth) development plan stresses the value of public investment as a means of preventing any further concentration of economic power in a few hands; whereas in Venezuela the role of public investment is mainly to support and facilitate private investment. In most tropical countries, however, the contribution of private investment to financial resources for development planning is insignificant, and any increases in this contribution are likely to result mainly from the general processes of economic development.

Whether public or private, the form of exchange in which the investment exists may be critical. A certain proportion of the available financial resources needs to be in foreign exchange, normally accumulated through exports, aid, or foreign private investment, in order that goods and skills not available locally can be imported. Foreign exchange, of course, is characteristically scarce in many tropical developing countries, and has in many cases formed an important obstacle to development.

There is, however, some controversy over the significance of capital resources to economic development. It is sometimes argued that shortage of capital is never a critical or decisive factor in the early stages of a country's economic progress: much more important is the capacity to absorb capital and to transform the economy. During the early stages of a country's economic development, it is argued, effective government, education, and social justice are the critical barriers to be overcome. As for effective government, it is particularly true of many Latin American countries that the political problem of securing governments willing and able to make the take-off into modernity seems often to be insoluble; and many writers argue for looking upon education as the most fundamental and important single factor in the early stages of economic development. Only when these social and political barriers have been removed and a fair measure of development achieved can anything really useful or permanent come either from capital investment or from technical assistance: 'capital becomes the touchstone of development, the limiting factor, only in countries that are well along the development line' (Galbraith, 1963: 21). Other writers go even farther, arguing that financial resources are exaggerated in many development analyses in developing countries and contending that such resources receive far more attention than they deserve (Cairncross, 1962; Nevin, 1961; Lewis, 1953). This tendency to give too much weight to capital resources in development is possibly due to the fact that economics has relatively little developed systematic theory regarding the factors responsible for development but already has a well-developed capital theory (Villard, 1963).

Many authorities, however, conclude that real weight should be given to capital as occupying the central position in economic development theory. It is argued that an injection of financial resources may 'set alight' or 'prime the pump' of development. Financial resources, according to this viewpoint, are of great importance in many developing countries in enabling them to break out from the vicious circle of low purchasing power and savings capacity, leading to a low rate of capital formation, lack of capital, low productivity, low real income, and so back to low purchasing power and savings capacity. This view of the vicious circle, in which an economy is imprisoned in its own shortcomings, is regarded by some economists as central in a description of what ails developing countries (Mydral, 1956). Furthermore, as noted earlier in this book, capital can substitute for resources and for labour. Yet the necessary degree of increase in savings and capital formation in low-income countries is very difficult to achieve. In most tropical countries annual savings rarely amount to over 6 per cent of the national income, as against over 20 per cent in the United States. Partly for this reason, it is argued, external or international aid is an essential ingredient of the economic development planning of any tropical country.

International aid. As will have emerged from the discussion in the previous section of this chapter, the argument for emphasizing external capital is both simple and attractive. The low average income of the inhabitants of tropical developing countries enforces a low level of consumption per head and reflects a low level of productivity. This low level of real output per head of population may be caused by a number of factors, including many of a social and psychological nature; but one factor is of outstanding importance – the lack of capital, including real capital equipment such as factories, machinery, or tools. According to this traditional analysis the rudimentary equipment available to the average worker in a developing country makes it impossible for him to increase his output; and for this reason the amount of capital available is critical in all attempts to increase substantially the level of productivity (Reddaway, 1966). Only a flow of external capital can help to break the vicious circle of poverty and provide the foreign exchange required to buy necessary imports of machinery and similar sophisticated goods without running into serious balance of payments difficulties.

A number of writers, however, have argued against this emphasis on the flow of external capital to help in accelerating the development of these countries. First, there is the simple fact that the total amount of such external capital is unlikely ever to be of the scale to allow even a moderate rate of growth in developing countries. Foreign capital contributions may be of real importance as 'seed corn'; but as a major contribution to development, a much larger expansion of foreign aid than now appears probable would be needed. The World Bank is becoming more and more convinced that the problem of the next decade is how to see that aid flows more freely, without tying up the poorer countries with impossible debt burdens, and how to ensure that the aid so given is used effectively. The developed countries must clearly contribute to any increased aid. One suggestion is for international agreement among the developed countries to give, say, one per cent of their gross national product each year to the developing countries on terms that do not place a heavy burden of debt on the recipient country. A figure of one per cent would represent an increase of about half over the current average level of 0·73 per cent and it remains to be known whether the developed countries with large military expenditures could do this without increasing taxation. Borrowing by the developing countries is already made easier, especially through the Development Assistance Committee (DAC) and the International Development Agency (IDA), an offshoot of the World Bank; these agencies produce 'soft' loans, a matter of great significance because over 15 per cent of the export earnings of the poorer countries today are being used as debt repayments. Secondly, available evidence seems to suggest that external capital should only be thought of as but one factor in a detailed overall plan. Certainly the mere provision of external capital does not automatically stimulate advance in other sectors of the economy, nor can one assume that supplies of the complementary factors will necessarily be available. As Reddaway (1966) argues, the 'shortage of capital' thesis both exaggerates and at the same time makes it appear too easy. Much more emphasis should be placed on increasing the capacity of a country to absorb aid effectively and on self-help, involving the better use of existing or new capital by the developing countries themselves; and this often means in practice that attention should be concentrated on agriculture rather than on industrialization, because it is on agricultural development – by the introduction of better methods and additional equipment – that existing capital can be most effectively utilized in increasing productivity. Thirdly, there is the common argument that many developed countries really cannot afford as a regular commitment such altruistic gestures as the giving of aid to the developing countries of the world. It is frequently held, in fact, that the most important though indirect means of assistance to developing countries is the stabilization of high levels of employment in the developed countries. This contributes to the steadiness of prices and value of exports of primary products in developing countries and to the stability of the availability of private capital, much of which is dependent for its investment in developing areas on the expansion of markets in developed areas (Kindleberger, 1966: 377).

As for aid in kind, in which the United States is easily the most important participant, this is, of course, very much bound up with the wider question of international trade. Something was said about this in Chapter 13, where it was suggested that present trading policies are slanted against the developing countries and that international action for evening out the advantages of such trade needs to be given great prominence. Assistance in kind is normally in food, and the most striking instance of this sort of aid in recent years has been the movement of grain to India from the United States. This type of movement also implies surpluses in the producing countries of the developed world. Yet even within the tropics there are many cases of surpluses being wasted or not ever being produced because the existing pattern of trade or trans-port facilities makes such trade or production either impossible or unprofitable.

As for aid in the form of technical assistance, this is perhaps particularly important in that any financial assistance is unlikely to be fully effective unless combined with the provision of tech-nical experts. According to some authorities, notably Schumpter

Q

(1949), technical change is the central aspect of economic development. Yet investment in human resources is usually a lengthy
process; and to be economically effective it may require far-
reaching social changes which are also likely to take much time.
Kindleberger (1966: 136) has pointed out that it used to be believed that technical assistance – the transfer to developing countries of advanced technological methods and ideas such as longer
hoes, row planting, improved seed, and the diffusion of agricultural
techniques through extension services – would by itself result in
economic development. This is now known to be untrue. No such
development will take place unless technical assistance also 'sets
in motion an indigenous cumulative process of innovations and
capital formation . . . this implies changes in attitudes, institutions,
organizations, and social relationships' (Belshaw, 1956: 103). It
may be, as some writers have argued, that technical assistance to
tropical countries should come primarily from those countries
which have only recently reached developed status. Countries like
Japan, especially, are perhaps better able to give technical assistance than America or Western Europe because of their much
narrower cultural and technical gaps. Even within the developing
countries of the tropics, too, technical assistance can be given – for
instance from relatively developed India to Indonesia, or from
Venezuela to Nigeria.

Whether aid takes the form of grants or loans, kind or technical
assistance, a good deal of controversy exists over the extent and
even the desirability of such aid for the developing world today.
To many recipient countries in the tropics, especially in Africa,
all aid is interpreted as a form of neo-colonialism, more especially
when this aid is bilateral and 'tied' in a number of ways – by projects or by countries. Many tropical countries, indeed, continue to
adopt a restrictive attitude towards private foreign investment to
an extent that is clearly holding back development. In the donor
countries, too, there seems to be an increasing reluctance to provide
assistance that so often appears to be wasted, misused, or little
appreciated; and certainly, private investment is not encouraged
by recurrent political upheavals. In Nigeria it is estimated that the
1966–1967 series of coups and wars resulted in a loss of investment

opportunities of over £100 million. Some doubt is now felt, too, about the validity of the 'economic self-interest' argument for giving aid on the part of the developed world. Most authorities now find it hard to make the case that the development of tropical countries carries economic benefits for the developed countries which justifies their assistance: 'the argument that no country can be prosperous in a world where there are countries which are not prosperous is rhetorical nonsense' (Kindleberger, 1966: 365). Certainly the whole question of aid to the developing countries has been brought under severe scrutiny where economies in public expenditure in the donor countries are being practised. It is becoming increasingly apparent that many of the old assumptions about aid do not bear examination. It seems likely that multilateral aid will slowly replace bilateral aid as the chief vehicle for expressing the developing world's concern at the low levels of production and consumption in the tropics. Nevertheless, on humanitarian and on social and political, if not economic, grounds, the arguments for international aid to the developing world are decisive. As a number of writers have emphasized, the arguments for aiding the development of the developing countries 'rest less on economic and short-run political grounds than on the long-run political. Rising national expectations must see some prospect of satisfaction, or low-income countries are likely to be prey to economic, political, and social breakdown, with convulsive results' (ibid.: 379). Without substantial and continuing aid from outside it is difficult to see how development in tropical countries can ever be achieved at the rate demanded by the circumstances. Rostow's estimate of sixty years and even Dumont's figure of twenty years before underdevelopment can be conquered refer to time scales longer than anything acceptable to the peoples of the tropical world today.

Although it may seem as yet little more than a dream that developed countries should contribute multilaterally through some international body perhaps one or even two per cent of their national income to the developing countries of the world, the urgent and obvious need for some such substantial, regular, equitable and, to the recipient countries, anonymous contributions is becoming more generally accepted. A good deal of literature now exists on the ways in which the giving of aid for developing countries might most fairly be shared out among the developed countries. It is suggested, for instance, that countries with higher *per capita* incomes should give higher rather than equal percentage contributions of national income, compared with those countries with lower *per capita* incomes (Rosenstein-Rodan, 1961). Given adequate safeguards about the kind of aid to be given and about the capacity of recipient countries to absorb such aid effectively, substantial multilateral aid is now at least a practical proposition, although as much as 90 per cent of current aid to developing countries is still bilateral. Yet even a dramatic increase in aid will make little impression on the problem unless it is accompanied by trade liberalization and by the encouragement of industrial exports from the developing world along the lines suggested in the previous chapter. So long as the present structural imbalance of trade exists, the gap between the rich and poor nations will continue to widen and the demands for aid will continue to mount.

Conclusions

The dangers of generalizing about tropical development. Much of the current thinking about tropical development is characterized by a tendency to oppose tropical and non-tropical lands in a most misleading way. Thus it is sometimes suggested that there are specifically 'tropical' problems or that the tropics have their own peculiar – and usually, by implication, inferior – physical and human geography. It is to be doubted, however, whether any useful generalizations of this kind can be made about the tropics and their development problems any more than they can be made about the temperate lands. Indeed, it will have become apparent that to write about 'tropical' as quite distinct from any other kind of development is impossible; and very little of what has been written here about the processes of economic development could not also be written of developing countries in the arid tropics, sub-tropics, or temperate lands of the world. Furthermore, in their natural and human characteristics tropical countries differ widely from one another, and each country embraces that unique complex of natural and human circumstances which provides the only realistic territorial framework for development planning. In this sense the resource bases of Brazil, Nigeria, and India differ as widely as do those of Great Britain and Ghana. Whether they occur in tropical or in non-tropical areas, almost all applied problems of economic development are regional or local problems; and the specific areal setting in which they occur is likely to reveal a unique combination of natural and human circumstances.

It is similarly misleading to generalize rigidly about the whole developing world, of which the tropics forms by far the largest part, as if it were a separate and opposing entity for which a whole new set of concepts, ideas, and principles needs to be developed. There can be no single theory of economic development for any major part of the world, or for the whole world; nor can any one variable – capital, natural resources, scale, technology, human skills, or birth-control measures – ever provide the key to development. The processes of economic development are always immensely complicated. Moreover, the various countries of the developing world are clearly at different stages along a development line; and any attempt to devise a general formula on the basis of an economic theory that assumes otherwise is bound to lead to failure.

There is, then, as much variety in environments and in existing levels of achievement in the tropical developing world as there is in the developed world as a whole; and the distinction between developing and developed is as arbitrary and misleading in applied economic development studies as is the distinction between tropical and non-tropical lands.

Grounds for optimism. Seen in this light, there seems to be every reason for optimism about the *potential* for economic development in tropical countries. It is accepted as a necessary working hypothesis that the tropics possess no inherent disadvantages in natural or human resources compared with any other similarly large part of the earth's surface. This holds true both quantitatively and qualitatively. To suggest, for instance, that soils are especially limiting to agriculture in the tropics, that the climate is inimical to the growth of advanced civilizations, or that tropical peoples have a relatively low innate capacity for participating in the more complex forms of social, economic, or political endeavour: all such viewpoints are rejected. Rather is it accepted that the natural and human resources of the tropics are as varied – as 'good' and as 'bad' – as in any other large region, and that these resources are certainly not especially limiting to development, given adequate knowledge about the resources and their utilization and given also a readiness to adapt economic planning to the opportunities and limitations set by them. Substantial difficulties in the understanding and utilization of the resource base do exist; but these difficulties commonly derive from a lack of information, experience, and training, and so are not of the kind to inhibit permanently the economic development of the tropical world.

Further grounds for optimism about tropical development are provided by the growing awareness among the countries of the developed world that the economic problems of tropical countries can never be understood, let alone solved, out of the context of the total world economy, and in particular out of the context of existing international trading relations. The provision of aid, whether financial, in kind, or in technical assistance, is undoubtedly important. But perhaps even more critical is the need for larger and wider trading and marketing opportunities in the developed world. Present international trading relations perpetuate the traditional exchange of Western manufactures in return for raw materials and make very difficult the kind of rapid economic advance based upon overseas markets that played so large a part in the growth of prosperity at earlier stages in the economic history of most countries in the developed world. Apart from common humanitarian motives, there are strong practical arguments for providing better trading and marketing opportunities for tropical countries, including the fact that vast potential markets in the developing world itself can never be tapped while the purchasing power of the mass of the population there remains so low: the prosperity of Great Britain as a great trading nation, for instance, must in the long run depend on the continuous expansion of world markets, and in particular on the growth of new markets for sophisticated products in the poorer countries. Furthermore, the developed countries are becoming increasingly aware that tropical developing countries now account for about two-thirds of the total voting strength of the United Nations; and the kind of political stability so urgently needed in these countries is unlikely to develop in a situation where economic instability and distress are endemic and where there continues to be little evidence of substantial improvements in living standards. While it may seem ingenuous to expect the developed world ever to indulge in the kind of economic altruism outlined in the latter part of this book, a great deal has, nevertheless, been accomplished in this direction over the last few years. Since 1964, in particular, the United Nations Conference on Trade and Development has gathered together a body of material and initiated a movement of world opinion already much closer to agreement on wider trading opportunities for developing countries than most observers would have thought possible only five years ago.

The increase of production. In trying to identify the many and diverse problems of economic development in the tropical world, the central issue is taken to be what has been called in these pages the demographic–economic problem. This seems logical for many reasons, including the fact that economic development is defined, however crudely, as a rising *per capita* income and so can be considered to be a function of the changing relationship between national income and total population numbers. It is argued that in dealing with this demographic–economic problem the emphasis should not be placed upon trying to reduce the rate of population growth. While the demographic approach may have secular implications of some significance, to look upon birth control as a means of increasing *per capita* income is both to oversimplify economic development as a process and to exaggerate the role of the so-called 'population problem'. The real issue remains one of how to increase production at a rate substantially higher than the rate of growth of population.

In discussing, however selectively and briefly, some of the major issues relating to the increase of production in tropical countries, two main points have been made. First, it is misleading to isolate too sharply the supply and demand sides of production, and any applied problem of how to increase production must be seen in the context of the entire production–distribution–consumption process. Thus to increase the agricultural production of maize and cassava in an area involves considering all three aspects. At the production end there is the need to provide the appropriate fertilizers, together with information about farming methods and the cultivation cycle; and the successful introduction of such innovations implies also a host of other social, cultural, fiscal, administrative, and technological changes which are as yet perhaps little understood and require much deeper field experience and research. At the production end, too, the scope for applied scientific research into crops and their ecology – into better-yielding, disease-resistant, or pest-resistant varieties – is very wide indeed and is probably consistently underestimated in prognostications about production increases. But increased maize or cassava production in a country requires also that lines of distribution in terms of marketing organization, credit facilities, and good, cheap transport be made available. And finally, increased production cannot be expected to occur unless market opportunities are there and are seen to be there, either in the form of increased local food consumption; in new maize-processing or cassava-processing factories; or in larger overseas markets. All three aspects of the problem – at the production and consumption ends and in the distributive link – are closely related and together must always affect very deeply the individual farmer's motivation, incentives, and resistance to change.

A second point has been expressed in terms of a development continuum, in which all forms and levels of economic activity in tropical countries are seen as being at different stages along the same development line. In this context the problem in any particular case study is to locate the development stage and to analyse the existing tendencies to change within the economy. Only when this has been done should any attempt be made to accelerate, facilitate, or direct the economy along specific lines. This approach is likely to be more successful, and to have fewer ill-effects on indigenous societies, than the alternative approach: to consider a developing economy in the tropics as being essentially static, even stagnant; and to follow this up by trying to inject from outside a type of change which bears no relation to the spontaneous movements for improvement latent within all economies and societies. This notion also implies that the chief aim of economic policy must always be the increase of productivity by 'industrializing' all forms of economic activity, including agriculture; and by feeding back from industry into agriculture the results of applied research and technological advance.

The geographer and applied development studies in the tropics. It will be clear from the preceding pages that a great deal of research is now being directed into the field of tropical economic development studies. Since the early 1950s, certainly, there has appeared a spate of books and articles, only a fraction of which has been referred to in this short study. The amount of theoretical material alone is now formidable; and many physical and social scientists have greatly widened and deepened our understanding of the various countries and peoples of the tropical world.

Yet it is perhaps still true to say that one of the major difficulties with which development studies in the tropics have to cope is the paucity of ideas and case-study material. At the theoretical level, probably all economists would agree that development theory for developing countries still requires much refinement, although this is particularly difficult where the available statistical material is so limited. Existing data are usually too few and too crude to be subjected to the kind of refined techniques of statistical treatment now being adopted in the more advanced societies. There are few tropical countries, indeed, where even the basic data for development planning can yet be said to exist; and the need for more geological and topographical survey and mapping, climatological and biogeographical studies, land-use analyses, and population, settlement, and marketing studies is urgent and obvious everywhere.

Here, then, are two major kinds of research requiring continual and increasing attention in tropical development studies; and it is more especially in the second of these – in the collection and analysis of field data – that the geographer is already making significant contributions (Steel and Prothero, 1964).

But an equally urgent contemporary need is for the kind of 'grass-roots' case study of applied development in the field referred to on a number of occasions throughout these pages. In this kind of applied, essentially problem-oriented study, facts and theories are equally necessary. Furthermore, it demands an approach that is essentially interdisciplinary. Although the aim of economic development may be quite simply to bring about a cumulative increase in levels of consumption, it is now widely appreciated – by economists as well as by non-economists – that economic development is not simply an economic process, and that 'many if not most of the applied problems to which attention must be given if economic development is to be promoted, raise questions outside the field with which the economist is normally concerned' (Viner, 1953: 23). The range of factors operating in any specific situation in economic development reaches far beyond the confines of any one formal discipline or branch of knowledge. Especially in dealing with differences in qualities of economic factors between different regions, 'the economist is dealing with matters for whose detailed investigation other scientists – agronomists, political scientists, engineers, geographers, geologists . . . sociologists, and anthropologists – alone have the requisite professional qualifications and the economist must seek their counsel and borrow from them' (ibid.: 24).

This being so, the field study of applied problems of economic development has always to take into account the findings, methods, and viewpoints of a wide range of related disciplines. Real problems of economic development are no more 'geographical' problems than they are 'economic' or 'social' problems. Consequently it seems logical to insist that the questions a geographer asks himself about tropical development in his field studies must be examined and answered, not within any inhibiting framework of preconceived notions about what is or is not the proper scope of geography but simply with the aim of following all relevant lines of inquiry, wherever they might lead. The value and meaning of the geographer's contribution to development studies can only be demonstrated by the way in which geographers tackle their problems and try to answer their questions, and not by the way in which they stop their analysis every time it seems to go outside the legitimate field of geographical inquiry. In tropical development studies, as in perhaps all fields of applied knowledge, the scope of the inquiry must be defined only by the problem set.

References and Select Bibliography

ADAMSON, A. M. 1943. Termites and the fertility of soils, *Tropical Agriculture*, **20**.

ALEXANDER, J. B. 1964. The evolution of land suitability maps in the Federation of Malaya, *Journal of Tropical Geography*, **18**, 1–6.

ALLAN, W. 1965. *The African Husbandman*. London.

ALLEN, R. L. 1961. Integration in less developed areas, *Kyklos*, **14**, 315–36.

ARCHAMBAULT, J. 1960. *Les Eaux Souterraines de l'Afrique Occidentale*. Paris.

ARDENER, E. 1953. Oil palm and the Mba-Ise people, unpublished manuscript.

ARGAWALA, A. N. and SINGH, S. P. 1963. *The Economics of Underdevelopment*. New York.

ASHBY, D. G. and PFEIFFER, R. K. 1956. A limiting factor in tropical agriculture, *World Crops*, **8**.

AUBERT, G. 1954. La classification des sols utilisées dans les territoires tropicaux de l'union française, *Proceedings of the second Inter-African Soils Conference*, Leopoldville, **2**, 705–8.

AUBREVILLE, A. 1937. Les forêts du Dahomey et du Togo, *Bulletin Comité Etudes Historiques et Scientifiques de l'Afrique Française*, 1–113.

BAILEY, F. G. 1958. *Caste and the Economic Frontier*. London.

BAILEY, R. 1967. *Problems of the World Economy*. London.

BALDWIN, K. D. S. 1957. *The Niger Agricultural Project*. London.

BALDWIN, R. E. 1963. Export technology and development from a subsistence level, *Economic Journal*, 80–92.

BALOGH, T. 1966. *The Economics of Poverty*. London.

BARAN, P. A. 1957. *The Political Economy of Backwardness*. New York.

BARBOUR, K. M. 1966. Facility profiles as criteria for the geographical assessment of development schemes, unpublished manuscript.

BARNETT, H. J. and MORSE, C. 1963. *Scarcity and Growth: The Economics of Natural Resource Availability*. Baltimore.

BATES, M. 1952. *Where Winter Never Comes*. New York.

BAUER, P. T. 1957. *Economic Analysis and Policy in Underdeveloped Countries*. London.

1961. *Indian Economic Policy and Development*. London.

1963. *The Study of Underdeveloped Economies*. London.

1963b. *West African Trade*. Cambridge.

BAUER, P. T. and YAMEY, B. S. 1957. *The Economics of Underdeveloped Countries*. Cambridge.

BECKFORD, G. L. F. 1964. The growth of major tropical export-crop industries, *Social and Economic Studies*, **13**, 413–29.

1964b. Secular fluctuations in the growth of tropical agricultural trade, *Economic Development and Cultural Change*, **13**, 80–94.

BECKINSALE, R. P. 1957. The nature of tropical rainfall, *Tropical Agriculture*, **34**, 76–98.

BEGUIN, H. 1964. *Modèles Géographiques Pour l'Espace Rural Africain*. Brussels.

BELSHAW, D. G. R. 1964. Agricultural settlement schemes on the Kenya highlands, *East African Geographical Review*, **2**, 30–6.

BELSHAW, H. 1956. *Population Growth and Levels of Consumption*. London.

BENHAM, F. and HOLLEY, H. A. 1960. *The Economy of Latin America*. London.

BERG, E. J. 1961. Backward-sloping labour supply fluctuations in dual economies: the Africa case, *Quarterly Journal of Economics*, 468–92.

BERNARD, E. 1945. *Le Climat Ecologique de la Cuvette Central Congolaise*. INEAC, Brussels.

BERRILL, K. (ed.). 1965. *Economic Development with Special Reference to East Asia*. London.

BHAGWATI, J. 1966. *The Economics of Underdeveloped Countries*. London.

BHAT, L. S. 1963. Regional contrasts in population density and growth in India, 1951–61, *Geography*, **48**, 313–16.

1964. Aspects of regional planning in India, in R. W. Steel and R. M. Prothero (eds), *Geographers and the Tropics*, London, 297–322.

BLANCKENBURG, P. VON. 1962. *Rice Farming in the Abakaliki Area*. Ibadan.

BOEKE, J. H. 1942. *The Structure of Netherlands Indian Economy*. New York.

1953. *Economics and Economic Policy in Dual Societies*. New York.

1954. Three forms of disintegration in dual societies, *Indonesie*, **7**, 278–95.

BOHANNAN, P. 1959. The impact of money on an African subsistence economy, *Journal of Economic History*, **19**, 491–503.

BOHANNAN, P. and DALTON, G. 1962. *Markets in Africa*. Evanston.

BOSERUP, E. 1965. *The Conditions of Agricultural Growth*. London.

BRAMMER, H. 1956. *C. F. Charter's Interim Scheme for the Classification of Tropical Soils*. Kumasi.

BROOKFIELD, H. C. 1960. Population distribution and labour migration in New Guinea, *Australian Geographer*, **7**, 233–42.

BRUNT, D. 1943. The reactions of the human body to its physical environment, *Quarterly Journal of the Royal Meteorological Society*, **69**, 77–114.

1947. Some physical aspects of the heat balance of the human body, *Proceedings of the Physiological Society*, **59**.

BUCHANAN, K. M. 1964. Profiles of the third world, *Pacific Viewpoint*.

BUCHANAN, N. S. and ELLIS, H. S. 1955. *Approaches to Economic Development*. New York.

CAINE, SIR S. 1963. *Prices for Primary Producers*. London.

CAIRNCROSS, A. K. 1962. *Factors in Economic Development*. London.

CARROLL, T. F. 1961. The land reform issue in Latin America, in Hirschman, A. O. (ed.). *Latin American Issues*, New York.

CARTER, G. F. and PENDLETON, R. L. 1956. The humid soil: process and time, *Geographical Review*, **46**.

CHARTER, C. F. 1957. The aims and objects of tropical soil surveys, *Soils and Fertilisers*, **20**, 127–8.

CHENERY, H. B. 1955. The role of industrialisation in development programmes, *American Economic Review*, **45**, 40–57.

CHISHOLM, M. 1966. *Geography and Economics*. London.

CLARK, C. 1957. *The Conditions of Economic Progress*. London.

1967 *Population Growth and Land Use*. London.

CLARK, C. and HASWELL, M. 1964. *The Economics of Subsistence Agriculture*. London.

CLAWSON, M. 1964. *Natural Resources and International Development*. Johns Hopkins.

CLAYTON, K. 1963. *Economic Planning in Peasant Agriculture*. London.

1964. *Agrarian Development in Peasant Economies*. Oxford.

CONKLIN, H. C. 1961. The study of shifting cultivation, *Current Anthropology*, **2**, 27–61.

COPPOCK, J. T. 1966. Agricultural developments in Nigeria, *Journal of Tropical Geography*, **23**.

COULTER, J. K. 1964. Soil surveys and their application in tropical agriculture, *Tropical Agriculture*, **41**, 185–96.

CRIST, R. E. 1963. Tropical subsistence agriculture in Latin America, *Annual Report, Smithsonian Institute*, **1963**, 503–19.

CURLE, A. 1963. *Educational Strategy for Developing Societies*. London.

DALTON, G. 1962. Traditional production in primitive African economies, *Quarterly Journal of Economics*, **76**.

DAVEY, T. H. and LIGHTBODY, W. P. H. 1956. *The Control of Disease in the Tropics*. London.

DE CASTRO, J. 1952. *The Geography of Hunger*. Boston.

DE SCHLIPPE, P. 1956. *Shifting Cultivation in Africa*. London.

DE VRIES, E. 1954. *World Population Conference*. Rome.

DEBENHAM, F. 1948. *Report on the Water Resources of the Bechuanaland Protectorate*. H.M.S.O., London.

DOBBY, E. H. G. 1954. *South-east Asia*. London (6th edn).

DOOB, L. W. 1961. *Communication in Africa*. London.

DUBEY, V. 1963. The marketed agricultural surplus and economic growth in underdeveloped countries, *Economic Journal*, **73**.

DUMONT, R. 1962. *L'Afrique Noire est Mal Partie*. Le Seuil.
1966. *False Start in Africa*. London.

ECKAUS, R. S. 1955. The factor proportions problem in underdeveloped areas, *American Economic Review*, 45.
1966. Appendix on developmental planning, in C. P. Kindleberger, *Economic Development*, New York, 389–410.

ELLIS, H. S. 1965. *Economic Development for Latin America*. London.

EMERSON, SIR R. 1959. A project for extending the Nigerian railway into Bornu province, *Proceedings of the Institute of Civil Engineers*, **12**, 353–66.

ENKE, S. 1963. *Economics for Development*. New York.

EPSTEIN, S. 1962. *Economic Development and Social Change in South India*. London.

ERNLE, LORD. 1937. *English Farming, Past and Present*. London.

FAIR, T. J. D. 1963. A regional approach to economic development in Kenya, *South African Geographical Journal*, **45**, 55–77.

F. A. O. 1966. *The State of Agriculture*. New York.

FARMER, B. H. 1957. *Pioneer Peasant Colonization in Ceylon*. London.
1960. On not controlling subdivision in paddy lands, *Transactions, Institute of British Geographers*, **28**, 225–35.
1964. The extension of cultivation in underdeveloped countries, paper read at I.G.U. Conference, London.

FAYEMI, A. A. 1963. Effect of plant population and spacing on the yield of maize in the humid tropics, *Empire Journal of Experimental Agriculture*, **31**, 371–5.

FIRTH, R. 1946. *Elements of Social Organisation.* London.

FISHER, A. G. B. 1935. Economic implications of material progress, *International Labour Review*, July, 5–18.

1939. Production, primary, secondary and tertiary, *Economic Record*, 24–38.

FISHER, C. A. 1964. *South-east Asia.* London.

FLOYD, B. 1962. Land apportionment in southern Rhodesia, *Geographical Review*, **52**, 566-82.

1965. Soil erosion and deterioration in eastern Nigeria, *Nigerian Geographical Journal*, **8**, 33–44.

FORD, V. C. R. 1956. The trade of Lake Victoria and its marginal lands, in R. W. Steel and C. A. Fisher (eds), *Geographical Essays on British Tropical Lands*, London, 147–80.

FOSBERG, F. R., GARNIER, B. J., and KUCHLER, A. W. 1961. Delimitation of the humid tropics, *Geographical Review*, **51**, 333–47.

FRANKEL, S. H. 1953. *The Economic Impact on Underdeveloped Societies.* Oxford.

FREEMAN, J. P. 1955. *Iban Agriculture.* H.M.S.O., London.

FROELICH, J. C. 1949. Densité de la population et méthodes de culture chez les Kabré du Nord Togo, *Proceedings of the I.G.U., Lisbon*, **4**, 168–80.

FRYER, D. W. 1958. World income and types of economies, *Economic Geography*, **34**, 283–303.

1963. The development of cottage and small-scale industries in Malaya and in South-east Asia, *Journal of Tropical Geography*, **17**, 99–115.

1965. *World Economic Development.* New York.

FURNIVALL, J. S. 1948. *Colonial Policy and Practice.* Cambridge.

GALBRAITH, J. K. 1963. *Economic Development in Perspective.* London. 1967. *The New Industrial State.* London.

GALBRAITH, J. K. and HOLTON, R. H. 1955. *Marketing Efficiency in Puerto Rico.* Cambridge, Mass.

GARNIER, B. J. 1958. Some comments on defining the humid tropics, *Research Notes*, Ibadan, **11**, 9–25.

1960. Maps of the water balance in West Africa, *Bulletin, Institut Français Afrique Noire*, **22**, 709–22.

1961. The idea of humid tropicality, *Proceedings of the Tenth Pacific Science Congress*, Honolulu.

GAUSSEN, H. and LEGRIS, P. 1963. La délimitation des zones tropicales humides, *Annales Géographie*, **72**, 513–28.

GEDDES, W. R. 1954. *The Land Dyaks of Sarawak*. H.M.S.O., London.

GERSCHENKRON, A. 1962. *Economic Backwardness in Historical Perspective*, Cambridge, Mass.

GHOSH, D. 1946. *Pressure of Population and Economic Efficiency in India*. New Delhi.

GINSBERG, N. S. (ed.). 1960. *Essays on Geography and Economic Development*. Chicago.

1961. *Atlas of Economic Development*. Chicago.

GLASER, E. M. 1955. *Health in an Equatorial Climate*. Singapore.

GOLDSWORTHY, P. R. and HEATHCOTE, R. 1963. Fertilizer trials with groundnuts in northern Nigeria, *Empire Journal of Experimental Agriculture*, **31**, 351–66.

GOULD, P. 1964. A note on research into the diffusion of development, *Journal of Modern African Studies*, **2**, 123–5.

GOUROU, P. 1966. *The Tropical World*. London (4th edn).

GREGORY, S. 1964. Rainfall over Mozambique, in R. W. Steel and R. M. Prothero (eds), *Geographers and the Tropics*, London, 81–109.

GROVE, A. T. 1951. Soil erosion and population problems in South-east Nigeria, *Geographical Journal*, **117**, 291–306.

1951b. *Land Use and Soil Conservation in Parts of Onitsha and Owerri Provinces*. Geological Survey, Lagos.

1952. *Land Use and Soil Conservation on the Jos Plateau*. Geological Survey, Lagos.

1957. *Land and Population in Katsina*. Kaduna.

GROVE, D. and HUSZAR, L. 1964. *The Towns of Ghana*. Accra.

GUTMAN, G. O. 1957. A note on economic development with subsistence agriculture, *Oxford Economic Papers*, 323–9.

HAILEY, LORD. 1957. *Africa Survey, Revised 1956*. London.

HAIN, W. 1964. Die Landwirtschaft de Republik Guinea, *Geographische Berlin*, **9**, 178–93.

HANCE, W. A. 1964. *The Geography of Modern Africa*. New York.

HANSON, A. H. 1960. *Public Enterprise and Economic Development*. London.

HARBISON, F. and MYERS, C. A. 1964. *Education, Manpower and Economic Growth*. New York.

R

HARDY, F. 1951. Soil productivity in the British Caribbean region, *Tropical Agriculture*, **28**, 27–32.

HARROD, R. F. 1948. *Towards a Dynamic Economics*. London.

HASWELL, M. R. 1963. *The Changing Pattern of Economic Activity in a Gambia Village*. H.M.S.O., London.

HAUCK, F. W. 1966. Pilot schemes for fertiliser distribution in West Africa, paper read at second meeting of a Conference on Soil Fertility and Fertiliser Use in West Africa, F.A.O., Dakar.

HAUSER, P. M. (ed.). 1967. *Urbanisation in Latin America*. UNESCO, Paris.

HAWKINS, E. K. 1958. *Road Transport in Nigeria*. Oxford.

1962. *Roads and Road Transport in an Underdeveloped Country. A Case Study of Uganda*. H.M.S.O., London.

HAYEK, F. A. 1955. Comment on Kuznets, S. Toward a theory of economic growth, in R. Lekachman (ed.). *National Policy for Economic Welfare at Home and Abroad*. New York.

HAZLEWOOD, A. 1958. *The Economics of Underdeveloped Areas*. London.

1964. *The Economics of Development*. London.

HETZEL, W. 1965. Phosphatbergbau und -industrie in Togo, *Erde*, **96**, 136–47.

HIGGINS, B. 1956. The dualistic theory of underdeveloped areas, *Economic Development and Cultural Change*, **5**, 95–115.

1959. *Economic Development*. New York.

HILL, POLLY. 1963. Markets in Africa, *Journal of Modern African Studies*, **1**, 137–46.

1966a. Notes on traditional market authority and market periodicity in West Africa, *Journal of African History*, **7**, 295–311.

1966b. Landlords and brokers: a West African trading system, *Cahiers d'Etudes Africaines*, **6**, 349–66.

1966c. A plea for indigenous economics, *Economic Development and Cultural Change*, **15**, 10–20.

HIRSCHMAN, A. O. 1958. *The Strategy of Economic Development*. London.

HODDER, B. W. 1959a. *Man in Malaya*. London.

1959b. The growth of trade at Lagos, *Tijdschrift voor Economische en Sociale Geografie*, **50**, 197–202.

1961. Rural periodic day markets in part of Yorubaland, *Transactions, Institute of British Geographers*, **29**, 149–59.

1965a. The distribution of markets in Yorubaland, *Scottish Geographical Magazine*, **81**, 48–58.

1965b. Some comments on the origins of traditional markets in Africa south of the Sahara, *Transactions, Institute of British Geographers*, **36**, 97–105.

HODDER, B. W. and HARRIS, D. R. (eds). 1967. *Africa in Transition*. London.

HOSELITZ, B. F. (ed.). 1952. *The Progress of Underdeveloped Areas*. Chicago.

HUMPHREYS, R. A. 1946. *The Evolution of Modern Latin America*. Oxford.

HUNTER, J. M. 1966. River blindness in Nangodi, *Geographical Review*, **56**.

HUNTINGTON, E. 1915. *Civilization and Climate*. New Haven.

HUTCHINSON, SIR J. 1966. Land and human populations, *Advancement of Science*, **23**, 241–54.

INDIAN GOVERNMENT. 1961. *The Third Five Year Plan*. Planning Commission, New Delhi.

1964. *Memorandum on the Fourth Five Year Plan*. Planning Commission, New Delhi.

INDONESIAN GOVERNMENT. 1951 *Indonesïe*. Djakarta.

INTERNATIONAL BANK. 1954. *The Economic Development of Nigeria*. Washington.

1955. *The Economic Development of Malaya*. Washington.

1960. *The Economic Development of Venezuela*. Baltimore.

1961. *The Economic Development of Tanganyika*. Baltimore.

1962. *The Economic Development of Uganda*. Baltimore.

1962. *The Economic Development of Ceylon*. Baltimore.

1963. *The Economic Development of Kenya*. Baltimore.

JAGOE, R. B. 1952. Photoperiodism of Oryza sativa in Malaya, *Malayan Agricultural Journal*, **35**, 85–102.

JAMES, P. E. 1963. *Latin America*. New York.

JOHNSTON, B. F. and MELLOR, J. W. 1961. Agriculture in economic development, *American Economic Review*, **51**, 566–93.

JORGENSON, D. W. 1961. The development of a dual economy, *Economic Journal*.

KANEDA. H, and JOHNSTON, B. F. 1961. Urban food expenditure patterns in tropical Africa, *Food Research Institute Studies*, Stanford.

KENWORTHY, J. 1964. Rainfall and water resources in East Africa, in R. W. Steel and R. M. Prothero (eds), *Geographers and the Tropics*, 111–37.

KILBY, P. 1955. Industrial labour productivity in Nigeria, *Economic Journal*, **89**, 265–79.

KIMBLE, G. H. T. 1960. *Tropical Africa, Vol. 1*. New York.

KINDLEBERGER, C. P. 1966. *Economic Development*. New York.

KRISHNA, R. 1959. Agrarian reform in India: the debate on ceilings, *Economic Development and Cultural Change*, 7.

KUZNETS, S. 1959. *Six Lectures on Economic Growth*. New York.

LACOSTE, Y. 1965. *Géographie du sous-développement*. Paris.

LAUER, W. 1952. Humide und aride Jahreszeiten in Afrika und Sudamerika und ihre Beziehung zu den Vegetationsgurteln, *Bonner Geographische Abhandlungen*, **9**.

LEARMONTH, A. T. A. 1964. Applied geography in Mysore State, in R. W. Steel and R. M. Prothero (eds), *Geographers and the Tropics*, 323–48.

LEDGER, D. C. 1960. Aspects of Nigerian hydrology, *Nigerian Geographical Journal*, **3**, 18–27.

1961. Recent hydrological change in the Rima basin, *Geographical Journal*, **127**, 477–84.

1963. The Niger dams project of Nigeria, *Tijdschrift voor Economische en Sociale Geografie*, **54**, 242–7.

1964. Some hydrological characteristics of West African rivers, *Transactions, Institute of British Geographers*, **35**, 73–90.

LEE, Y. L. 1962. The population of British Borneo, *Population Studies*, **15**, 226–43.

LEIBENSTEIN, H. 1954. *A Theory of Economic–Demographic Development*. Ithaca.

1960. Technical progress, the production function and dualism, *Banca Nazionale de Lavoro Quarterly Review*, December, 3–18.

LEWIS, W. A. 1955. *The Theory of Economic Growth*. London.

LIM, J. J. 1954. Tradition and peasant agriculture in Malaya, *Malayan Journal of Tropical Geography*, **3**, 44–7.

LIM, T. B. 1956. Commentary in Thayer, P. W. and Phillips, C. (eds), *Nationalism and Progress in Free Asia*, Baltimore, 179–92.

LITTLE, I. M. D. and CLIFFORD, J. M. 1965. *International Aid*. London.

LITTLE, K. 1965. *West African Urbanisation*. Cambridge.

LLOYD, P. C. *et alia*. 1967. *The City of Ibadan*. Cambridge.

LORD, R. F. 1963. *Economic Aspects of Mechanised Farming at Nachingwea*. London.

MALAYAN GOVERNMENT, Institute of Medical Research, 1950. *Publication No. 25*. Kuala Lumpur.

MANDELBAUM, K. 1955. *The Industrialisation of Backward Areas.* London.

MARKHAM, S. F. 1947. *Climate and the Energy of Nations.* New York.

MARRIS, P. 1962. *Family and Social Change in an African City.* Evanston.

MARTIN, A. 1961. *The Economics of Agriculture.* London.

MASEFIELD, G. B. 1960. *Tropical Agriculture.* Oxford.

1962. Agricultural change in Uganda, 1945–1960, *Food Research Institute,* Stanford.

MCMASTER, D. N. 1956. The Owen Falls Dam, *Geography,* **41**.

1962. *A Subsistence Crop Agriculture of Uganda.* London.

1964. Uganda, *Focus.*

1966. Changes in the extent and the distribution of cultivation in Uganda, 1952–1958, *Uganda Journal,* **30**, 63–74.

MCPHEE, A. 1926. *The Economic Revolution in British West Africa.* London.

MEADE, J. E. 1955. *Trade and Welfare.* Fair Lawn.

MEEK, C. K. 1948. *Land Law and Custom in the Colonies.* London.

MILLS, C. A. 1942. *Climate Makes the Man.* New York.

MILNE, G. 1935. Some suggestions for classification and mapping, particularly for East African soils, *Soil Research, Berlin,* **3**.

MIRACLE, M. P. 1958. Seasonal hunger: a vague concept and an unexplored problem, *NISER Conference Proceedings,* 36–49.

MOHR, E. C. J. and VAN BAREN, F. A. 1954. *Tropical Soils.* The Hague.

MORGAN, W. B. 1959. Agriculture in southern Nigeria, *Economic Geography,* **35**, 138–150.

MORTIMORE, M. J. and WILSON, J. 1965. Land and people in the Kano close-settled zone, *Occasional Papers,* **1**, Zaria.

MOSS, R. P. 1963. Soils, slopes and land use in a part of south-western Nigeria, *Transactions, Institute of British Geographers,* **32**, 143–68.

MOUNTJOY, A. 1963. *Industrialisation and Underdeveloped Countries.* London.

MYINT, H. 1964. *The Economics of the Developing Countries.* London.

MYRDAL, G. 1956. *An International Economy.* New York.

1957a. *Rich Lands and Poor.* New York.

1957b. *Economy Theory and Underdeveloped Regions.* London.

NASH, T. A. M. 1948. *The Anchau Settlement Scheme.* H.M.S.O., London.

NASH, T. A. M. and PAGE, W. A. 1953. The ecology of Glossina palpalis in northern Nigeria, *Transactions, Royal Entolomological Society,* **104**.

NEDECO. 1960. *The Improvement of Navigation on the Rivers Niger and Benue.* The Hague.

NELSON, R. R. 1956. A theory of the low-equilibrium trap, *American Economic Review*, **46**, 894–908.

NIGERIAN GOVERNMENT. 1962. *Federal Government Development Programme*. Lagos.

NJOKU, E. 1955. *Some Problems of Plant Life in a Tropical Environment*. Ibadan.

NURKSE, R. 1953. *Problems of Capital Formation in Underdeveloped Countries*. Oxford.

1959. *Patterns of Trade and Development*. Stockholm.

O'CONNOR, A. M. 1966. *An Economic Geography of East Africa*. London.

OJO, G. J. A. 1963. Trends towards mechanised agriculture in Yorubaland, *Nigerian Geographical Journal*, **6**, 116–29.

OOI, JIN BEE. 1955. Mining landscapes in Kinta, *Malayan Journal of Tropical Geography*, **4**, 1–147.

1959. Rural development in tropical areas with special reference to Malaya, *Journal of Tropical Geography*, **12**.

OWEN, W. 1959. Transportation and economic development, *American Economic Review*, **49**, 179–87.

PAGE, W. A. and MCDONALD, W. A. 1959. An assessment of the degree of man–fly contact exhibited by Glossina palpalis at water holes in north and south Nigeria, *Transactions, Tropical Medicine*.

PARKER, W. N. 1961. Comment in J. J. Spengler (ed.), *Natural Resources and Economic Growth*, Washington, 190.

PEDLER, F. J. 1955. *The Economic Geography of West Africa*. London.

PELZER, K. J. 1957. Agriculture in the humid tropics, *Proceedings of the Ninth Pacific Science Congress, Bangkok*, **20**, 124–43.

PHILLIPS, J. 1964. *Agriculture and Forestry Development in the Tropics*. London.

PIM, SIR A. 1946. *Colonial Agricultural Production*. London.

PREBISCH, P. 1949. *The Economic Development of Latin America*. New York.

PRESCOTT, J. R. V. 1960. Overpopulation and overstocking in the native areas of Matabeleland, *Geographical Journal*, **126**.

PROTHERO, R. M. 1966. *Migrants and Malaria*. London.

RADELL, D. R. 1964. *Coffee and Transportation in Nicaragua*. Berkeley.

RANIS, G. and FEI, J. C. 1961. A theory of economic development, *American Economic Review*, **51**, 533–65.

RAO, V. K. R. V. and DESAI, P. B. 1965. *Greater Delhi*. London.

REDDAWAY, W. B. 1963. The economics of underdeveloped countries, *Economic Journal*, 1–15.

1966. External capital and self-help in developing countries, *Progress*, **4**, 50–57.

REEVE, W. H. 1960. Progress and geographical significance of the Kariba Dam, *Geographical Journal*, **126**, 140–6.

RICHARDS, A. 1939. *Land, Labour and Diet in Northern Rhodesia*. London.

RICHARDS, P. W. 1952. *The Tropical Rain Forest*. Cambridge.

RICHARDSON, H. L. 1966. The F.F.H.C. – Five years of the F.A.O. fertiliser programme, *Outlook on Agriculture*, **5**, 3–16.

ROBINSON, E. A. G. 1960. *Economic Consequences of the Size of Nations*. 1964. *Economic Development for Africa south of the Sahara*. London. 1965. *Problems in Economic Development*. London.

ROBINSON, G. W. 1949. *Soils, Their Origin, Constitution and Classification*. London.

ROSENSTEIN-RODAN, P. N. 1961. Notes on the theory of the Big Push, in Ellis and Wallich (eds). *Economic Development for Latin America*. New York.

ROSTOW, W. W. 1953. *The Process of Economic Growth*. Oxford. 1956. The take-off into self-sustained growth, *Economic Journal*. 1960. *The Stages of Economic Growth*. Cambridge.

SARGENT, J. R. 1960. *Report on Transport Requirements in the Light of Economic Developments in North Borneo*. H.M.S.O., London.

SCHULTZ, T. W. 1961. Investment in human capital, *American Economic Review*, **51**. 1964. *Transforming Traditional Agriculture*. New Haven.

SCHUMPTER, J. A. 1949. *The Theory of Economic Development*. Cambridge.

SEMPLE, E. C. 1911. *Influences of Geographic Environment*. New York.

SHANNON, L. W. (ed.). 1957. *Underdeveloped Areas*. New York.

SIMEY, T. S. 1946. *Welfare and Planning in the West Indies*. Oxford.

SINGER, H. W. 1964. *International Development, Growth and Change*. New York.

SJOBERG, G. 1960. *The Pre-Industrial City*. New York.

SKINNER, G. W. 1964. Marketing and social structure in rural China, *Journal of Asian Studies*, **24–5**.

SPATE, O. H. K. *et alia*. 1967. *India and Pakistan*. London.

SPENGLER, J. J. (ed.). 1952. Population theory, in Haley, B. F. (ed.). *A Survey of Contemporary Economics*. Homewood. 1961. *Natural Resources and Economic Growth*. New York.

STALEY, E. 1954. *The Future of Underdeveloped Countries*. New York.

STAMP, L. D. 1964. *Our Developing World*. London.

STEEL, R. W. 1948. Some geographical problems of land use in British West Africa, *Transactions, Institute of British Geographers*, **14**.

STEEL, R. W. and FISHER, C. A. (eds). 1956. *Geographical Essays on British Tropical Lands*. London.

STEEL, R. W. and PROTHERO, R. M. (eds). 1964. *Geographers and the Tropics*. London.

TARDITS, C. and C. 1962. Traditional market economy in south Dahomey, in Bohannan, P. and Dalton, G. (eds). *Markets in Africa*, Evanston, 89–102.

TAYLOR, G. 1946. *Our Evolving Civilization*. Toronto.

TEMPANY, SIR H. and GRIST, D. H. 1958. *An Introduction to Tropical Agriculture*. London.

THOMAS, R. B. 1966. *Economics of International Migration*. London.

THOMLINSON, R. 1967. *Demographic Problems: Controversy over Population Control*. Prentice-Hall, London.

THORNTHWAITE, C. W. 1948. An approach toward a rational classification of climate, *Geographical Review*, **38**, 55–94.

TINBERGEN, J. 1962. *Shaping the World Economy*. New York.

TRICART, J. 1956. Les exchanges entre la zone forestière de Côte d'Ivoire et les savanes soudaniennes, *Cahiers d'Outre Mer*, **9**, 209–38.

TRINIDAD AND TOBAGO GOVERNMENT. 1963. *Draft Second Five Year Plan*. Port of Spain.

TROLL, C. 1963. Landscape, ecology and land development with special reference to the tropics, *Journal of Tropical Geography*, **17**, 1–11.

U. A. C. 1957. Industrialisation in West Africa, *Statistical and Economic Review*, **23**.

UDO, R. K. 1965. Sixty years of plantation agriculture in southern Nigeria, *Economic Geography*, **41**, 356–65.

UKWU, U. I. 1965. *Markets in Iboland*. Ph.D. thesis, Cambridge.

U.N. 1955. *Determinants and Consequences of Population Trends*. New York.

    1955. *Processes and Problems of Industrialisation in Underdeveloped Countries*. New York.

    1957. *Report on the World Social Situation, Including Studies of Urbanisation in Underdeveloped Areas*. New York.

    1963. *Fertiliser Use – Spearhead of Agricultural Development*. New York.

1964. *Towards a New Trade Policy for Development*. New York.

1966. *Committee for Industrial Development, Report on the Sixth Session, Supplement No. 6*. New York.

UNESCO. 1956a. *Social Implications of Industrialisation and Urbanisation in Africa South of the Sahara*. Paris.

1956b. *Social Implications of Industrialisation and Urbanisation: Five Studies in Asia*. New Delhi.

1958a. *Study of Tropical Vegetation*. Paris.

1958b. *Problems of Humid Tropical Regions*. Paris.

1963. *Enquête sur les Ressources Naturelles du Continent Africain*. Paris.

UPTON, M. 1966. Recent changes from subsistence to commercial agriculture in Nigeria, paper read at British Association for the Advancement of Science, Section E.

URQUIDI, V. L. 1962. *Free Trade and Economic Integration in Latin America*. Berkeley.

VAGELER, P. 1953. *An Introduction to Tropical Soils*. London.

VAN BATH, B. H. S. 1963. *The Agrarian History of Western Europe, A.D. 500–1850*. London.

VEYRET, P. 1952. L'élevage dans la zone tropicale, *Cahiers d'Outre Mer*, 70–83.

VILLARD, H. H. 1963. *Economic Development*. New York.

VINE, H. 1941. A soil catena in the Nigeria cocoa belt, *Farm and Forest*, 2, 137–41.

VINER, J. 1953. *International Trade and Economic Development*. Oxford.

WARD, B. 1964. *Towards a World of Plenty*. Toronto.

WARD, M. W. 1960. Recent population growth and economic development in Asia, *Pacific Viewpoint*, 1.

WATTERS, R. F. 1960. The nature of shifting cultivation: a review of recent research, *Pacific Viewpoint*, 1, 59–99.

WEINER, J. S. 1966. Aspects of adaptation, *Advancement of Science*, 23.

WHITE, H. P. 1956. The internal exchange of staple food crops in Ghana, *Economic Geography*, 58, 225–37.

1959. The movement of export crops in Nigeria, *Tijdschrift voor Economische en Sociale Geografie*, 54, 248–53.

WICKIZER, V. D. 1960. The smallholder in tropical export-crop production, *Food Research Institute Studies*, 1, 49–99.

WIKKRAMATILEKE, R. 1963. *South-east Ceylon: Trends and Problems in Agricultural Settlement*. Chicago.

WILLIAMSON, A. V. 1931. Indigenous irrigation works in peninsular India, *Geographical Review*, **21**.

WILLIAMSON, G. and PAYNE, W. J. A. 1959. *Animal Husbandry in the Tropics*. London.

WINTER, E. H. 1956. *Bwamba Economy*. Makerere.

WYCHERLEY, P. R. 1967. Indices of comfort throughout Malaysia, *The Meteorological Magazine*, **96**, 73–7.

YOUNGSON, A. J. 1959. *Possibilities of Economic Progress*. Cambridge.

ZIPF, G. K. 1949. *Human Behaviour and the Principle of Least Effort*. Columbia.

Index